C0-AVY-470

917.36   60597
  Ber

Berger.
The British traveller in America.

Date Due

The Library
Nazareth College of Rochester, N. Y.

PRINTED IN U.S.A.

STUDIES IN HISTORY, ECONOMICS AND PUBLIC LAW

Edited by the
FACULTY OF POLITICAL SCIENCE
OF COLUMBIA UNIVERSITY

NUMBER 502

THE BRITISH TRAVELLER IN AMERICA, 1836-1860.

BY

MAX BERGER

THE BRITISH TRAVELLER
IN AMERICA, 1836-1860

BY

MAX BERGER, Ph.D.

Lecturer in History, Wagner College
Principal, Metropolitan Vocational High School
New York City

GLOUCESTER, MASS.

PETER SMITH

1964

DISCARDED

60597

Copyright, 1943 by
COLUMBIA UNIVERSITY PRESS

Reprinted 1964 by Permission of
Max Berger, Ph. D.

17.36

Ber

INTRODUCTION

AT a time when Americans are observing their English ally more closely and more critically than ever before, it is interesting to turn back the pages of history and see what Englishmen thought of America a century ago. At that time America was still very much a New World, a land of promise with new men and new ideas, a slowly awakening colossus. Proudly it proclaimed to a doubting and hostile world its belief that " all men are created equal."

To this land of equality flocked emigrants and visitors; the former to settle, the latter to investigate. Here was a New Order, a social system at variance with the established customs of the Old World. America's fascination to the foreign traveller a century ago was similar to that which drew clouds of tourists to the Soviet Union during the late 'twenties and early 'thirties of the present century. In both cases some visitors approved what they saw, others did not.

Europe between 1836 and 1860 was in the throes of one of its recurrent turmoils. The revolutions of 1830 were still bright in the memory of man when a new crop broke out in 1848 like a sporadic rash. Although relatively immune from these troubles, England was not entirely unscathed. Conservatives had scarcely become reconciled to the Reform Bill of 1832, when Chartism began sending chills down their spines. It was a period of change, of uncertainty, of hope, and of fear. Seeking a guiding star by which to steer safely through this troubled sea, many Englishmen turned their eyes overseas towards the distant and semi-fabulous Republic.

Granting that travel accounts of America had a vital interest for Europeans of that day, is there anything they can offer to the historian and scholar of a later period? The travel book fur-

5

nishes, primarily, a source for data not elsewhere obtainable.[1] Things too commonplace for a native to mention often appear sufficiently bizarre to the stranger to merit notation and investigation. New light may thus be cast upon a subject otherwise hackneyed. Foreign travel accounts not only provide an additional check upon native viewpoints and prejudices, but often expose those held by the visitor as well. To the extent to which such viewpoints are typical of the group from which the traveller comes, they furnish a perspective upon his own country and civilization. Nor should it be forgotten that in the past, when communication was poor and transportation slow, the people of one nation all too often arrived at their knowledge of another, largely on the basis of reports brought back by travellers.

Man has always been an inquisitive animal. Lands beyond the horizon have never ceased to intrigue him. From the days of Herodotus onward, travellers' tales have always found a ready audience. European ideas of America have undoubtedly been affected in this way. A popular travel book might have an influence out of all proportion to its true worth. In any case travel accounts furnish a ready arsenal from which each side can cite precedents as to the relative advantages or disadvantages of proposed reforms, whether political, social, or economic.

In considering the role of the travel book, its weaknesses should not be overlooked. Chief among these is the limited knowledge of many travellers. This frequently causes them to draw generalizations from a few isolated incidents, generalizations which may not be typical. Another weakness is the tendency to emphasize the unusual and to ignore the commonplace. Most travel books are written for sale. Hence, sensational matter is welcomed rather than deprecated. Last but not least, the traveller has preconceptions and prejudices that consciously or unconsciously affect his reporting.

---

1 Thus, for example, W. B. Adams, a leading authority in his field, considers travellers' accounts as the best source of information on the Irish in America during the period 1830-1847. W. F. Adams, *Ireland and Irish Emigration to the New World from 1815 to the Famine*, 434.

This work is intended to reveal what the British traveller saw in America during the period 1836-1860 and to analyze his viewpoint so far as is possible. Jane L. Mesick's *English Traveller in America, 1785-1835* has already covered the travellers who visited this country during the first half-century of our national existence. The period 1836-1860 forms the next logical unit. Jacksonian Democracy based upon universal (white) male suffrage had by this time triumphed over all opposition. A new era opened which was to last until the outbreak of the Civil War.

The British travellers and former emigrants who published travel books on America during this period discussed a multitude of topics. Almost every conceivable aspect of American life came under the scrutiny of one or another of them. To consider all of these topics in a single volume would be inadvisable, if not entirely impossible. It has been necessary, therefore, to limit ourselves to a treatment of such subjects as were of paramount importance to the British visitor. The necessity for omitting many subjects is obvious, but the omission of separate treatments for agriculture, commerce, and industry may appear strange. The first of these subjects interested only a limited number of agricultural scientists and emigrants. Discussions by the former were highly technical, of value to experts only, and largely of antiquarian interest today. Data that interested the emigrant has been included so far as possible in the chapter on Emigration. As regards commerce and industry, but few English visitors showed any concern. In most cases they simply jotted down statistics from American newspapers, almanacs, or government reports. Personal observations were strictly limited. Hence, the data quoted were of doubtful validity, especially since documentation was almost always lacking. There is, therefore, no logical basis for including these subjects when space is limited, even though the topics may appear important when viewed in retrospect from an economic-minded age. To the British traveller of 1836-1860, such matters as democratic government, slavery, manners and customs, national character, the voluntary support of religion, popular education, and emigration prospects were the topics of outstanding importance. Not only did these topics cover the salient features of American life, but they were also the subjects that were being debated by reformers and reactionaries at home.

An attempt has been made to provide sufficient data concerning the traveller, himself, to furnish an adequate background and perspective for his observations and conclusions. Readers desiring more data on any traveller than is given in the narrative, are directed to the Critical Bibliography where the salient facts concerning each traveller's background are summarized, and where each travel book is briefly evaluated. The concentration of such material in the bibliography not only makes it readily available to the reader, but also prevents the narrative from being overwhelmed with lengthy footnotes on each traveller's background, viewpoint, and reliability.

The author is greatly indebted to Professor Henry S. Commager of Columbia University for reading the proofs, and for numerous suggestions in planning this work. Professors Allan Nevins and John A. Krout were also most helpful.

TABLE OF CONTENTS

	PAGE
INTRODUCTION	5

CHAPTER I
The Traveller 13

CHAPTER II
The Face of America 25

CHAPTER III
Customs and Character 54

CHAPTER IV
Democratic Government 86

CHAPTER V
Slavery 108

CHAPTER VI
Religion 129

CHAPTER VII
Education 147

CHAPTER VIII
Emigration 162

CHAPTER IX
Conclusion 183

CRITICAL BIBLIOGRAPHY 189

INDEX 231

"No one who writes about the United States should be considered an oracle."

T. C. GRATTAN, *Civilized America,* I, v.

"How shall a man, to whom all characters of individual men are like sealed books ... decipher from his four-wheeled vehicle, and depict to us the character of a nation? He courageously depicts his own special delusions; notes this to be incomprehensible, that other to be insignificant; much to be good, much to be bad, and most of all indifferent; and so, with a few flowing strokes, completes a picture, which, though it may not resemble any possible object, his countrymen are to take for a national portrait."

HARRIET MARTINEAU, *Society in America,* I, iv.

CHAPTER I
THE TRAVELLER

ENGLISH travellers to the United States between 1836 and 1860 were a motley lot. Jackson's administration was drawing to a close when Harriet Martineau, after a youth devoted to social reform and religious writings, crossed the Atlantic " to compare the existing state of society in America with the principles on which it was professedly founded." [1] She found a land of corduroy roads and canal boats, with travel conditions so primitive that for the first time in her life her inability to hear, taste, and smell became positive assets. A bare quarter-century later the Prince of Wales was whisked around the nation in a specially constructed railroad car to receive the plaudits of curious throngs. Between the two there passed in kaleidoscopic array, authors, journalists, lecturers, scientists, businessmen, clergymen, soldiers, politicians, artists, promoters, actors, songwriters, and sportsmen—to mention but a few.

Practically all of them came from middle or upper class backgrounds. There were a few exceptions to this, of course. They were chiefly Britons who had come to America as emigrants, only to return to their homeland, unsuccessful, but anxious to capitalize on their experiences by publishing advice for others. In this group belonged men like Casey, who claimed that his book at least had the merit of viewing America from " between decks " (emigrant quarters). Thomson, a Scotch weaver who came to America in the hope of alleviating his tubercular condition, was likewise without riches. He saw America as an itinerant worker. But not all English emigrants or prospective emigrants were poor. Beste, after wandering around the West with a wife and eleven children, finally settled on the banks of the Wabash. Conditions failing to prove sufficiently attractive, the entire family returned to England. Despite the huge travel expenses of so large a group, never once was he without

1 Harriet Martineau, *Society in America*, I, iv.

adequate funds. Although this could not by any means be regarded as typical of the financial position of the emigrant group, yet, most emigrants who wrote travel books did come from middle-class backgrounds. Bookwriting was not a proletarian pastime. The poor and uneducated remained more or less inarticulate. The upper strata of British society, on the other hand, were well represented. Messrs. Marryat, Warburton, Mackinnon, Sullivan, Maxwell, and Ranken were members of the aristocratic military set. C. A. Murray, Gladstone, and Berkeley were active at Court. Lyell, Johnston, and A. M. Murray were outstanding scientists. Business interests were represented by Chambers, Baxter, Moore, and Watkin.

The total number of Englishmen who came to visit America during these years can never be estimated accurately, since no statistics of this type were kept by either the British or American governments. However, the number appears to have been quite large. Of these, approximately two hundred and thirty published accounts of their travels.[2]

They came for many reasons and saw many things.[3] If Combe came to spread the gospel of phrenology, Caird was chiefly interested in promoting Illinois farm lands. While Buckingham lectured on the Holy Land, Lyell sought geological data. Crossing the continent by stage-coach on his way back to England from Australia, Tallack took time out to investigate denominational disputes among the Quakers. Berkeley, speeding westward to hunt buffalo, thoroughly enjoyed snubbing the "riff-raff" he claimed to have encountered on the trains. Harvey was busily painting American landscapes at the very moment that Thomson was trudging through the Midwest seeking employment as a weaver.

Many Britons came to America on special missions. Young Lord Acton was a government representative to the New York

2 The method whereby this number has been determined is explained in the Bibliographical Note.

3 A brief description of each traveller and a critical evaluation of his book is provided in the bibliography.

Exhibition of 1853. Grattan, though he grew to detest America thoroughly, nevertheless was compelled to remain as British Consul in Boston from 1839 to 1846. Practically all the ministers who visited America (and they were numerous) were members of deputations sent to attend one or another of the many denominational conventions.

British civil and military officials stationed in Canada, usually spent their vacations in the United States. Except for Maxwell, who was a friend of Grattan and hence gravitated towards Boston, most of these men preferred " roughing it " in the West. Thus, Kennedy first became interested in Texas while vacationing from his Canadian post. Similarly, Oliphant, Superintendent of Canadian Indian Affairs, took a busman's holiday and explored the Indian lands of Minnesota by canoe. These officials were highly trained men whose observations were worthy of attention.

As transportation facilities improved in speed and comfort, tourists too began coming to America. Typical of these were the Turnbull sisters who travelled over 26,000 miles in the United States, Cuba, and Canada between 1852 and 1857. Such, also, was the youthful Mrs. Bishop who began a lifetime of travel with a journey to America in 1854. When Mrs. Trotter made a Grand Tour in 1858 from Boston to St. Louis and return, accompanied by a brother, a husband, and a complete retinue of servants, it was evident that tourism was here to stay.

The cheapness of American travel probably constituted an attraction for many visitors, though few Britons would admit that money affairs worried them. Sir Arthur Cunynghame, who made a whirlwind tour of the United States while on leave from his regiment in Canada, boasted that he had covered 5300 miles in 53 days at a total expense of £53. A businessman shortly thereafter, in remarking upon the cheapness of American travel, set it at about one-half of what it would be in Britain.[4] The Jamaican missionary, Phillippo, went even

4 James Robertson, *A Few Months in America*, 159.

further, advising Englishmen that a trip to the United States, including a visit to every state in the Union, and the return to England, would cost less than a two-month tour of the British Isles, and " with the same amount of comfort." [5]

This circumstance helped attract voyagers to America who were travelling to recuperate from illness or overwork. Sometimes such visitors found that the medicine was worse than the disease. Mrs. Maury had hoped that the sea voyage would improve her health. Instead, she caught small-pox. Convalescents usually remained in the seaboard cities, for earlier travellers who had been to the South and West had warned that only the strongest constitutions could withstand the countless fevers and diseases of those unhealthy regions.[6]

Especially in the 'fifties, it was not unusual for Britons to come overseas ostensibily to visit relatives. The latter, however, seldom received more than a line in the Preface. Once in the New World, the visitor found too many factors of interest to care to devote more than an absolute minimum of time to relatives.

Mention has already been made of those who came to America as emigrants. Not alone the poor, but the heads of large middle-class families, such as Mrs. Maury and Beste, came to investigate the opportunities that the Great Republic could offer their offspring. Businessmen, like James Robertson, Hancock, and Prentice were interested in America as a place for investments and commercial enterprises. The Irish Famine and the Revolutions of 1848, of course, were responsible for the bulk of the emigration of this period. However, many Englishmen and Scots emigrated to America at this time also. The movement was further accelerated by the California Gold Rush which drew adventurers from all walks of life and from all parts of the globe.[7]

5 J. M. Phillippo, *The United States and Cuba*, 96.

6 The chapter on Emigration discusses western health conditions as reported by travellers.

7 The Census of 1860 placed the number of emigrants from Great Britain and Ireland during the period 1830-1860 at 2,629,047.

Travel accounts naturally reflected the special interests of their authors. The Reverend George Lewis devoted most of his book to American churches; Tremenheere to schools; Rhys to the theatre; Berkeley to hunting; Captain Mackinnon to the Navy; and the Reverend F. J. Jobson to Methodism. " Bleeding Kansas " found its spokesman in Gladstone, feminism in Mrs. Finch, negro slavery in Fanny Kemble. Satiated with the mysteries of Africa and Arabia, Burton came to Utah to write about the Mormons. Oliver, an untutored emigrant, wrote a little-known but unexcelled booklet on western agriculture. As for the Far West, Ruxton told of his adventures with the Indians and fur-trappers of the Rockies, while Kelly described life in the roaring mining camps of California. America was sufficiently vast and varied to allow each to find what he sought.

Not all travel books were specialized, however. On the contrary, a great many were devoted to a general discussion of American institutions and customs. Into this group fell some of the most famous accounts, including those by Miss Martineau, Dickens, Grattan, Buckingham, Marryat, and Mackay. Finally, there were many visitors, like the Turnbull sisters, who were content to present merely a personalized diary of their day-by-day experiences.

The number of travellers to America increased rapidly after 1848. Instead of the handful of adventurous souls who had dared the rigors of America prior to that date, the period between the Mexican and Civil Wars witnessed the entry of a veritable horde of visitors. Travel to America was changing from the spectacular to the commonplace. Though improved diplomatic relations between England and America may have partially accounted for this, improvements in transportation facilities provided the key to the situation. The speedy Collins Line established in 1847, followed shortly thereafter by the luxurious Inman Line, brought a new era of steam, speed, and comfort into transatlantic travel. The steamer was displacing the sailing packet so rapidly that by the 'fifties even emigrants were

using the former. The first Cunarder in 1841, though of only
1100 tons displacement, was double the size of the sailing ships
of the 'thirties. Improvements were constantly being made so
that the *Persia,* a 3300-ton vessel which won the Blue Rib-
bon in 1856, crossed the Atlantic in nine days, as compared with
the sixty to ninety day voyages not infrequent two decades
earlier.[8] Within the boundaries of the United States, too, travel
conditions were improving rapidly. Although the stage-coach
was still the mainstay of transportation in the more remote
regions of the South and the West, the railroad was rapidly
displacing both stages and canals throughout the East. The
country's railroad mileage which had been only 1,098 in 1835,
had grown to 30,626 by 1860, with a line extending as far
west as St. Joseph, Missouri.[9] Transport by river steamer,
always a favorite on the western rivers, became less hazardous
as a result of mechanical improvements and federal safety
regulations. The vast increase in emigration in the late 'forties
was also influential in making American travel more commonplace. Finally, the Gold Rush opened up new routes across the
Continent to California and the Pacific Coast. Thus, although
Charles A. Murray in 1836 had only to cross the Mississippi to
be beyond the pale of civilization, less than two decades later
many of his countrymen were jogging across the deserts of
Utah and Arizona. The country was expanding westward at a
tremendous rate. As one Englishwoman observed, "Every year
a tide of emigration rolls westward . . . forming a tangled web
of races, manners, and religions which the hasty observer cannot attempt to disentangle." [10] Whereas Harriet Martineau had
regarded Illinois as a rather wild place in 1836, only a decade
later this area was being recommended as suitable for those
emigrants desiring farms in an established community.

But as transportation facilities improved and travel became
simpler, the length of time spent in the United States by the

8 F. C. Bowen, *A Century of Atlantic Travel: 1830-1930,* 15-95.

9 *United States Statistical Abstract,* 1921, table 239, p. 376.

10 Mrs. I. L. Bishop, *An Englishwoman in America,* 322.

individual traveller tended to grow shorter. Buckingham had spent four years in America; Harriet Martineau, Captain Marryat, and C. A. Murray, two years each. Maxwell, in 1840, had apologized for presuming to write a book on America, based upon " a journey made at railroad speed." [11] But after 1848 only those who actually settled in the United States as emigrants or for business reasons, spent more than a few months here. Conditions had changed so greatly by 1859 that Sir G. C. G. F. Berkeley, Conservative Member of Parliament, after a hunting trip to the West, urged his colleagues to take a similar trip as a vacation between Parliamentary sessions. It was certainly a long way from the days when Buckingham had jolted over endless corduroy roads in dusty, uncomfortable stage-coaches, to those when the Prince of Wales toured the United States by rail, including stops at Detroit, Chicago, St. Louis, Richmond, Washington, New York, and Boston— all within a sojourn of two months.

As travel conditions changed, so to a large extent did the type of traveller coming to the United States. On the whole, British travellers in America before 1848 appear to have been more serious and of greater ability than those who came between that date and the Civil War. Miss Martineau, Buckingham, Dickens, Combe, Lyell, Marryat, and Alexander Mackay, to mention but a few of the better known authors, all belonged to the earlier group. No travellers between 1848 and 1860 could compare with them either in power of description or of analysis. The weighty subjects that filled the ponderous tomes of these writers found no counterpart in the comparatively scanty works of their successors.[12] It was unusual in 1840 for an author to admit as great an interest in the " delicacy " of the Astor House chambermaids as in the demeanor of the President.[13]   But a scant fifteen years later it was common-

11 A. M. Maxwell, *A Run through the United States*, I, vii.

12 Buckingham wrote eight volumes on the United States; Martineau, six; Lyell, four; Combe and Mackay, three each. All were compact, containing a minimum of " padding."

13 A. M. Maxwell, *op. cit.*, II, 48-50.

place to find statements in the Preface to the effect that the sole aim of the book was to be amusing. If Marryat had crossed the ocean in 1837 ostensibly to discover whether " the faults of a people arise from the peculiarity of their constitutions, or from the nature of their governments," [14] two decades later an actor admitted that he had crossed the Atlantic merely to win a bet.[15] By 1848 England had become flooded with travel books on America. " We are no longer to be told that ' Boston is a beautiful city built on a hill' and so on . . . We know almost as much about Boston as we do about Manchester and Leeds," commented one visitor at this time. " I have taken it for granted that every reader . . . will have already gone through many books . . . on the United States. I have consequently excluded everything in the shape of statistics or information." [16] Although not all travellers in the 'fifties were this drastic, the reading public very definitely demanded a lighter fare. Lady Stuart-Wortley's book on her American travels had a wide circulation chiefly because it aimed " to amuse that large class to whom gossip is welcome." [17] But while these later works were lighter and briefer, they also revealed a greater catholicity of interest. Less attention was devoted to political and governmental matters, more to other aspects of American life.

As Britons became more familiar with American ways, there also came about a growing understanding and tolerance. The days of Mrs. Trollope and Basil Hall were past. Not even Marryat, Warburton, or Mrs. Houstoun, all of whom had a deadly hatred for democracy, could be compared in virulence with their forerunners in the early 'thirties, and still less with those of the years following the War of 1812.[18] This did not

14 David Hannay, *The Life of Frederick Marryat*, 98.

15 Capt. H. Rhys, *A Theatrical Trip for a Wager through Canada and the United States.*

16 J. D. Lewis, *Across the Atlantic*, ix.

17 Lady E. C. E. M. Stuart-Wortley, *Travels in the United States*, iii.

18 See J. L. Mesick, *The English Traveller in America: 1785-1835.*

mean that all criticism of America ceased—far from it. But there was a greater tendency to be fair, and to award both praise and criticism where due. On the interpretation of these last three words, travellers differed widely. But if the Briton was more reasonable in his criticism of America than he had been in the past, this was not due entirely to an increased knowledge. An ever larger number of travellers came from middle-class backgrounds, and were naturally less hostile to democratic innovations than would be true of the upper classes. The lessening in diplomatic tension between the two countries after 1848 also helped to pare down antagonisms. Nor should it be overlooked that the Revolutions of 1848 had pushed America into second place as the home of disorder and revolutionary demons.

Books on America streamed from the presses at an ever-increasing rate. It almost seemed that no sooner had an Englishman set foot on American soil than he rushed into print. Certainly, Americans came to take this for granted by the 'fifties. No one would believe Thackeray when he insisted that he was not going to write a book on America. For once American skepticism was unjustified; Thackeray kept his word. But his companion, Eyre Crowe, finally succumbed to the temptation, and a half-century later belatedly brought out a volume on the trip.

Granted that there were many excellent reasons for a journey to United States, why should so many visitors rush into publication? Too many of them modestly assured the reader that they had been forced to reveal their private notes and reminiscences to public gaze at the insistence of friends. Some, of course, had " axes to grind." Thomas Brothers, for example, admitted that his principal purpose was to prove that democracy could have " as much oppression, poverty, and wretchedness as any other form of government." [19] D. W. Mitchell was equally frank in revealing that he proposed to

---

[19] Thomas Brothers, *The United States of North America, as They Really Are*, 260.

defend the southern position that had led to the outbreak of the Civil War. Most travellers, however, were less outspoken and more devious. Theatrical manager Bunn tried to coax the reader into a " cozy chat." True to her sex, Lady Stuart-Wortley offered some gossip. Most ingenious of all was the excuse given by the Reverend F. J. Jobson, who averred that if he were to answer personally the innumerable questions asked him about his American trip, he must neglect his ministerial duties.[20] Regardless of the reason put forward by the traveller, the chief motive for publication was financial. A tremendous market existed at the time for books on America, as is evidenced by the fact that Vere Foster's nineteen-page pamphlet sold over a quarter-million copies.[21] As one Irishman was candid enough to admit concerning his American travels, " neither the journey nor the book was undertaken under any philanthropic enterprise." [22]

The attitude of travellers towards each other was amusing. Marryat's frank confession that " all I have yet read by English travellers is absurd," [23] was typical. Each visitor delighted to list the errors of his predecessor, emphasizing by implication his own superiority.[24] Admitting that " a reliable book on the

20 Alfred Bunn, *Old England and New England*, I, xv; Lady E. C. E. M. Stuart-Wortley, *op. cit.*, iii; F. J. Jobson, *America and American Methodism*, viii.

21 Vere Foster, *Work and Wages*. This pamphlet contained information for emigrants on such matters as transportation facilities, exchange, manners and morals, health conditions, and emigrant prospects. It sold for one penny.

22 William Kelly, *A Stroll through the Diggings of California*, 239.

23 Mrs. Florence Marryat, *Life and Letters of Captain Marryat*, I, 26.

24 Travel books on America by Continental authors such as Tocqueville and Bremer were regarded no differently than British accounts, by the English travellers of this period. Tocqueville was cited probably more often than any other Continental writer. In at least one instance, an author (C. A. Murray) admitted that he thought so highly of Tocqueville as to omit the chapter on American political institutions that he, himself, had planned to include, inasmuch as he could not improve upon the latter. However, this was exceptional. Other travellers did not hesitate to criticize Tocqueville, while the vast majority omitted all mention of him.

United States yet remains to be written," [25] one young lady blithely went on to write an account which the reader might assume would fill this need. Grattan, who stated that no one should be considered an oracle on the United States, did not mean to apply the statement to himself. Nor did Harriet Martineau refrain from analyzing American national character after she had very clearly shown the impossibility of doing so adequately.[26]

Travellers' protestations of impartiality were not to be taken too seriously either. It was quite unusual for a visitor to realize that he viewed America " with that amount of prejudice which seems the birthright of every English person." [27] Consciously or unconsciously, each traveller had preconceptions, or a tendency to think along certain lines. In proclaiming that he intended describing American conditions just as they appeared, " whether for good or evil," Buckingham forgot to mention that he did not have an entirely open mind on such subjects as liquor, tobacco, and slavery. Nor did he regard it as important to mention that he had just completed a five-year term in Parliament as a Whig; nor that (as a youthful editor in India) he had staked all on an unsuccessful struggle to expose the tyranny of the East India Company; nor that he had devoted his entire life to the fight for social reform. It was hardly to be expected that George Lewis, a Scotch Presbyterian minister, would view the Irish emigrant in the same light as William Kelly, an Irish Catholic. How could Tremenheere, a Tory poor law inspector, see democratic America with the same eyes as social reformer Harriet Martineau? Could either be absolutely impartial and objective? Chandless and Burton both wrote about Mormonism in Utah. The latter was a world renowned scholar; the former, a teamster. But the futility of accepting an author's own self-estimate was best illustrated by

25 Mrs. I. L. Bishop, *op. cit.*, 321.

26 T. C. Grattan, *Civilized America*, I, v; Harriet Martineau, *op. cit.*, I, iv.

27 Mrs. I. L. Bishop, *op. cit.*, 3.

Captain Marryat. This gentleman confided to his mother that unlike other travellers who had written disparagingly of the Americans, " he, at least, would do them justice." [28] Yet, his work turned out to be the most scathing indictment of the American way of life that was written during the entire quarter century between 1836 and the Civil War.

Actually then, far from being models of impartiality and scientific objectivity, the travel accounts reflected the interests, the biases, the preconceptions, and the viewpoints of their authors. The traveller saw new scenes, but through his old spectacles. As a result, all too often it came about that the Tory found American institutions intolerable; the Whig reported them with sympathy; and the Radical used them as ammunition for attacks upon conditions at home.

28 Mrs. Florence Marryat, *op. cit.*, I, 26.

CHAPTER II

THE FACE OF AMERICA

THE main gateway into the United States at this time was New York. Boston, Baltimore, and New Orleans were also large but secondary ports, while even minor ports such as Natchez received a share of the transatlantic traffic. New York, however, remained paramount and handled not only most of the traffic between England and America, but also that between England and Canada. For navigation on the St. Lawrence was still based upon the charts made by General Wolfe's expedition in 1759, and this made it too dangerous for more expensive ships, especially steamers, to enter the channel.[1] At any one time, New York harbor might contain scores of ships bound for England, dozens for France, many for the Baltic, several for Spain, a few for Africa, numbers for India, China, the Sandwich Islands, and the South Seas. The city side of the East River was covered as far as eye could see with a forest of masts and rigging, as dense and tangled in appearance as a cedar swamp, while the overflow could be seen moored across the river on the Brooklyn shore.[2]

Although there was yet no Statue of Liberty to greet the stranger as his vessel came up the bay, the green shores of Staten Island were a welcome sight after the grueling sea voyage. No sooner had the ship touched dock, than the Customs officials swarmed on board. Quickly but courteously they checked through the baggage. In a very short time the visitor found himself setting foot on American soil. Jumping into a carriage (or a sleigh if there was snow on the ground), he was driven at breakneck speed to his hotel. In the 'thirties and 'forties, the Astor House far up Broadway (now City Hall Plaza) was "the place" at which to stop. Grattan, who had

1 F. C. Bowen, *A Century of Atlantic Travel, 1830-1930*, 63.

2 Alexander Mackay, *The Western World*, I, 78-80.

just left the Belgian Court to accept appointment as British Consul in Boston, called it " a really magnificent hotel." [3] But later the St. Nicholas Hotel was opened and outdid it in splendor.

Accustomed to the small quiet inns of their homeland, the English were distinctly surprised by the great American hotels. A wealthy Englishman declared that the St. Nicholas was more like the palace of an Eastern prince than a hotel. " Every chimneypiece and table slab is of marble, every carpet is of velvet pile; chair covers and curtains are made of silk or satin damask ... the embroidery on the mosquito nettings, itself, might be exhibited to royalty." [4] To live in such opulence cost but $2.50 per day in the North, and $3 per day in New Orleans, where living costs were higher. Nor was the St. Nicholas unique; it had its counterpart in the Tremont House of Boston, the St. Charles in New Orleans, the Mansion House in Philadelphia, and Barum's in Baltimore.

Aside from the richness of the furnishings, these palace hotels provided so many conveniences that Americans, it was said, travelled without even combs or razors. In some New York hotels, travellers were amazed to learn, shirts could be laundered while the guest took his bath. [5] With his every want thus anticipated, travel in America at first seemed to be far easier than the Englishmen had been led to expect.

Hardly had the visitor recovered from his first astonishment, when the peremptory crash of a gong, which Grattan mistook for thunder, summoned the guests to dinner. Instead of the quiet service in the guest's own room that was customary in the better English hotels, the traveller found it necessary to eat in one vast dining salon in common with all the other guests. Furthermore, since there were no reserved places, a mad rush for seats ensued as soon as the dining-room doors

3 T. C. Grattan, *Civilized America*, I, 17-21.

4 W. E. Baxter, *America and the Americans*, 33-34.

5 Mrs. I. L. Bishop, *An Englishwoman in America*, 102.

were opened. Those who could not be accommodated at the first seating, waited till someone arose, and then rushed for his place. Visitors could see no distinctions as to class or occupation in the seating. A general might sit next to a workingman, and neither feel discomfited. Food was plentiful and good. But table manners were not up to English standards. Waiters rushed madly to and fro carrying huge platters of food, which the patrons endeavored to gobble down as quickly as possible. Not a word was spoken at the table. Just as soon as he finished eating, each guest rose precipitately and fled to his work. One British businessman tried to rationalize such conduct on the ground that time was precious to business people who were in town at great expense for only a day or two.[6] But few other visitors could see any justification for bolting down a full course dinner in ten minutes, as frequently happened.

After dinner the visitor went out to see the sights. In 1837, with a population of only 300,000, New York was already " the busiest community that any man could desire to live in. In the streets all (was) hurry and hustle; the very carts, instead of being drawn by horses at a walking pace, (were) often met at a gallop and always at a brisk trot." [7] New York was also a city of contrasts. Buckingham asserted that nowhere else in the world had he seen so many expensively dressed women as daily promenaded on Broadway. " Rich and bright coloured silks, satins . . . ermine-lined coats, and the most expensive furs " were to be seen in profusion on all sides.[8] Yet in that same year Combe found that once away from the bright lights of Broadway, the streets were narrow, dirty, poorly paved, ineffectively policed, unlighted at night, and " adorned with fat swine." [9] Reverend R. H. Collyer, a year previously, had ventured one evening into the Five Points slum area, between

6 J. G. Taylor, *The United States and Cuba*, 37.

7 J. S. Buckingham, *America*, I, 53.

8 *Ibid.*, I, 54.

9 George Combe, *Notes on the United States of North America*, I, 23.

Broadway and the Bowery. He was horrified to find human beings crowded into dens that " would have been spurned by the swine." What he saw there, caused the impressionable clergyman to conclude that New York led the world in vice.

The principal streets at night are filled with courtesans dressed in gay and flaunting dresses, noisy and boisterous in their conduct; the bars abound with them, the oyster shops swarm with them; the theatres are disgraced by them . . . in some streets nearly every house is one for harlots.[10]

Englishmen, who after reading this, expected to find New York a second Gomorrah, were speedily disillusioned upon arrival. For though vice did exist here as elsewhere, it was under cover, and not to be seen by casual visitors.

But there was no denying either the presence of pigs in the streets, or the existence of slums inhabited by free negroes and Irish emigrants. Charles Dickens, whose interest in the conditions of the poor led him to visit the slums, climbed up the rickety stairs to the attic of a dilapidated tenement one evening. Entering the attic, he lit a match.

The match flickers for a moment, and shows great mounds of dusky rags upon the ground. . . . Then the mounds of rags are seen to be astir, and rise slowly up, and the floor is covered with heaps of negro women. . . . They have a charcoal fire within; there is a smell of singeing clothes, or flesh, so close they gather round the brazier; and vapours issue that blind and suffocate. . . . Where dogs would howl to lie, women and men and boys slink off to sleep, forcing the dislodged rats to move away in quest of better lodgings.[11]

Conditions in the Irish quarter, where the filth stood four feet deep in the streets, were no better.

But the average tourist was not interested in slumming, and seldom even heard of Five Points. A carriage ride uptown into the country, a boat trip to Staten Island, a sightseeing tour to

10 R. H. Collyer, *Lights and Shadows of American Life*, 7.

11 Charles Dickens, *American Notes*, 273.

the Passaic Falls in New Jersey, or an excursion to Brooklyn were far more to his taste. Then in the evening there were the theatres, the bars, and above all the brilliantly lighted oyster saloons for which New York was famous.

As time passed and the city grew, many of the conditions that had offended earlier visitors were corrected. Mrs. Maury, in 1845, noted the gradual disappearance of pigs from the streets, adding unwittingly that now the streets were " not quite so dirty as those of Paris." The most striking feature of the town, she felt, was its bright cheerful appearance which provided a welcome change from the soot and dingy walls of Liverpool.[12] This was, of course, true of other American cities as well, except for Pittsburgh which already had a complexion as sable as that of Sheffield.[13] New York was expanding rapidly. Hancock, upon returning in 1854 after a two year absence from the city, was startled to find that the fashionable shops had moved uptown a half mile.[14] Lord Acton thought the site of the Crystal Palace Exhibition of 1853 too far out-of-town (42nd Street). Yet by that year the best residential areas had already been moved up to Fifth Avenue.[15] The growth of the city necessitated better transportation facilities, and led to the introduction of the horse-car. It was the latter, rather than the pigs, that confronted later travellers. Unlike the porker, it received high praise.[16] By 1860, Broadway was declared equal to any street in Europe " in grandeur and richness of appearance." [17]

If after a day of strenuous sightseeing the visitor retired with expectations of a quiet restful night, he was quickly disillusioned. Hardly had he closed his eyes than his slumbers were shattered by the clang of fire bells and the shouts of volun-

12 S. M. Maury, *An Englishwoman in America*, 163-175.

13 Lady E. C. E. M. Stuart-Wortley, *Travels in the United States*, 90.

14 William Hancock, *An Emigrant's Five Years in the Free States of America*, 29.

15 J. E. E. D. Acton, "Lord Acton's American Diaries," *Fortnightly Review*, CX, 732.

16 Walter Thornbury, *Criss-Cross Journeys*, I, 301.

17 Hugo Reid, *Sketches in North America*, 222, 226.

teer firemen tearing through the streets with their apparatus. Fires were extremely frequent in all American cities and particularly in New York. Britons were amazed to learn that two or three fires a night were regarded as quite ordinary. They had only to ascend to the roof of their hotel to see the glow of nearby blazes.[18] Tavern-keeper Brown estimated that fifty per cent of these fires were of incendiary origin. Others agreed that arson alone could explain their frequency. In rural areas, Brown charged, it was customary for quarreling farmers to threaten to burn down each other's barns. In such cases each farmer would sit up nightly for months thereafter to guard his property.[19] In the cities, discontented Irish employees were often accused of arson. Though fires caused little loss of life, property damage was very high. Harriet Martineau witnessed the Great Fire of 1835 which burned down over fifty acres in the heart of New York. It was not so much the blaze that impressed her as the fact that even before the embers had cooled, the merchants were rushing plans for bigger and better shops.[20] This " Go Ahead " spirit typified America.

Fire fighting in America though not especially efficient was very picturesque. In New York, the location of a fire was indicated by a crimson ball or lantern suspended from the cupola of the City Hall. The position of the ball to the cupola indicated the direction of the fire. Mrs. Felton narrates that on one night fires were discovered in three separate locations. The lantern was shifted from one location to another with the result that the firemen raced around in circles till messengers were sent out to direct them.[21] The installation of a telegraphic fire alarm system in Boston in 1854, which Britons regarded as characteristic of American readiness for innovation, was certainly a most necessary improvement.[22] Immediately the alarm was given,

18 S. M. Maury, *op. cit.*, 174.

19 William Brown, *America*, 24.

20 Harriet Martineau, *Society in America*, II, 70-74.

21 Mrs. Felton, *American Life*, 52.

22 C. R. Weld, *A Vacation Tour in the United States and Canada*, 382.

volunteer firemen would rush to the engine houses for their
apparatus and race to the fire. It was established practice for
the first brigade to reach the scene to be in command. This
produced keen competition. The engines were pulled through
the streets by companies of from twenty to one hundred men.
Persons in the way, even stumbling firemen, were ruthlessly
run over. So great was the rush to arrive first, affirmed British
visitors, that firemen ran out dressed only in boots and over-
coats, and finished their wardrobe at the fire. Should two companies arrive at the same time, a bloody battle quite frequently
ensued between them while the flames raged unchecked. After
the fire, or in the event of a false alarm, the firemen adjourned
to a tavern and made a night of it.[23]

However interesting it was to watch the firemen, travellers
soon became as jaded with this sight as with many other
novelties in New York that had first surprised them. The visitor
turned next to the hinterland. Thenceforth, itineraries tended
to take on a rather individual character.

The tremendous growth of the country, and the rapid advances in road, canal, and railroad building were constantly
opening up new routes between 1836 and 1860.[24] Hence, by
the 'fifties, the British traveller had an infinite combination
of routes available to him. In general, as has been pointed
out in the preceding chapter, the traveller endeavored to see
as much of America as his time and purse would permit.
The continual extension of stage, steamer, and rail lines (especially the last) enabled him to see more and more of the
country, till it became almost a commonplace by 1860 to cross
the continent. Similarly, as the speed of travel increased, and
more of the country became easily accessible, travellers tended
to spend less time in any one locality, or for that matter in
all America.[25]

23 Alexander Majoribanks, *Travels in South and North America*, 432-433.

24 See J. L. Mesick, *The English Traveller in America, 1785-1835* for
descriptions of the travel routes during the half-century preceding 1836.

25 See the chapter on The Travellers for further treatment of this problem,
as well as the annotation for each traveller in the bibliography.

Those who had special missions or particular interests, naturally made up their itineraries with this in mind. Burton, who came to investigate Mormonism, did not go to Florida; nor did Amelia Murray, who sought sub-tropical flora, go to Utah. Ruxton did not trap game in Boston; nor did Combe lecture the Apache on phrenology. Lecturers had their tours pretty well laid out for them. Prospective and actual emigrants naturally hastened to those regions which they regarded as most suitable for their purposes. The numerous preachers who came to attend church conventions usually went directly to the cities in which these were held. In addition to these visitors with definite goals and itineraries, there were still a very large number not tied down to any one route or program, but simply interested in seeing America. Furthermore, a great many of those with special programs were sufficiently curious to turn aside and observe what they could. Thus, although Sir G. C. G. F. Berkeley crossed the Atlantic chiefly to hunt buffalo, he recorded his impressions of his journey to and from the Plains. Burton was interested in Mormonism, but he included observations on California. Grattan was a British consul assigned to Boston, yet he frequently visited Washington, and did not hesitate to make sharply critical observations on many aspects of American life. As for the clergymen, once their conferences were over, they endeavored to make as many side-trips as possible. Between them, British travellers by 1860 had covered practically every part of America—from Maine to California, Florida to Oregon, and Texas to Minnesota.

For those who had the time, the interest, and the money, there were three great tours of America. The longest of these, which may be called the Grand Tour, consisted of a circular route commencing in the Northeast and heading south along the seaboard to New Orleans, then north up the Mississippi, and finally east via the Ohio Valley or the Great Lakes. A second and shorter tour included the Northeast and the Midwest only. Visitors following this itinerary went as far south as Washington and then swung westward to the Ohio Valley, following this to the Mississippi. They returned to the East along or on the Great Lakes. The third tour was the shortest of all. It consisted of a circular route around the Northeast from Boston to Washington to Niagara. A variety of routes existed between any two points on any of these tours. Furthermore, a great many side-trips were also available. Thus, Englishmen desiring to go from Washington to New Orleans could either go south along the seaboard as far as Georgia and then west along the Gulf Coast, or else southwest by stage through the interior via the Blue Ridge Mountains, Natural Bridge, and Birmingham, or else directly west over the Alleghanies by stage, canal, or rail to the Ohio and then south through the Mississippi Valley. Finally, some travellers boarded a ship for Havana at Charleston and then continued by ship to New Orleans from Cuba. Similarly in the North, side-trips to Montreal or the Maritime Provinces were frequent. An infinite combination of routes was possible by the 'fifties in touring the Ohio Valley. Yet, in the main, most tourists followed the general plan of one or another of the three tours outlined above.

From New York it was customary to start out with a trip to New England. A fast little steamer took the visitor up Long Island Sound to Norwich, Connecticut, where connection was made with the Boston train. Transit facilities in this part of the country were good. Even in Miss Martineau's day the trip took only twenty hours. The punctilious Maxwell was moved to exclaim that " everything is arranged like clockword; you start to the minute and you arrive exactly at the time named." [26] At Norwich the traveller made his first acquaintance with American railroads. Immediately upon arrival at the station a porter would take over his baggage and issue a small brass check to him. For the remainder of his journey the railroad

26 A. M. Maxwell, *A Run through the United States*, I, 80; Harriet Martineau, *op. cit.*, I, 80.

cared for the baggage, including transfers between trains. To
be relieved of this burden while travelling, and to secure one's
luggage at one's destination simply by handing the check to
the hotel porter, seemed truly an admirable American innovation.

In buying his ticket, however, the Briton was surprised to
learn that there were no first, second, or third class accommodations. Instead, one class travel for all was the fixed rule. The
thought of literally rubbing shoulders for several hours with
any riff-raff that might come aboard, was not particularly pleasant. Even that staunch friend of American democracy, Alexander Mackay, felt that this was carrying the doctrine of
equality too far. Why not just as well have one class steamers
or one class hotels, he demanded.[27] The chief effect of one class
travel, so far as the English could see, other than discomfort
for the genteel, was that " the rich pay less and the poor more
than they ought." [28] Although the practice might be necessary
in the United States, where all pretended to be on a footing of
equality, it was definitely not recommended by travellers for
adoption in Britain.

The trains, too, were unlike those in England. Although the
earliest cars had been little more than stages with flanged
wheels, a definite American-type car, similar to our present
coaches, developed very quickly. Its chief innovation from British practice was the long center aisle with seats placed crosswise
on either side. In the center stood a stove, which glowed red-
hot in winter. Nearby passengers roasted, while those at the
ends of the car froze. Needless to say there was a mad scramble
for seats in the temperate zone, though Britons preferred to
take their chances of freezing on the periphery rather than endure the odors and coal vapors near the stove.

Down the middle aisle tramped the conductor, a personage
very different from his British equivalent. He wore no uniform,

27 Alexander Mackay, *op. cit.*, II, 250-251.
28 Alexander Majoribanks, *op. cit.*, 297.

did no menial work, and so far as visitors could see, was usually engaged either in conversing with the passengers or else in staring at foreign travellers. He was master of the train and bore his office with great dignity. Britons who addressed him as they would an English railroad " guard," soon learned this to their embarrassment. British visitors did not take kindly to him. Baxter went so far as to accuse conductors of overcharging passengers and then fleeing to the West with their ill-gotten gains.[29]

But the visitor soon forgot about the conductor as he noticed the continuous streams of saliva that every male was expectorating on the floor, on the stove, into corners, or at any other likely spot. When the windows were open in warm weather, a constant barrage of spit and tobacco juice was laid down on the surrounding countryside. The effects of rounding a sharp curve were disastrous upon the passengers of the following car. In winter the stove became the chief spittoon, each male endeavoring to hit that target with a louder report than the others. The English gentleman's first horror gave way to petrified rigidity as his neighbors spat over his shoulder or between his legs. Luckily for him, their aim was usually accurate.[30]

Meanwhile the passengers kept up a running fire of conversation. Politics was an eternal subject for discussion. Crop reports came a close second. In New England, especially in winter, the status of the shoe market frequently took priority. For practically every farmer in this area supplemented his income by having his family work at home, under a " putting-out system," making shoes for contractors. All other topics failing, there was always the weather.

All of this was sufficiently novel and interesting to take up the full attention of the visitor. Longer journeys and greater familiarity with American railroads would bring other factors,

29 W. E. Baxter, *op. cit.*, 45.

30 See the chapter on Customs and Character for more detailed treatment of this habit.

such as construction and safety, to his attention. For the moment, however, the lights of Boston appeared all too soon. Happy, but tired, he drove to the Tremont House. American travel was really not so bad after all, it seemed.

Sallying forth into Boston, most visitors thought it a beautiful city. Even the satirical Dickens was moved to remark that " the private dwelling houses are, for the most part, large and elegant; the shops are extremely good; and the public buildings handsome." [31] Its atmosphere was more English and less foreign than that of New York. Though known as the intellectual center of America, its streets were filled with tall, bony Yankees, few of whom looked especially intellectual. Rather, their every move seemed marked by perseverance, activity, determination, and a suspicious taciturnity.[32]

A visit to Bunker Hill and other historical sites was in order, to be followed by attendance at the sermons of Dr. Channing and other well-known clergymen. British lecturers, like Combe and Lyell, found here their most receptive audiences.

But his long sojourn in New York had familiarized the visitor with the salient features of American urban life, so a short stay in Boston soon satisfied his curiosity about that city. The next step in his itinerary was a side-trip to the nearby mill towns.

American industrialism was still in its infancy. Both employer and employee were less than a generation removed from the counting-house and the farm. Accustomed to thinking of industrial towns in terms of dirty, sooty, poverty-stricken Manchester and Sheffield, foreigners were tremendously impressed by the mill towns of New England. Lowell, the principal mill center, seemed a model city—clean, fresh, neat. The mill employees were girls recruited from nearby farms. They remained at their jobs a few years, saved some money for a dowry or to pay off family debts, and then left to marry. The girls worked

31 Charles Dickens, *op. cit.*, 210.

32 D. W. Mitchell, *Ten Years in the United States*, 194.

only twelve hours a day, then attended lectures and classes in
the evening. On the Sabbath they went to church and Sunday
School. British visitors were amazed at their fine clothing, their
healthy complexions, their clean well-ordered workrooms. The
matrons of their boarding houses had to furnish character references and submit to mill supervision. Immorality among the
girls was practically unknown, the slightest trace of suspicion
leading to discharge. The town had many schools and excellent
hospital facilities. Harriet Martineau, though a staunch advocate of social reform, gasped when she saw factory girls going
to work carrying umbrellas.[33] Buckingham, who offered them
cut-rates to his lectures, was totally unprepared for the storm of
protest evoked by his attempt to be considerate. A committee
of girls called to inform him that " they would be put on the
same footing as other ladies, or not attend at all." [34] Dickens
assured his English readers that he was telling only the truth
when he stated that these factory girls had pianos and libraries
in their boarding houses, and savings accounts amounting to
$100,000. They even issued a literary periodical, *The Lowell
Offering,* in their spare time.[35] So long as these conditions prevailed, Lowell was one of the show places of America. Reformers of every stripe flocked there to observe and report home,
with appropriate implications, the wonders of American industrialism. But the flower began fading all too soon. By the 'fifties,
the Irish were replacing the native girls, since they were willing
to work more cheaply. Mill conditions became progressively
worse, until the black van of the employee solicitor moved like
a hearse through those remote poverty-stricken areas where
girls were still willing to sign up. Lowell faded into the background. Slowly but surely it became just another mill town.

After their side-trip to Lowell, most travellers returned to
New York, but some of the hardier ones turned westward over
the Berkshires to Albany, or northward through the White

33 Harriet Martineau, *op. cit.,* I, 12.

34 J. S. Buckingham, *Eastern and Western States,* I, 234.

35 Charles Dickens, *op. cit.,* 249-253.

Mountains to Lake Champlain and Montreal. From New York, a trip to Niagara Falls was almost inevitably the next step on the program.

The most popular method of ascending the Hudson was on the river sloops. These steamers " rushed up " the Hudson at twelve miles per hour. They were luxuriously furnished, and equipped with life-boats, life preservers, and fire pumps.[36] During the 'thirties and 'forties, they provided a pleasing contrast to the ramshackle railroads running towards Albany. Reid, as late as 1860, was convinced that these lines were in cahoots with the hotel owners at transfer points, so regularly did the trains miss connections.[37]

From Albany onward there was a choice between canal, stage, or railroad transport. Canal boat travel was never popular among English visitors. Its slowness was an obvious handicap in a country where a premium was placed upon speed. In the daytime, passengers were forced below deck or else flat on their backs every time the boat passed under one of the innumerable bridges. At night, forty or fifty people were cramped into the small, dirty, foul-smelling cabin. On the first evening he spent on a canal boat, Dickens descended to the cabin to fetch something. " I found suspended on either side of the cabin, three long tiers of hanging book shelves, designed apparently for volumes of small octavo size ... I descried on each shelf a short of microscopic sheet and blankets." [38] These were the sleeping quarters. Small wonder that Dickens decided to stay on deck as long as possible. Hours later, weary from pacing the deck, he finally entered the cabin again. To his horror, it was full of sleepers in every stage, shape, attitude, and variety of slumber. Men were sleeping in the berths, on the chairs, on the floors, on the tables, and particularly round the stove. Finally discovering an empty berth, he undressed, putting his clothing on the

36 George Combe, *op. cit.*, I, 31; Alfred Bunn, *Old England and New England*, 145.

37 Huge Reid, *op. cit.*, 28.

38 Charles Dickens, *op. cit.*, 332.

floor for lack of hangers, and getting both his hands and his clothes full of spit in the process. After long minutes of agony, weariness overpowered him and he slept until the bustle of dressing people awoke him in the morning. Washing facilities for the fifty men consisted of two towels, three small wooden basins, a keg of water with a ladle, a small looking-glass, two pieces of soap, a common comb and brush. The women's quarters were no better, being separated from the men's by a temporary curtain only.[39]

Small wonder that Miss Martineau preferred the stage-coach. No doubt Combe, who took the railroad, must have envied her choice, since his train broke down after a few miles. The passengers alighted and pushed the entire train to a station a third of a mile back. There one horse was obtained which pulled the train on towards Schenectady.[40] Yet, Marryat called this the best and speediest railroad in the United States at that time (1837).[41] Train service improved rapidly, however, until it usurped most of the traffic that had formerly gone to the canals and stage-coaches. After 1848, only the poverty-stricken emigrants still used canal transport, because of its cheapness.

When the traveller finally arrived at Niagara, all the hardships he had endured in getting there seemed inconsequential. Standing at the foot of the rushing torrent, deafened by its thunder, wetted by its spray, the Englishman became " rapt, motionless, speechless, entranced with wonder." [42] The Falls were one of the few things in America that never disappointed the visiting Briton.

From Niagara, several alternate routes were again open. The first was to return to New York; the second was to continue westward via the Great Lakes; the third to descend the St. Lawrence to Montreal and then circle back to New York via

39 *Ibid.*, 315.

40 George Combe, *op. cit.*, II, 313.

41 Capt. Frederick Marryat, *Diary in America*, second series, I, 28.

42 Charles Casey, *Two Years on a Farm of Uncle Sam*, 73.

Lake Champlain. In the 'thirties and early 'forties, the first
and third alternatives were the most popular. Later, as travel
facilities west of the Alleghanies improved, and as the tide of
emigration streamed into the Midwest, it became more customary to continue westward from Niagara on a loop tour of the
Ohio Valley-Great Lakes Region.

Most travellers, however, preferred to see more of the East
before heading westward. These visitors continued southward
from New York to Philadelphia or Washington. Routes were
available to the West and South from both these cities.

Southbound travellers from New York took a steamer down
the harbor to New Brunswick or Amboy, where connections
were made with the Philadelphia train. The ride through the
Jersey meadows was dull, particularly in winter. Sometimes,
however, snowdrifts were piled so high that trains stalled and
passengers spent a day or two in the cars shivering round the
stove, singing to keep up their spirits till help arrived to clear
the track.[43]

After such an experience, Philadelphia seemed very wonderful and welcome. The rectangular pattern of its streets, the
canopy of foliage formed in summer by the trees lining the
streets, the exterior cleanliness of the dwellings, the well-kept
brick buildings with their marble doorsteps, gave it an air of
somewhat monotonous elegance. The splendid buildings of
Girard College, the defunct Bank of the United States, the
waterworks in Fairmount, and the new prison on the outskirts
of town, were all duly visited and commented upon with favor.
The Quaker spirit was no longer outwardly evident, but after
the hurly-burly of New York, Philadelphia's air of historic tradition and settled respectability was decidedly soothing.

From here, unless he turned westward over the famous port-
age canal which crossed the Alleghanies on inclined planes, the
traveller's next major stop was made at Washington. Departing
from the City of Brotherly Love, the railroad cars were drawn
by mules through the streets to the city's outskirts. Here the

43 Alexander Mackay, *op. cit.*, I, 128-131.

locomotive was attached.[44] The train picked up speed (14-18 miles per hour) and rushed southward through villages and past small farms to Baltimore, which had given itself the title, " The Monumental City." Visitors thought this strange, considering the fact that it had only three.[45] But then there were many strange things in this land. Few of them, however, stopped off here for more than a moment. Washington drew them on like a magnet.[46]

Few railroad trips as long as this were without incident. Grattan's train on this very route had run over a horse and buggy containing two women, and had sped on without stopping. Later the conductor casually informed him that one woman had been killed and the other seriously injured. The indifference of the passengers and trainmen shocked Grattan.[47] Other Britons had similar experiences. Bunn, in 1853, noted that there had been forty railroad accidents in the preceding four months, resulting in 12 deaths and injuries to 200 others.[48] Yet nothing was done about it. What was the cause for this terrific toll? Prentice, in 1848, had blamed it on faulty construction. He claimed that the railroads were poorly built, with short and frequent curves, without proper gradients and ballast, and with rails made of strips of iron nailed to horizontal sleepers.[49] Robertson some time later, however, showed statistically that fully fifty per cent of the fatalities were caused by persons being in the path of the trains or else jumping from them.[50] Obviously, therefore, equipment alone was not to blame. Carelessness and indifference were equally responsible. The testimony

44 Alexander Majoribanks, *op. cit.,* 296.

45 Mrs. M. C. J. F. Houstoun, *Hesperos,* I, 217.

46 See the chapter on Democratic Government for the traveller's impressions of Washington.

47 T. C. Grattan, *op. cit.,* I, 161-162.

48 Alfred Bunn, *op. cit.,* 151.

49 Archibald Prentice, *Tour in the United States,* 65.

50 James Robertson, *A. Few Months in America,* 162-163.

of travellers bore this out. Baxter saw mere children in charge of switches at the passing of express trains. One night when his train broke down in a wood with a thousand passengers on board (so he claimed) and another train coming up a few miles behind, the conductor did not even place a signal light on the last car.[51] Weld's cab driver in Cincinnati insisted upon racing a train to a crossing. Weld escaped death by a hair.[52] Practically every Briton admitted his fright the first time his train charged over the shaky trestles or ramshackle piles sunk precariously into some river bed. Yet despite rickety roadbeds and innumerable accidents, trainmen, with the full approval of the passengers, still insisted on racing at the locomotive's maximum speed, upgrade or down. "Go Ahead" rather than the British "All Right" was the password of American railroads. Why were Americans so indifferent to human life? Why was safety sacrificed to speed? The true cause, said the Briton, lay in the fact that money-making was the all-absorbing purpose of American life. The pursuit of Mammon left no time for thought of anything else. Those who were killed could not speak; those who lived were too busy seeking wealth to pause and worry about anything else.[53]

Although American railroad and other travel facilities were dangerous, no British traveller ever appears to have been stopped by that factor. Surprisingly few travellers were actually involved in accidents. This may prove that the number of accidents and fatalities were exaggerated. It is also possible, however, that many of those actually involved in mishaps never lived to tell the tale. In any event, no Briton ever admitted staying out of any part of the United States solely because travel facilities were poor, and especially not from the South, where travel conditions were notoriously primitive.

51 W. E. Baxter, *op. cit.*, 45.

52 C. R. Weld, *op. cit.*, 221.

53 Lady E. C. E. M. Stuart-Wortley, *op. cit.*, 19; Capt. Frederick Marryat, *op. cit.*, second series, I, 91; see also the section on American indifference towards human life in the chapter on Customs and Character.

Grattan declared the South to be " almost a paradise,"[54] but he never went beyond Richmond. Those who did, thought otherwise. They generally agreed with Buckingham's statement that travel conditions in the South were the worst in the entire country.[55] The further south one went, the worse they became.

No sooner was the Mason and Dixon Line crossed than poverty, decay, and retrogression stared the traveller in the face. Unpainted houses, broken windows, sloth, filth, and inertia appeared on every side. The Earl of Carlisle called the South " the Ireland of America." " Everything appears slovenly, ill-arranged, incomplete, windows do not shut, doors do not fasten." [56] " Where slavery sits brooding," added Dickens, " there is an air of ruin and decay abroad, which is inseparable from the system. The barns and outhouses are moldering away; the sheds are patched and roofless; the log cabins are squalid to the last degree . . . Gloom and dejection are upon all." [57]

Arriving at Richmond, travellers were amazed by what they saw. The city presented the appearance " so unusual in America of retrogression and decay." [58] The great Charleston of which they had heard so much, turned out to be equally disappointing to most visitors. It resembled a West Indian port rather than an American city, with its wooden buildings painted white, its large verandahs, and its Venetian blinds. The buzzards scavenging in the streets completed the picture. At night, the streets were unlighted and so full of holes as to be impassable.[59] New Orleans likewise failed to impress Britons. During summer months, malaria, yellow fever, and cholera made it a pesthole. In winter, it was filled with gamblers and desperadoes. After dark the streets were infested with slimy rats the size of young

54 T. C. Grattan, *op. cit.*, II, 180.

55 J. S. Buckingham, *Southern or Slave States*, I, 190.

56 Earl of Carlisle, *Travels in America*, 55.

57 Charles Dickens, *op. cit.*, 318-319.

58 J. R. Godley, *Letters from America*, II, 193.

59 J. S. Buckingham, *op. cit.*, I, 48; F. A. Kemble, *Journal of a Residence on a Georgian Plantation, 1838-1839*, 21.

pigs.[60] Carlisle asserted that the only good thing New Orleans contained, was the St. Charles Hotel.[61] However, the French Quarter with its bars, gambling dens, and octaroon prostitutes provided excellent " copy " for home consumption. No chapter on New Orleans was therefore complete without some attention to these lurid details. Characteristic practices, such as the burial of the dead above ground (owing to inability to dig proper graves in the mucky soil), also proved of interest to visitors.[62]

Travel facilities reflected the undeveloped condition of the South. Harriet Martineau, in 1836, had found only a few miles of local railroads in the entire South. The roadbeds were poor, the boilers leaked, the trains arrived hours late. When her train stalled for the night in a swamp outside of Charleston, she shuddered at the thought of what would have happened if this had occurred during the malaria season. On another short trip, cinders from the locomotive burned thirteen holes in her gown.[63] Travel conditions were scarcely better a generation later. The promise held forth by the extensive railroad construction of the late 'thirties failed to bear fruit. Instead, the South became rapidly outdistanced by the North and Midwest in respect to mileage and equipment. In 1855 Baxter reported that on one occasion in Georgia he had found his train awaiting its passengers " in the midst of a field of Indian corn, no edifice of any sort being in sight." [64] Southern railroad mileage remained inadequate right down to the Civil War, and the lines that did exist, were notoriously poor.

Hence, stage-coaches remained the chief form of transportation in the South, along with the steamers on the great rivers of the Mississippi Valley. American coaches, like railroad cars,

60 Sir E. R. Sullivan, *Rambles and Scrambles in North and South America*, 207.

61 Earl of Carlisle, *op. cit.*, 61-62.

62 Lady E. C. E. M. Stuart-Wortley, *op. cit.*, 126; Sir E. R. Sullivan, *op. cit.*, 206.

63 Harriet Martineau, *op. cit.*, II, 10-11.

64 W. E. Baxter, *op. cit.*, 43.

differed from their English counterparts. Unlike the latter which rested on springs, the American coach was suspended by leather straps from the axles. When roads were bad (and they usually were in the South), the motion of the coach was similar to that of being tossed in a blanket. The coach ordinarily accommodated nine to eleven persons inside, arranged in three parallel rows, plus one or more persons outside with the driver. Ventilation was provided by a window in the door. In summer the dust was choking; in winter the bad air stifling. Worse than the ventilation, however, was the incessant jolting of the carriage. The corduroy roads and bridges of the South twisted every muscle in the body, complained Buckingham.[65] Considering the number of bumps on one's head from hitting the roof of the coach, added Lady Stuart-Wortley, "if there be any truth in phrenology, what changes in character must be wrought during a journey across the Alleghanies."[66] Miss Martineau told how her companions bought some eggs for supper. To prevent them from breaking, each passenger rode for the rest of that day holding an egg in each hand.[67]

When the roads became impassable, coaches left the highway and wound through woods and swamps. Under such conditions, accidents and breakdowns were frequent. The British were always surprised at the good nature with which Americans took these mishaps. Rarely did they report hearing a word of complaint. In the event of breakdowns, mirings, or bridge washouts, the passengers dismounted and the men pitched in to get the coach under way again. Sometimes this took hours. In such cases, travel would continue far into the night over pitch-black roads, the passengers shifting their weight from side to side to prevent the coach from overturning as it struck unseen ruts.

Coach travel was bad, but to stop at a Southern wayside inn for refreshment or rest was even worse. The best of them had no bells, no bed curtains, no basins with jugs, no clothes pegs

65 J. S. Buckingham, *op. cit.*, I, 237.
66 Lady E. C. E. M. Stuart-Wortley, *op. cit.*, 88.
67 Harriet Martineau, *op. cit.*, I, 239.

or mirrors.[68] Marryat had heard of a Mississippi inn where the kitchen floor had been used as a bed for both travellers and the proprietor's family, amounting to seventeen persons in all, both sexes " turning in " together. Though sharply hostile towards America, he had to admit that nothing in his own experience had been quite that bad.[69] But not unusual was Miss Martineau's experience when (after riding all night) her coach stopped at a Kentucky inn for refreshment. The place consisted of two rooms and a hall. Upon requesting water and towels to wash up, they were given one shallow tin dish of water for the entire company. Towels or napkins were not to be had.[70]

If lodgings were bad, food at these inns was even worse. The South so far as the traveller was concerned, was very definitely not the answer to a gourmet's prayer. Buckingham, who was an experienced and sympathetic traveller, and whose long years in the Orient had eliminated any fastidiousness on the subject of food, complained repeatedly about the rusty forks and knives, the rancid butter, and the unappetizing food in Georgia restaurants. As the climate got warmer, sanitation became worse instead of better.[71] Nor was poor food restricted to Georgia, alone. Stopping for a meal along the Cumberland, the passengers of a coach were served a dish which none could identify. " The dish from which I ate was according to some, mutton; to others, pork; my own idea is that it was dog," [72] commented Miss Martineau, a member of the party. If this woman, who could neither taste nor smell, arrived at this opinion, the dish must have been truly awful. Private cooking was undoubtedly better than the food served at the public inns. But few travellers had the opportunity of being invited into the better Southern homes. Those who did, failed to cele-

68 J. S. Buckingham, op. cit., I, 245.

69 Capt. Frederick Marryat, op. cit., second series, I, 105.

70 Harriet Martineau, op. cit., I, 214-215.

71 J. S. Buckingham, op. cit., I, 190, 245.

72 Harriet Martineau, op. cit., I, 192.

brate the excellence of such food sufficiently to overcome popular belief in the wretchedness of Southern cooking.

Following experiences such as these, the traveller was only too glad to board a stately Mississippi steamer and turn northward again. The river boats with their wide decks and spacious superstructures seemed positively luxurious after weeks of stage and rail travel. But this first feeling of relaxation soon gave way to anxiety as the Briton realized that almost everyone on board either carried a life-preserver, or kept one handy. Fires, explosions, and shipwrecks, it appeared, were exceedingly frequent occurrences. Marryat warned that although steamer travel was the most comfortable, yet it was also the most dangerous. Having passed several wrecks in the river, Harriet Martineau, for once, was in agreement with him.[73] Yet her own ship had made ninety-six trips without mishap. Federal laws providing for safety inspection improved the situation but slightly. According to one hostile visitor, no sooner did the inspector come on board than he headed straight for the ship's bar and remained there until sailing time.[74] Competition between the river boats was keen. If one grounded, others steamed past without stopping, while passengers and crews cheered. As in the case of the railroads, the public appeared to accept accidents and wrecks with equanimity. Casey spoke to two survivors of a steamer that had blown up, killing sixty people and scattering wreckage for acres around. The two men had just been fished from the river. Casey asked one of them if he didn't feel thankful for so wonderful an escape. The man replied, " Wall yes! I guess it was a pretty bad fix—won't you pass those mutton chops? " [75] On the steamers, as on the railroads, visitors attributed the high accident rate to carelessness and the desire for speed. Dionysus Lardner, a well-known British authority on rail and steamer transport, was appalled by the high accident rate on the Mississippi steamers. Poor boiler construction was partially to blame, he stated, but the chief cause lay in the premium placed upon speed with in-

73 *Ibid.*, II, 23.
74 Mrs. M. C. J. F. Houstoun, *op. cit.*, II, 27.
75 Charles Casey, *op. cit.*, 310.

difference to human safety. The apathy of Congress towards preventive legislation struck him as "a disgrace to humanity." [76] But as far as Britons could see, Americans appeared perfectly satisfied to risk being blown to smithereens for the sake of getting to their destination a few hours earlier.[77] The Britons themselves always kept an uneasy eye on the boilers. Added to this was the fear of the epidemics that periodically swept through the steamers, and of the quarrelsome, quick-shooting gamblers who infested the salons. As a result the British traveller found little occasion to relax and enjoy the trip.

The chronic sightseers disembarked on the Kentucky shore to take the stage to that newly opened wonder, the Mammoth Cave. It was on this trip that Harriet Martineau was shown an "unshaded meadow where the grass had caught fire every day at 11 o'clock the preceding summer," thus demonstrating the need for shade in this clime.[78] If this widely travelled lady accepted this statement unquestioningly, how many errors did not less critical travellers repeat to their credulous countrymen back home.

Most visitors went ashore at St. Louis. Their feelings about this city changed with time. Buckingham had found it a quiet little place. He thought its site well chosen; its climate healthy and cooler than that of the great seaboard cities.[79] Evidently he had not been there in summer. A few years later Dickens described the place as an unhealthy swamp.[80] As it grew in size, it became dirtier. Baxter, who saw it in the middle 'fifties, avowed that he had lived there for three days under the impression that the streets were unpaved, until a heavy rainstorm washed away the tons of dirt atop the pavements. Its streets could "scarcely claim equality with the foulest towns of South-

76 Dionysus Lardner, *Railroad Economy*, 382-383.

77 See the Chapter on Customs and Character for further data on the apparent disregard for human life in America.

78 Harriet Martineau, *op. cit.*, I, 306.

79 J. S. Buckingham, *Eastern and Western States*, III, 117.

80 Charles Dickens, *op. cit.*, 360.

ern Europe," he affirmed.[81] The city's chief interest to English-men lay in its large Catholic population, dating back to French days and recently added to by German and Irish emigration. Its famous Cathedral and its equally well-known Jesuit College led many a Protestant to fear that it would some day become the Rome of America. During the Gold Rush, of course, St. Louis had a more immediate significance, for it was the starting point for the overland caravans. " California fever met you here at every turn, every corner, every dead well; every post and pillar was labelled with California placards. The shops seemed to contain nothing but articles for California." [82] Advertise-ments and extracts from prospectors' letters filled all the news-papers. Everyone asked, "Are you for California?" It seemed as though the entire city were about to pick itself up bodily and leave for the West.

More than one Englishman was caught up by the fever. Chandless went so far as to take a job as a teamster with a wagon-train bound for Salt Lake. No Englishman who got as far as that Mormon haven was willing to pass it by without at least a short sojourn in a polygamous household, attendance at a service in the Tabernacle, and an introduction to Brigham Young. After departing from Salt Lake City, whose long sym-metrical rows of small houses always reminded foreigners of a vast overgrown village, the caravans continued westward over deserts and mountains to the gold fields of California.

For a mile outside of Sacramento there was a suburb of snow-white tents. At the height of the Rush, fully nine-tenths of the entire town was constructed of canvas. Goods were piled high in the streets, the fear of summary punishment preventing thefts. Town lots, 25x25, were selling for $3,000-$5,000. The visitor was even more amazed to find boardinghouses charging $25 a week for meals, with sleeping quarters provided at a dol-lar a night extra on the hay-covered floor of a large adjoining

81 W. E. Baxter, *op. cit.*, 24-25.

82 William Kelly, *Across the Rocky Mountains from New York to California*, 36.

apartment. Here, the traveller discovered, since all did not go to bed at the same time, "you were subject to having your snoring interrupted by the iron heel of a huge boot on your nose, or the knee of a staggering emigrant . . . in the pit of your stomach; nor was it unusual in the morning to find a congealed tobacco spittle on your cheek." [83] Kelly claimed that one night he had two judges, five ex-governors, three lawyers, three doctors, plus a smattering of blacksmiths, tinkers, and tailors for bedfellows.

But the full madness of the Rush became apparent only when the visitor got to San Francisco. Russians, Swiss, Spaniards, Swedes, French, Italians, Hindus, Turks, Indians, Malays, English, Scots, as well as Americans, thronged the streets. Every incoming ship disgorged newcomers. There was scarcely a country on the face of the globe which did not have a delegate present. Ships, whose crews had deserted, were beached and used as shops and boarding houses. The city was full of saloons and gambling dens, located in the most prominent spots, open twenty-four hours a day, from which the loud crash of music emanated almost constantly. No expense, Kelly found, was spared to get the best musicians. Women were also used to entice the innocent. Kelly attested that he had seen a monte dealer in one of these dens deliberately shoot a young lad honestly scuffling for his stake, and "then with the most perfect sang-froid, call the 'coroner' whom he recognized amongst the bystanders to hold an inquest." [84] It took place on the spot in the presence of the murderer. A volunteer jury of pals returned a verdict of "accidental death" almost before the victim had breathed his last.

If such perfidy revolted the law-abiding Englishman, the arduous work of "the diggings" was not to his taste either.

83 William Kelly, *A Stroll through the Diggings of California*, 47. Kelly's account, though occasionally over-emphasizing the more sensational aspects of California life during the Gold Rush, is a well-written and honest attempt at presenting a fair picture. It is the best account on the subject by a contemporary British traveller.

84 *Ibid.*, 182.

Kelly, on the basis of his own experience, warned his country-men that only those accustomed to strenuous manual labor should try mining; others would be better off at home. If come to California they must, let them stick to their old trades.[85]

Should the Briton decide upon returning home after all, it was customary to go by ship via Panama or Cape Horn. How-ever, regular coach service to the East, over the Plains, was not long in developing. Tallack, who used it all the way from California to Missouri in 1860, left a vivid portrait of the Cali-fornia Overland Express, the longest stage ride in the world.

Most English travellers were less venturesome, however, and were quite content to leave California and the Plains out of their American itinerary. After departing from St. Louis these visitors continued up the Ohio by steamer, or else by stage and rail to Chicago. Transit facilities in the Midwest, especially after 1845, though not as good as in the East, were still superior to those in the South. Unlike the South, everything here was growing and improving with gigantic strides. While Marryat had complained, in 1838, of the difficulty of securing a bed to himself at the overnight stage stops,[86] two decades later sleeping cars were available on the better railroads. These cars accommo-dated seventy passengers on three tiers of padded shelves at an additional charge of only 50c. a night.[87]

Unlike the South where progress crawled, here it appeared to gallop. The Midwest was a boom area during this period. Emigrants from Europe and the East were grabbing up all available farm land. The ever lengthening fingers of the railroad and the steamer were bringing larger and larger areas closer to the markets of the East. Travellers felt that a new empire was being created under their very eyes.

Nowhere did this appear more evident than in Chicago. When Miss Martineau visited the place in 1835, it had only a couple of thousand inhabitants. Troops were still stationed near-by to ward off Indian attacks. The town looked bare and raw,

85 *Ibid.*, 196.

86 Capt. Frederick Marryat, *op. cit.*, second series, I, 105.

87 John Macgregor, *Our Brothers and Cousins*, 128; Hugo Reid, *op. cit.*, 26.

the houses insignificant. Yet she had never seen a busier place. The streets were crowded with land speculators hurrying from one sale to another.

A negro dressed up in scarlet, bearing a scarlet flag, and riding a white horse with housings of scarlet, announced the times of sale. At every street-corner where he stopped, the crowd flocked round him and it seemed as if some prevalent mania infected the whole people. . . . As the gentlemen of our party walked the streets, storekeepers hailed them from their doors with offers of farms and all manner of land plots.[88]

A lawyer in her party made $500 a day for merely drawing up land titles. The Panic of 1837 put a temporary stop to this speculative mania, however, and shortly thereafter Buckingham found it a quiet healthy town of about 4,000 inhabitants, with bright future prospects.[89] His expectations were realized. A decade later the town had grown to 20,000, its waterfront lined with fine villas. In the next five years it grew to almost 100,000. Yet the original blockhouse of Fort Dearborn was still standing in the center of the town. But drainage and sewage disposal, that bane of large American cities, had failed to keep pace with the tremendous growth of the city. Whenever the wind blew from the Lake, the odor was asphyxiating. " Skunks Hole," the Indian equivalent of Chicago, struck travellers as particularly appropriate.[90]

The " booster " spirit, speculation, and faith in rapid growth received but a temporary setback in 1837. Soon it dominated the entire area again. Oliphant, Canadian Superintendent of Indian Affairs, was shown some lots in a prospective city, during his trip through Wisconsin in 1854. Led by the salesman, he wrote, " we commenced cutting our way with bill-hooks through dense forest, which he called Third Avenue, or the fashionable quarter, until we got to the bed of a rivulet, down

88 Harriet Martineau, *op. cit.*, I, 259-260.

89 J. S. Buckingham, *op. cit.*, III, 262-281.

90 L. B. Mackinnon, *Atlantic and Transatlantic Sketches*, I, 180; James Stirling, *Letters from the Slave States*, I; and C. R. Weld, *op. cit.*, 195.

which we turned through tangled underwood (by name West Street) until it lost itself in a bog, which was the principal square, upon the other side of which, covered with almost impenetrable bush, was the site of our lots." [91] Needless to say, Oliphant did not buy. But that night he had cause for meditating about American optimism as he slept on the bare floor of a nearby inn with thirty frontiersmen, carrying pistols and knives in their belts, for bedfellows.

Yet, was this optimism not justified? There were Chicago, Cleveland, Sandusky, and dozens of other flourishing cities which had been only villages a generation ago. Returning to the Midwest in 1854, after an absence of twelve years, the Reverend Henry Caswall could scarcely recognize the places he had known so well during his residence from 1828 to 1842, so great were the changes.[92]

Cincinnati, where Mrs. Trollope had opened her ill-fated Bazaar, furnished another example of this growth. In 1842 Dickens had called it a beautiful, cheerful city full of neat, elegant, private residences.[93] In the next few years it became the Porkopolis of America. Mrs. Houstoun, in the late 'forties, declared that every third person and every third house was in the pork trade. By 1854 at least a half-million hogs were being slaughtered here annually. The streets were so full of loose pigs, scavenging in the dirt, that whenever their number reached 6,000, Weld reported, they were rounded up and disposed of by the city at public auction.[94]

When the traveller wearied of the Midwest, it was a comparatively simple matter to return to the East over one or another of the many available routes via the Great Lakes or the Ohio Valley. After a short rest, the visitor embarked for England to write the inevitable book on his American experiences.

91 Lawrence Oliphant, *Minnesota and the Far West*, 159-160.

92 Henry Caswall, *The Western World Revisited*, 214-219.

93 Charles Dickens, *op. cit.*, 347.

94 Mrs. M. C. J. F. Houstoun, *op. cit.*, I, 284; C. R. Weld, *op. cit.*, 195.

NAZARETH COLLEGE
LIBRARY

CHAPTER III

CUSTOMS AND CHARACTER

MOST prominent of the many impressions of America that Britons took back with them was the aggressive egalitarianism of the people. A tailor had refused to come to Marryat's hotel room to measure him for a coat on the ground that " it wasn't republican." Buckingham had been present at a Buffalo hotel when General Scott had sat down to dinner next to a mechanic, and no one had even looked up. The Reverend F. J. Jobson had been offended by the failure of coachmen to tip their hats when he " tipped " them. Sir Charles Lyell had been startled to learn that two female travelling companions in his coach were servants on vacation. In these and countless other ways, the American spirit of equality was constantly being impressed upon visitors.[1]

Thomson, a weaver seeking employment, called at the home of a Southern mill owner. He was ushered into the parlor amidst the family. Though unable to offer him work, the employer talked to him politely, invited him to visit the plant, and finally gave him a " lift " back to town.[2] Actions such as these convinced the very conservative Mrs. Houstoun that in America " a man is equally civil to the President of the country or to the Irish gentleman who acts as his servant." [3]

Nowhere was this egalitarianism more apparent than in the West. Oliver knew a major who had received and accepted an invitation to a corn-shucking.[4] Another Englishman had sat

1 Capt. Frederick Marryat, *Diary in America*, first series, II, 155; J. S. Buckingham, *Eastern and Western States*, III, 450; F. J. Jobson, *America and American Methodism*, 27; Sir Charles Lyell, *Second Visit to the United States*, I, 93.

2 William Thomson, *A Tradesman's Travels in the United States and Canada*, 18-19.

3 Mrs. M. C. J. F. Houstoun, *Hesperos*, I, 177.

4 William Oliver, *Eight Months in Illinois*, 120.

down to a meal in a Kansas hotel with a backwoodsman at his right, and a man without stockings, covered with rags and dirt, on his left. This, Macregor felt, was carrying equality too far.

In trains, on boats, in the stages, there was but one class travel. In politics, many a son of toil held high office. The mighty and the humble rubbed shoulders periodically at the Presidential levees. All (except the negro) were equal before the law.[5] Travellers could see no distinction between the clothes worn by the various classes. All who had the means bought the best articles. Clerks wore as fine a broadcloth as their employers. Nor could that painstaking reporter, James S. Buckingham, see any perceptible difference between the dress of the wife of a $1,000 a year clerk and the daughter of a $5,000 a year banker.[6]

Such a condition, wherein both the loftiest and the lowliest were placed on the same level of equality, seemed " strange and objectionable " to persons accustomed to the various gradations of European society.[7]

Of course this egalitarianism was not entirely a product of Jeffersonian or Jacksonian philosophy. Foreigners realized that it was made possible by the general well-being of the people. The extremes of wealth and poverty common to the Old World were lacking. Poverty and beggary were unknown except among newly arrived emigrants. Bunn expressed the general sentiment of travellers when he said that the poor would starve or steal, but never beg.[8]

The doctrine of equality had many ramifications, some of which were distinctly annoying to travellers. One of these was the servant problem. Domestics in the past had been recruited from the slaves. This was still true in the South. Hence, to the average American, domestic service had slave connotations to

5 See the chapter on Slavery for the status of the free negro.

6 J. S. Buckingham, *op. cit.*, III, 5-6.

7 *Ibid.*, III, 451.

8 Alfred Bunn, *New England and Old England*, 231.

which he would not lower himself. Few Americans cared to become servants. Those who did, insisted not only on high wages and good treatment, but on many special privileges as well.

In the first place, they were not " servants," but " help "; and they worked for " employers " or " bosses," not " masters." They carried their independent attitude much further. One Englishman had heard of a female servant who refused to permit her mistress to ring for her unless she in turn could ring for madam when she desired " to have speech " with her.[9] In the cities, Britons were informed, it was customary for female help to specify that the mistress share certain housework with them. Cooks, particularly, were independent. Grattan was advised that the slightest deviation from the usual arrangement, which might interfere with her plans for attending a meeting or lecture, might lead the cook to quit her job without notice, even if dinner were half-done and company arriving. His own cook used the kitchen as headquarters for the meetings of the local chapter of an Irish revolutionary society, although he was the British Consul. She must have been a good cook, for he laughed off the incident when he learned of it, instead of discharging her.[10] Britons were shocked to learn that servants would borrow their mistresses' clothing to attend parties. In some instances servants were even permitted to use the best rooms in the house to hold parties of their own.[11]

Visitors were highly amused when they heard of instances where both master and servant belonged to the same militia company, with the latter an officer and the former a private. In one such case the servant became a colonel while the master remained a private. At public functions the former served as chairman, while his master sat at the foot of the table. The fol-

9 T. C. Grattan, *Civilized America*, I, 268.

10 *Ibid.*, I, 265.

11 *Ibid.*, I, 266. Grattan has a good chapter devoted entirely to the servant problem.

lowing morning saw the colonel once more serving his master, the private.[12] All this seemed ridiculous to the Englishman.

Bad as it was in the cities, the servant problem was definitely worse in the rural areas. Travellers heard that in the latter, servants insisted upon absolute equality, even to sitting with the family at the same table. On the farms, the farmer and his help worked together, ate together, and occasionally slept together.[13] Previous travellers had reported their shocked horror at such intimacy, and later visitors were prepared for the worst. But the latter found their fears largely unjustified. Buckingham, for example, came across only one instance of a servant sitting at the same table as the guests. This was a demure little girl of fifteen, at an inn situated in the White Mountains.[14]

The dislike shown by native Americans for domestic service compelled the use of free negroes and Irish emigrants. As early as 1837 the latter were rapidly taking over the domestic service. By the 'fifties they dominated the field, particularly in the great Northern hotels. But in the eyes of British visitors, the cure seemed to be worse than the disease. For the Irish were not only stupid and dirty, but far too prone to take up American ways of independence and equality. To travellers constantly in contact with servants at hotels, inns, and the private homes they visited, the problem loomed large. Many of them had been accustomed to servants at home. A few, such as Major Warburton and Mrs. Trotter, took the warnings of earlier travellers to heart to the extent of bringing their own servants with them. Those who hired American help were driven frantic. Beste, ordinarily a mild person, cursed the Irish as "beggars on horseback," while Mrs. Maury became so be-devilled that she hailed slavery as the best solution for the problem. Oldmixon went so far as to attribute the American tendency to live in

12 George Combe, *Notes on the United States of North America*, I, 143; T. C. Grattan, *op. cit.*, I, 267.

13 Alexander Mackay, *The Western World*, I, 225.

14 J. S. Buckingham, *America*, III, 207; see also Alexander Majoribanks, *Travels in South and North America*, 167.

boardinghouses to the attempt to avoid the plague of the servant problem. Amelia Murray, a scientist who should have known better, reduced the argument to absurdity when she alleged that polygamy among the Mormons was doubtless caused by the nuisance of keeping servants.[15]

Just as Americans refused to lower themselves to work as servants, they likewise refused other menial work. It was left to the free negro, the Irish emigrant, and to a lesser extent the Chinese " coolie " (in California) to be the hewers of wood and the drawers of water. Travellers often wondered who would have built the canals, railroads, and public works if these peoples had not been around.[16]

Alexander Mackay, sympathetic towards practically everything American, insisted that the spirit of equality existed not only in politics and before the law, but also in private social practice.[17] Insofar as this was restricted to servant-master relations, other Britons agreed with him. But that it applied equally to all social relationships, they denied almost unanimously. Americans, they insisted, though aggressively egalitarian in their public relations with each other, were quite the contrary in their personal relations in private life. The theory of equality and of a classless society became a farce when applied to the latter, according to British visitors. Instead, they avowed, a strong aristocratic feeling existed. In some it was pride of learning, in many the pride of riches, and in not a few even pride of family.

One had only to visit Philadelphia to see this. The ladies of Chestnut Street would not speak to those of Arch Street, since the latter's money came from their fathers, while the former's came from their grandfathers. Its society, thought Miss Mar-

---

15 J. R. D. Beste, *The Wabash*, I, 74; S. M. Maury, *An Englishwoman in America*, 193; J. W. Oldmixon, *Transatlantic Wanderings*, 37; A. M. Murray, *Letters from the United States, Cuba and Canada*, 176-177.

16 See the chapter on Emigration for further treatment of the role of emigrant labor.

17 Alexander Mackay, *op. cit.*, I, 198.

tineau, was the most aristocratic in the country.[18] Boston was not far behind, however, and its upper class seemed even more snobbish. While visiting a girls' school, Miss Martineau was informed that the daughters of merchants would not speak to those of grocers, and neither would accept a lottery runner's daughter into their set.[19] Women seemed especially prone to set up and enforce social differentiations. Dr. Collyer avowed that nowhere in the world had he witnessed such a feeling of aristocracy as in this city of bluebloods.[20] Although this statement was as exaggerated as everything else the doctor wrote, it contained some truth insofar as it applied to high society. To Grattan, familiar with the courts of Europe, such pretensions by Americans seemed sheer mockery. He denounced as effrontery any attempt at setting up a pseudo-aristocracy in the Republic.[21] Other Britons, however, were overjoyed at these very pretensions, since they regarded them as proof that the doctrine of democracy was unworkable and contrary to human nature. New York, too, had its high society, composed, it was said, largely of merchants who had made their fortunes in the South. In the late 'forties there was even a regular " Court-Guide " selling for 10c. which contained the names, addresses, businesses, and fortunes of the local aristocracy. Social climbers paid $20-$25 to have their names listed in it, and thus secure an invitation to high society. Some of them may have been disappointed, however, for Mrs. Bishop, who was impressed most highly by New York society, reported that she knew of invitations being refused to millionaires, yet granted to poor men of intellectual distinction.[22]

18 Harriet Martineau, *Society in America*, II, 173; W. E. Baxter, *America and the Americans*, 191, 200; Earl of Carlisle, *Travels in America*, 34.

19 Harriet Martineau, *op. cit.*, II, 172.

20 R. H. Collyer, *Lights and Shadows of American Life*, 27.

21 T. C. Grattan, *op. cit.*, I, 118-119, 202-204.

22 Mrs. I. L. Bishop, *An Englishwoman in America*, 374-375. See also Mrs. M. C. J. F. Houstoun, *op. cit.*, I, 173; W. E. Baxter, *op. cit.*, 92.

But this was most unusual as she, herself, later admitted when she declared that " Mammon is the idol which the people worship." [23] Most travellers agreed with this statement. Harriet Martineau pointed out that wealth, which she characterized as the most important object in American life, was used chiefly to outshine one's neighbors. This resulted in an aristocracy of wealth that was " vulgar in the extreme." [24] Logan added that rich Americans affected airs of superiority and treated their menials with far more haughtiness than would a rich Englishman. In such circumstances, he felt, liberty and equality were mere shibboleths.[25]

But it appeared that not even the money worshippers were able to root the basic respect for rank out of their natures. Though they ridiculed aristocratic titles, Englishmen affirmed, Americans did this merely to cover up their true desires. Actually, they said, no people bent the knee lower at the shrine of hereditary rank. Coats of arms whose flamboyance would put British coats to shame, were widely used. To claim kinship with an ancient and honorable family, Britons stated, was an American's greatest boast.[26] His love of titles, they affirmed, was greater than that of any Englishman. Nor was anyone content until he had obtained some rank. This was inevitable in any democracy, concluded the aristocratic Major Warburton, since the frustration of the basic human desire for some vain symbol of superiority resulted in a wild scramble for titles whenever class institutions were absent. Everyone seemed to be a captain, a colonel, a general, or a judge. Such titles sounded imposing but meant little, visitors warned. Warburton had met a " general," so-called because he was an animal trainer. H. A.

---

23 Mrs. I. L. Bishop, *op. cit.*, 326.

24 Harriet Martineau, *op. cit.*, II, 141, 144, 168.

25 James Logan, *Notes of a Journey through Canada, the United States and the West Indies*, 195.

26 Mrs. M. C. J. F. Houstoun, *Texas and the Gulf of Mexico*, 179; Mrs. M. C. J. F. Houstoun, *Hesperos*, I, 176, 178; C. R. Weld, *A Vacation Tour in the United States and Canada*, 367.

Murray countered with a " judge " who had received the title because he was a wine connoisseur.[27] So profuse were such titles in America that one traveller, normally reliable, professed to believe that in the South all tall men were generals, all stout men judges, and all men of medium proportions captains and colonels.[28]

Family, too, was beginning to mean something in democratic America, though not nearly as much as wealth. Buckingham claimed that the phrase " they are people of no family " conveyed as much odium to an American as to an English ear.[29] But this attitude, he felt, was still largely restricted to the upper circles of Philadelphia and Boston.

In any event American society, at least in its private relations, seemed very clearly to belie the public lip-service paid to equality. It was useless for Alexander Mackay to affirm that the love of titles was not inconsistent with republicanism, but simply a manifestation of the universal love for distinction; that the love of money was not restricted to America; that the fear of the political power of poorer neighbors restrained any aristocratic impulses on the part of the wealthy.[30] It was even more useless for Chambers to assert that in America distinctions of wealth and refinement were merely respected, not worshipped.[31] The great mass of English visitors were convinced that there was a fundamental conflict between the aristocratic pretensions of high society and the public theory of equality.

But to suggest this to Americans was unthinkable, for they were the proudest and most boastful people on earth. They would brook no criticism from foreigners. Visitors complained of being denounced as slanderers for merely writing or repeat-

27 G. D. Warburton, *Hochelega*, II, 224; H. A. Murray, *Lands of the Slave and the Free*, 357.

28 James Robertson, *A Few Months in America*, 107.

29 J. S. Buckingham, *America*, II, 81.

30 Alexander Mackay, *op. cit.*, I, 190, III, 338-339.

31 William Chambers, *Things as They Are in America*, 341.

ing what was openly heard on all sides.[32] In this attitude, America reminded foreign observers of an adolescent boy who felt he was not quite a man, but desired everyone else to think so. An American would hear no disparagement; he would admit no inequality. All classes, said Buckingham, regarded their country as the most free, the most intelligent, and the most powerful nation under the sun. Marryat was amused at the tickled expression on American faces when he praised their country, and the writhing at any disparagements he might make. Britons assumed that this was due to the fact that the American had been educated to despise all other countries as slaves to despots, while his own alone was free.[33] One American had actually told Marryat that "in a short time England would only be known as having been the mother of America."[34] Utterly ridiculous! If Americans were so anxious to whip the whole world, he demanded, why hadn't they been brave enough to come out from behind those cotton bales at New Orleans and fight in the open?[35] A Yankee had assured Mitchell with firm conviction that history did not record bigger battles than the assault on Chapultepec, nor mightier campaigns than that which had conquered Mexico.[36] No European worried half so much about his country's fame as did the American, thought the traveller. Each American spoke as if he had a personal stake in his country's fortune. Small wonder, then, that the standard phrase of every American was, "We are a great people." His country was the greatest in the world, his countrymen the most gifted, his government the best, his laws the purest, his institu-

32 J. S. Buckingham, *Eastern and Western States*, I, 452; Alexander Mackay, *op. cit.*, III, 321.

33 Sir E. R. Sullivan, *Rambles and Scrambles in North and South America,* 182; Alfred Bunn, *op. cit.*, 13; J. S. Buckingham, *op. cit.*, I, 456; Capt. Frederick Marryat, *op. cit.*, second series, II, 80-82.

34 Capt. Frederick Marryat, *op. cit.*, second series, II, 89.

35 *Ibid.*, second series, II, 95-103.

36 D. W. Mitchell, *op. cit.*, 53.

tions the wisest, his shipping the finest. In fact, snickered one Briton, everything about America was beyond compare.[37] Few travellers could rise above such sarcasm. One of those who did was C. A. Murray, master of Queen Victoria's household. He was tolerant enough to grant that American vanity and pride were no worse than British. " If I were an American," he added, " I confess I should be proud of my country—proud of its commercial enterprises—of its gigantic resources, of its magnificent rivers and forests and scenery—still more proud should I be of its widely diffused education and independence." [38] Such tolerance, however, especially from a member of the British court, was quite unusual.

Americans were undoubtedly filled with pride in their own ways, yet they betrayed a remarkable curiosity concerning the foreigner. Dickens complained that people kept sticking their heads into his railroad car to stare at him. Privacy was denied him even in his hotel room because small boys shinned up the rain-pipe and spent hours staring at him. He had never been conversant with the American tendency to " lionize " celebrities, and hence could not understand the cause for such annoya Buckingham had better grounds for complaint when fellow passengers on a Southern river steamer kept interrupting his writing in order to go through his papers or borrow his books without permission. Only by locking himself into his narrow bedroom, could he avoid this nuisance. Evidently, bowie knives, pistols, and dice were more familiar sights aboard these ships than a pen. Other travellers had their complaints also. It appeared as if the asking of all sorts of impertinent questions was practically a national trait. No offense was intended; mere curiosity was to blame. To conceal something was considered a sign of aristocratic exclusiveness.[39] One Englishman, Gladstone, who had lived among the frontiersmen, explained this attitude

37 Alfred Bunn, *op. cit.*, 301-302.

38 C. A. Murray, *Travels in North America, 1834-1836*, II, 220.

39 Charles Dickens, *American Notes*, 299; J. S. Buckingham, *Southern or Slave States*, I, 469; G. D. Warburton, *op. cit.*, II, 225.

on the ground that the Westerner was ready to offer anyone the use of anything he had, and felt the same way about the property of others. Though annoying to most visitors, a few of them conceded that the fault was not entirely one-sided. Americans, they maintained, were no more curious, prying, or impertinent than the foreign traveller who was constantly sticking his nose into all sorts of places and asking questions. Rubberneck tourists were certainly in no position to complain about the inquisitiveness of others.[40]

If American inquisitiveness was annoying, the widespread use of chewing tobacco was positively disgusting. It was undoubtedly the most revolting custom to be encountered in America. Wherever the visitor turned, this practice forced itself upon his attention. Inasmuch as most men chewed at all times and in all places, it seemed to most visitors as if all America was covered with a carpet of spit. House floors, costly rugs, public conveyances, grates, streets, and shop floors were covered with expectorations. Men spit even in theatres, in Congress, and at meals. However, the accuracy with which spitters hit their targets could not but evoke admiration.[41] In the very courts, Dickens complained, " the judge has his spittoon, the crier his, the witness his, and the prisoner his." [42] Of course, the jury and the spectators were similarly provided. He avowed that Americans even spit in their sleep. All night long in the canal boat cabins " there was a perfect storm and tempest of spitting, once my coat being in the very centre of a hurricane sustained by five gentlemen." [43] Grattan found words inadequate to express his loathing for the practice. How could any woman kiss a man who chewed tobacco, he wondered. Buckingham denounced the vested interests that supported the custom, but hoped that the

40 T. H. Gladstone, *An Englishman in Kansas*, 109; J. G. Taylor, *The United States and Cuba*, 32; S. M. Maury, *op. cit.*, 213.

41 Alfred Bunn, *op. cit.*, 267.

42 Charles Dickens, *op. cit.*, 297.

43 *Ibid.*, 333.

upper classes would lead the masses away from it. Lyell found such a trend already under way in the South. He submitted the fact that tobacco chewing was no longer tolerated in Southern drawing rooms. But apparently the Southern gentleman had no restraints elsewhere as regards this vile habit, for while sailing up Lake Champlain, the eminent geologist observed a Southerner strolling 'round the deck, followed by a boy with a swab who cleaned up the trail of spit that the latter left behind him. Other passengers were amused, and the Southern gentleman highly indignant when he realized what was happening.[44] Most Britons took a pessimistic view of the situation, however, and agreed with Grattan that it was impossible to change or eradicate so deeply engrained a habit.

Americans were also accused of drinking to excess. Bars were the universal meeting places. Nothing could be done without a drink. " If you meet, you drink; if you part, you drink; if you close a bargain, you drink." [45] Drams of liquor were swallowed by half the stage passengers at every stop. In the West, Marryat stated, the greeting was, " Stranger will you drink or fight?" Despite great difficulty in refusing these invitations without incurring the consequences, he found it necessary to do so in order to avoid being perpetually drunk.[46] Southerners were even more addicted to liquor. The fame of the mint julep and other American drinks was fast spreading overseas. Many a traveller included the recipe of the latest " sling " in his travel account. The quality of American liquor drew no complaints. Furthermore, it was said, America was a drinking but not a drunken nation. Except among the Irish emigrants, drunks were rarely seen by travellers. An ardent temperance man, the Reverend Jabez Burns, reported that he had seen not a single drunk in Boston, Philadelphia, or Albany, and only

44 T. C. Grattan, *op. cit.*, I, 67; J. S. Buckingham, *America*, I, 466; Sir Charles Lyell, *Second Visit to the United States*, II, 358.

45 Capt. Frederick Marryat, *op. cit.*, second series, I, 124.

46 *Ibid.*, second series, I, 126; see also G. D. Warburton, *op. cit.*, II, 275.

two in New York. In Vermont and New Hampshire, he added, one could travel for days without seeing a drunk.[47] Other temperance-minded visitors agreed with him.[48] Yet the opportunity for drunkenness was ever present, and the vast quantities of liquor which Americans imbibed, awed the traveller. Furthermore, although few natives succumbed to drink, this could not be said of the emigrants. Buckingham, a temperance advocate, estimated the average life span of Irishmen in the South at three years, because of excessive drinking.[49] This, of course, was an absurd exaggeration. But the " drunken Irishman " was a by-word throughout America. The Reverend Robert Everest, who disliked Catholics intensely, estimated that in New York City alone, in 1855, there were 7,130 liquor shops, 2,327 of which were owned by the Irish. Prejudice may have misled the clergyman, but the following year a more sympathetic observer placed the number at double this figure.[50] Even if these statistics were only rough approximations, yet for a city with a population of less than 600,000, they seemed inordinately high. Practically every grocery sold liquor. Drunken election bouts were common. In Irish work-camps throughout the country, payday was inevitably followed by drunken sprees. German emigrants, though more temperate than the Irish, were heavy drinkers. Sir Charles Lyell told of seeing a German emigrant in Alabama drunk for two whole days. At the end of that time he was lost in the woods, and his womenfolk were scouring the thickets for him.[51] Instances of this kind led visitors to warn prospective emigrants not to set out for the New World unless they were absolutely sober.[52] Such instances also furnished fuel for the temperance movement which had gotten under

47 Jabez Burns, *Notes of a Tour in the United States and Canada*, 172-173.

48 Joseph Sturge, *Visit to the United States*, 214.

49 J. S. Buckingham, *Southern or Slave States*, I, 169.

50 Robert Everest, *Journey through the United States and Canada*, 150; D. W. Mitchell, *op. cit.*, 144.

51 Sir Charles Lyell, *op. cit.*, II, 67.

52 See the chapter on Emigration.

way in the 'thirties. Always strongest in New England, the temperance movement effected the passage of the " fifteen gallon law " in Massachusetts in 1838. This law prohibited the sale of hard liquor in taverns for beverage purposes. Although the act aroused great opposition and was finally repealed in 1840, other states passed similar " gallon " laws. Finally, in 1851, Maine adopted a Prohibition Law forbidding the manufacture and sole of intoxicating beverages. By 1855, thirteen states in the North and West had prohibited the unrestricted sale of alcoholic stimulants. Englishmen were particularly interested in this attempt at compelling temperance through state action. Inquiry convinced them that the prohibition acts had been passed by minority pressure, and were not supported by public opinion. They discovered that the typical male attitude was reflected in the tale of the fellow who when asked to join a temperance society replied that water was " very good for navigation." [53] Evasion of the law was therefore inevitable. The first American " speakeasy," as described by British travellers, consisted of a booth advertising a marvelous striped pig. Admission was equivalent to the price of a glass of rum. Having paid the fee, the alleged spectator entered the booth, and found therein a clay pig with painted stripes. A glass of rum stood on the counter, to which the spectator, of course, was free to help himself. Combe, though a temperance advocate, admired the ingenuity of the scheme.[54] This and other methods of evasion led travellers to denounce the laws as ineffectual and hypocritical. The rich man could still secure liquor, they charged, while the poor man was hard hit. The sole result, as far as they could see, was that there was much more drinking being done one the sly.[55]

---

[53] Capt. Frederick Marryat, *op. cit.*, second series, I, 125.

[54] George Combe, *op. cit.*, I, 87.

[55] A. M. Murray, *Letters from the United States, Cuba and Canada*, 151; Alfred Bunn, *op. cit.*, 44; J. E. E. D. Acton, "Lord Acton's American Diaries," *Fortnightly Review*, CX, 735.

Another characteristic of America was the apparent tendency towards lawlessness. The first newspaper the visitor picked up on his arrival gave him a shock. Column after column, page after page, was devoted to sordid crimes of violence. Murders, shootings, knifings, duels, and even occasional lynchings were featured in every issue of the press. The latter, never very sedate according to British standards, was in its most sensational period at this time. Travellers failed to realize this. They assumed, instead, that it provided a true portrait of American life. Men who should have known better, like Buckingham, reprinted page after page of newspaper excerpts in their travel books.

But it was not alone on the basis of newspaper stories that visitors concluded Americans to be a lawless people. Stirling contrasted the British respect for law as embodying the best elements in British civilization, with the American tendency to regard it as an instrument of a meddling despotic executive.[56] Nowhere was there a well-organized police force; nowhere did they appear to be respected. The chief occupation of New York's policemen, badges dangling from frayed buttonholes, appeared to be the handing of ladies over the crossings on Broadway. No policeman would wear a uniform. That was livery, fit only for slaves.

Laws were plentiful, but were not enforced. Stirling was present in New Orleans during the Know-Nothing riots of 1854, when the Attorney General reported that there was a general sense of insecurity in the community, but that the populace was convinced that to lodge a complaint would lead to assassination.[57] Murder and assassination were daily occurrences in "Bleeding Kansas," also. Here, too, Gladstone alleged, whoever dared report a case to the authorities would probably be dead by evening. He had known of a Leavenworth attorney who had protested the validity of a local election to the Governor. The attorney, thereupon, was " notified " to leave the ter-

56 James Stirling, *Letters from the Slave States*, 145-147.

57 *Ibid.*, 141.

ritory. Upon his refusal, he was kidnapped by border ruffians, carried into Missouri, and there tarred, feathered, and sold at a mock auction presided over by a negro. Not only was no punishment meted out to the culprits, but a week later the community adopted a resolution commending them.[58]

The very first object of Americans after a law had been passed, said the Briton, was to find a way of evading it. The failure of safety legislation on the river steamers was cited as an example of this. The terrific toll of steamboat accidents had led to the passage of federal inspection regulations. The penalty for navigation without a Certificate of Inspection was $500. Despite the fact that it was to the passengers' own advantage to see that the law was enforced, they cooperated in its evasion. Marryat witnessed one instance in which the passengers raised $250 by a collection, and turned it over to the captain. The latter then informed on himself, and received back his own half of the $500 as the informer. The ship sailed without papers.[59]

Dueling, of course, constituted a still more spectacular disregard for law. To Marryat, " dueling always has been and always will be, one of the evils of democracy." [60] Others, however, usually blamed it upon the survival of frontier traditions or the headstrongness associated with slavery. The bloodthirstiness revealed in American dueling appalled the Briton. An eyewitness told Lady Stuart-Wortley of a duel in a Kentucky market place. One man had a pistol, the other a sixshooter. The first shots went wild, whereupon the latter fellow emptied his remaining five bullets into his opponent. Everyone just stood around and watched.[61] Fanny Kemble told of another duel, this time between two neighboring planters over a piece of land. Notice appeared in the local newspaper to the effect that the winner would have the privilege of cutting off his oppo-

58 T. H. Gladstone, op. cit., 69, 99-100.

59 Capt. Frederick Marryat, op. cit., first series, III, 195-196.

60 Ibid., first series, II, 16.

61 Lady E. C. E. M. Stuart-Wortley, Travels in the United States, 104.

nent's head and sticking it on a pole in the center of the disputed land. She neglected to mention whether the threat was carried out.[62]

Southern feuds, usually confused with dueling by travellers, also seemed to illustrate this bloodthirstiness. A lady in Montgomery informed Miss Martineau that not a day passed without shootings. That very afternoon a lawyer with whom Miss Martineau was chatting, was called to take the deposition of a man dying from gunshot wounds inflicted by three men, hiding behind trees, while he sat eating lunch with his family.[63]

Although the rough free-for-alls, with the gouging and strangling that had adorned travellers' tales earlier in the century, were no longer in evidence, the savagery of personal quarrels was still noteworthy. While Buckingham was in Louisville, a fight broke out with bowie knives between three natives and three Mississippians, including a judge. Two of the former were killed, leaving one with his bowels protruding from his body on the barroom floor, and the other weltering in his own blood from wounds in the back inflicted by the hand of the judge. The latter defended himself in court on the ground that he had the right to wipe out an insult with death. Small wonder that Buckingham after this experience warned that "no one can approach the frontier settlements . . . without being struck with the lawless spirit . . . everywhere manifested by the inhabitants." [64] But visitors could see similar occurrences in the civilized East, as well, though with less frequency. Weld saw a Southern doctor kill a man with a sword-cane at the bar of the ultra-fashionable St. Nicholas Hotel in New York. He received only a four-year sentence. The judge's comment was startling: "Killing is excusable when committed, first by accident and misfortune; second, in the heat of passion; third, upon a sud-

62 F. A. Kemble, *Journal of a Residence on a Georgian Plantation, 1838-1839*, 250.

63 Harriet Martineau, *op. cit.*, I, 229.

64 J. S. Buckingham, *Eastern and Western States*, III, 194, also 31-32.

den combat; fourth, without any undue advantage being taken; fifth, without any dangerous weapon being used; sixth, not done in a cruel and unusual manner." [65]

More potent than individual crimes in demonstrating the general lawlessness, were the cases of mob violence. In the North, mob action during the 'thirties and 'forties was directed chiefly against the abolitionists. Harriet Martineau saw a mob stone Garrison. Next day an eminent lawyer told her: " There was no mob, I was there myself and saw they were all gentlemen." [66] Such incidents convinced her and other English abolitionists that in America mobocracy was a weapon of the upper class against the lower—the reverse of the European situation. A quarter-century later another British traveller, Reid, denounced the abolitionist mob that had freed a Mr. Sanborn who had been arrested for refusing to testify against John Brown.[67] The tables had turned, but mob rule seemed still triumphant.

Nowhere was it stronger than in the frontier areas. In these regions, however, Englishmen were prone to regard it as justifiable on the ground that it was the only means available for suppressing lawless elements. They pointed to the case of Vicksburg, infamous as the den of gamblers and desperadoes until the citizenry, goaded to desperation, hanged the leaders and drove out the small fry.[68] Other examples were also cited of justice enforced by the mob. In Natchez, a young husband had flogged his wife to death. Inasmuch as only negroes had seen the act, and these could not testify against a white man, the husband was freed. Thereupon he was " seized, tarred and feathered, scalped, and turned adrift in a canoe without paddles." [69] The lynching of negroes was rare, though widely

65 C. R. Weld, *op. cit.*, 360.

66 Harriet Martineau, *op. cit.*, I, 129.

67 Hugo Reid, *Sketches in North America*, 56-58.

68 William Thomson, *op. cit.*, 157.

69 Capt. Frederick Marryat, *op. cit.*, first series, III, 237-238.

publicized by the abolitionists. In St. Louis, a free negro had been burned to death by a mob over a slow fire. Miss Martineau was horrified, but Marryat defended it on the ground that the negro was of bad repute, had killed one man, and attempted to murder two others.[70] Mob rule was not always restricted to individuals or even movements. Thomson watched a Cincinnati mob level a number of shin-plaster banks that could not meet payment on their notes. The first bank was protected by a squad of soldiers who fired on the mob. This only infuriated the mob the more. The troops were swept aside, and the bank torn to the ground. Four other institutions of the same type were razed in rapid succcession, but sound banks were left unmolested. Once opposition was overcome, the mob worked efficiently but in good humor. In the evening, everyone, even children, raced through the streets scattering bundles of paper money. Like other Britons, Thomson had had sad experiences with American paper money. As a result, he enjoyed the spectacle immensely.[71] Evidently, mob violence estranged visitors only when its object displeased them.

Non-violent crimes were widespread enough to attract attention, also. Although Grattan doubted if the same temptation for petty crimes existed as in Europe, many travellers complained of being cheated with worthless or counterfeit paper money.[72] Sharp business practices were admired by Americans, they noted. It was " slick " to outdo the other fellow. Oliver mentioned the fact that in the Midwest the expression for having been cheated was " yankeed." Similarly, any worthless thing which was tinselled or varnished, was said to have been " yankeed over." [73] The Mormons theoretically did not tolerate thievery, but Chandless heard Brigham Young complain publicly at church services about the theft of clothing from his

70 *Ibid.*, first series, III, 238-240.

71 William Thomson, *op. cit.*, 163-168.

72 James Stirling, *op. cit.*, 365; C. R. Weld, *op. cit.*, 217; Alfred Bunn, *op. cit.*, 281-282.

73 William Oliver, *op. cit.*, 68.

closets by people who came to see him at his home.[74] Majoribanks cited the report of the Boston Night Watch for 1850 as proof of the prevalence of petty crime. The Watch had arrested 3,355 persons in the previous quarter alone, including such offenses as street-walking (73), larceny (88), and fornication (18).[75] He neglected to point out, however, that the great majority of the offenders were Irish emigrants who were notorious for disorderliness and criminality in both Old World and New. The extraordinary number of fires in the cities was attributed largely to arson, sometimes for the insurance money, sometimes to destroy records of obligations, and sometimes for plain looting. Buckingham was present at a fire that burned sixty houses in the dead of winter. The origin of the blaze was subsequently traced to looters.[76] Such occurrences caused misgivings, but it took the mass bankruptcies and debt repudiations accompanying panics, such as that of 1837, to cause Britons to declare that in no country of Europe were there " so many fraudulent transactions, so many unprincipled extortionists, so many unfulfilled contracts and money obligations " as in the United States.[77]

What were the causes for this widespread lawlessness and crime? Abolitionist sympathizers blamed the evil influence of slavery. In the South, it bred headstrongness, lack of restraint, and disregard for human rights; in the North, it incited violence between factions.[78] Temperance advocates, like Buckingham, blamed drink. Conservatives regarded lawlessness as " the pestilent symptom of the gangrene of ultrademocracy," and the natural fruit of mob rule.[79] They were happy to point out that

74 William Chandless, *A Visit to Salt Lake*, 187-188, 197, 206.

75 Alexander Majoribanks, *op. cit.*, 202.

76 J. S. Buckingham, *America*, I, 165.

77 J. S. Buckingham, *Eastern and Western States*, III, 28.

78 Joseph Sturge, *op. cit.*, 215; Harriet Martineau, *op. cit.*, I, 122; T. H. Gladstone, *op. cit.*, 100.

79 James Stirling, *op. cit.*, 144.

Baltimore, a leading city in this land of Golden Opportunity, had forty-six per cent more crime than London, judging by arrests alone.[80] How could there be respect for law when everyone in authority was looked upon with suspicion? The tradition of lawlessness went back to colonial times, they stated, as demonstrated by the Revolution. It had been nourished and kept alive by the independence and self-sufficiency generated by the frontier. It was a permanent rather than a temporary feature of American life.[81] Furthermore, how could there be respect for law when judges were underpaid, and dependent upon the populace for their election? When lawyers in New York made $3,000-$5,000 a year, what type of person could be secured for a judiciary which paid only $1,600-$3,000? In the South, a similar situation existed. Judges in Mobile received $2,500-$3,000 while good lawyers made as high as $14,000. So low had the judiciary fallen that a Mississippi judge had been known to wander from tavern to tavern soliciting votes for reelection.[82] The robes and other insignia of office which gave dignity to English justice were discarded as too aristocratic. Instead, " the judge on his bench sits half asleep, with his hat on, and his coat and shoes off; his heels kicking upon the railing or table which is as high or higher than his head; his toes peeping through a pair of old worsted stockings, and with a huge quid of tobacco in his cheek." [83] Was this the majesty of the law? Although such scenes were prevalent only in the West, justice was no better, they said, in the more civilized East. Wealth, influence, and bribery procured acquittals even more easily than in aristocratic England. Punishment, visitors charged, seldom overtook the rich.[84] There was the case of the Southern boy sent

80 H. A Murray, *op. cit.*, 367.

81 Hugo Reid, *op. cit.*, 55, 65, 68.

82 J. S. Buckingham, *America*, I, 186; Sir Charles Lyell, *op. cit.*, II, 88, 213.

83 Capt. Frederick Marryat, *op. cit.*, first series, III, 197-198.

84 W. E. Baxter, *op. cit.*, 100.

to a Connecticut academy, who killed an old man sitting on the school steps, for not immediately obeying his order to get up. The family of the boy, it was said, packed the jury, with the result that he received only a six-month sentence for a murder in cold blood.[85] To such charges the few defenders of the popular election of judges could only reply that in general the system must work well or the people would not reelect the same judges year after year.[86]

Tied up with the problem of lawlessness was the general disregard for human life that Britons had so frequently encountered in their American travels. It was revealed in dueling, in the ever-ready bowie knife, in the itching trigger finger, in the Southern blood feuds. It was reflected in the nonchalance with which murders were reported in the press, in the evasion of safety laws on steamers, and in the rickety construction of railroads. If these things did not impress visitors sufficiently, personal incidents of a more gruesome character were not lacking. There was the case of the stableman who found a severed hand grasping a horsebrush, not far from Thomson's home in Cincinnati. Thomson saw the hand himself. It was evident that a murder had recently been committed in the stable. Yet no one except himself appeared in the least concerned. No investigation was made, and not even the newspapers mentioned the incident.[87] Buckingham had a still more shaking experience. At Louisville he saw a well-dressed man fall from an overcrowded steamer, struggle in the water for almost ten minutes, and finally drown. Absolutely no attempt was made by anyone to save him. Was it to be wondered that Buckingham concluded that the loss of a life did not excite as much attention in America as did the death of a dog in England.[88]

85 James Logan, *op. cit.*, 189-190.

86 George Combe, *op. cit.*, III, 113; J. F. W. Johnston, *Notes on North America*, I, 151. See also the section on the judiciary in the chapter on Democratic Government.

87 William Thomson, *op. cit.*, 151-152.

88 J. S. Buckingham, *Eastern and Western States*, III, 39.

Indifference to the loss of human life was ascribed even to the American woman [89] — of whom the average Briton was quite fond. If not already familiar with the fact, British visitors soon learned that they would encounter American women, ordinarily completely unchaperoned, almost everywhere in their travels. Women were absolutely safe from molestation wherever they went, be it to the corner grocery or across the continent. Mrs. Bishop, then a girl of twenty-three, travelled over 7,000 miles through America, most of it alone. Yet never did she experience any discourtesy. She could not help but contrast this with the impossibility of a woman travelling alone in second or third class trains in England.[90]

Women were able to go everywhere in safety because American men assumed an attitude of quixotic chivalry. A woman entering a railroad car with a young man had merely to point out the seat she desired, and her escort would calmly request its occupant to vacate it for the lady. Should the woman be alone, the nearest male would spring to his feet, and offer his place. Sometimes the English gentleman was not quite so chivalrous himself. Mayne, an organist from India, endeavored to assist a woman boarding a New York omnibus by getting up and paying her fare. When he turned back to his seat, he found her calmly occupying it. Considering the position of women in India, it is small wonder that he was half-amazed, half-amused by the " cool impudence " of American women.[91]

Englishmen were fascinated by the attention accorded the American girl. But Englishwomen were more critical. That prim old maid, Miss Martineau, thought the chivalry overdone. Many women, she declared, were selfish enough to take advantage of it. Tl ᶜ was particularly true in the South. Once, in Virginia, five men had ridden on the top of a coach, at the risk of life and limb, so that a young girl could stretch out her feet

89 Capt. Frederick Marryat, *op. cit.*, second series, II, 17.

90 Mrs. I. L. Bishop, *op. cit.*, 94.

91 J. T. Mayne, *Short Notes of Tours in America and India*, 78.

on the seats inside. Miss Martineau wondered angrily why the girl did not hire a separate coach if she could not travel like other people. The travelling manners of women, she thought, were anything but amiable. They acted like spoiled children, either screaming and trembling at danger, or else accepting the best of everything with cool selfishness and never a word of thanks.[92]

If Miss Martineau had been a male, she would probably have forgiven all these faults. For travellers were unanimous in declaring that the American girl was beautiful to behold. " In the classic chasteness and delicacy of the features and the smallness and exquisite symmetry of the extremities," she was seldom equalled, and never surpassed.[93] Though she might fall short of the Englishwomen in regularity of teeth, brilliance of color and complexion, in the development of the bust and figure, yet her delicate languid beauty was most enchanting. Alas, visitors lamented, she blossomed and faded all too soon. While an Englishwoman did not reach her prime until close to thirty-five, American girls, it was alleged, were apt to look faded and haggard at twenty, while one of twenty-five was definitely passé. But so long as they were young, they were very beautiful. Even Englishwomen admitted this.[94]

A minor battle raged among Englishmen as to the city that had the most beautiful women. Baltimore held first place. Many Britons agreed with Buckingham that " few if any cities in Europe could produce so many handsome women." [95] But Marryat chose Cincinnati, and others preferred the Creole women of New Orleans.[96]

92 Harriet Martineau, *op. cit.*, 214-216.

93 Alexander Mackay, *op. cit.*, I, 227-228.

94 J. M. Phillippo, *The United States and Cuba*, 408; Mrs. I. L. Bishop, *op. cit.*, 362; W. E. Baxter, *op. cit.*, II, 59; S. M. Maury, *op. cit.*, 208-209; C. A. Murray, *op. cit.*, II, 214.

95 J. S. Buckingham, *America*, I, 456.

96 Capt. Frederick Marryat, *op. cit.*, second series, II, 31.

One characteristic of American women caused much comment among travellers. This was their delicacy and poor health. Some visitors attributed this to the dry heat of American homes, which enervated the constitution; others to the thin fluffy clothing so popular among American women. Baxter blamed it on lack of physical exercise. The idea of walking or of doing similar physical activity would shock the American belle, he said.[97] Early marriages were also considered as a cause for the pallor and poor health of American women. Occasionally speculation on this subject took a completely ridiculous turn. Logan, for example, ascribed their poor health to the fact that American women took a great deal of opium and laudanum. Regardless of its cause, Thomson could not refrain from reflecting upon the trouncing American women would receive from their English sisters if the two should ever come to blows.[98]

On the other hand, American women were generally regarded as well-read, and as animated conversationalists. They gave the impression of intelligence. The naïveté and liveliness of the younger girls reminded travelers of the French. The education of well-to-do girls was quite similar to that in England, the chief aim being conversational ability. After a coeducational primary education, girls were sent to academies. Here they learned a wide variety of subjects superficially. But after marriage, their leisure gave them greater opportunity than their menfolk for cultural refinement. Reading was popular among them, and languages were much cultivated. Miss Martineau met many women who read Latin; some who read Greek; others who knew Hebrew and German. In music and the arts, however, visitors judged them to be inferior. C. A. Murray thought American women to be better in metaphysics and poorer in dancing than Englishwomen. But at social affairs, single girls barely out of school eclipsed the more cultured married women.

97 W. E. Baxter, *op. cit.*, 96.
98 William Thomson, *op. cit.*, 32.

Sweet young things of sixteen and seventeen held the center of attention while more attractive mature women were relegated to the background.[99]

Young women were no more chaperoned in their private engagements than in their public activities. Marryat thought this attributable to the fact that mothers were busy at home, and fathers absorbed in business.[100] Whatever its cause, there was no doubt that the absence of chaperoning led to an air of independence, an absence of bashfulness, and a degree of self-reliance on the part of young women that was most striking to foreigners. C. A. Murray deplored the freedom from chaperonage during courtship on the ground that love, like religion, burned most brightly when fanned by persecution.[101] Yet he, himself, married an American girl! Despite the opportunities for waywardness and promiscuity among unchaperoned youngsters, it was generally agreed that the virtue of American womanhood was above question, more so than was true of European women.[102] Sturge pointed out that immorality was almost unknown even among mill hands. There had been only one case of an illegitimate birth in five-and-a-half years among the 950 girls employed by one Lowell firm, and that by an Irish emigrant girl.[103] Marryat, of course, with his usual cynicism, sneered that it was contrary to human nature for so many girls at Lowell, all able to afford silks, to be virtuous. He thought that scandals were simply hushed up. On the other hand, he mused, perhaps American women remained virtuous more out of necessity than choice, for the men were unable to stay away from work long enough to have an affair without being

99 W. E. Baxter, *op. cit.*, 98; Mrs. I. L. Bishop, *op. cit.*, 365; Harriet Martineau, *op. cit.*, 215, 228, 256; C. A. Murray, *op. cit.*, II, 214-215; Alexander Mackay, *op. cit.*, I, 216.

100 Capt. Frederick Marryat, *op. cit.*, second series, II, 3-4.

101 C. A. Murray, *op. cit.*, II, 218.

102 Harriet Martineau, *op. cit.*, II, 243; C. A. Murray, *op. cit.*, II, 216.

103 Joseph Sturge, *op. cit.*, 179.

missed.[104] Evidently Marryat thought American men did nothing but sleep after working hours. That there was vice and prostitution under the very moral surface of American society was apparently unknown to most foreigners. Only a few visitors who had lived in the seaboard cities for some time were cognizant of the problem. But even these, with the exception of Bell, swore that conditions were not nearly as bad as in England.[105]

One reason for the absence of vice, they believed, was the early age at which marriages took place. After twenty an American girl was passé, and at twenty-five an old maid. In the South, marriages often occurred when the girl was no more than fourteen. Visitors thought the tendency towards early marriage to be admirable, especially in a land where the young man had ample employment opportunities to support a family. But the child marriages of the South were criticized as going too far.[106] The young folks, rather than their parents, chose their mates. " If there is any country on earth where the course of true love may be expected to run smooth, it is America," [107] said Miss Martineau. Unfortunately, this was not always the case. For one thing, there was a disproportion of men and women in certain areas. Thus, in New England where the younger men had been drawn off by westward emigration, there were large numbers of women married to men old enough to be their fathers.[108] In the West, on the other hand, the situation was reversed, and women attained " a famine price." Majoribanks wondered how the Mormons were lucky enough to get several wives in a region where women were so scarce that others had trouble finding even one.[109] In the older sections of

104 Capt. Frederick Marryat, *op. cit.*, second series, II, 15, 35-53.

105 Andrew Bell, *Men and Things in America*, 235.

106 Harriet Martineau, *op. cit.*, II, 237.

107 *Ibid.*, II, 236.

108 *Ibid.*, II, 242.

109 Alexander Majoribanks, *op. cit.*, 189; see also J. F. W. Johnston, *op. cit.*, II, 461.

the country, mercenary marriages were numerous, visitors believed. In too many instances, they felt, marriage was a matter of business to the male, coquetry to the female, and an affair of calculation to both. Although there was no dowry, each side took a gamble on getting a share of the inheritance. Flirtations, engagements, and marriages seemed to be regarded far too lightly by Americans. " No native ever died of love in this country," grumbled Her Majesty's consul, Grattan.[110] Luckily, he said, the girls selected their own husbands. This made for marriages ostensibly happy, since the woman would endure anything rather than admit she had made a bad choice. Yet, in the end, even Grattan admitted that they made good housewives. As for the men, they were back at work the morning after marriage, as business claimed priority over everything.[111]

After marriage it was customary for urban couples to move to a hotel or boardinghouse. It became their home until such time as they set up housekeeping on their own. This might not occur for years. To the English visitor, married life in a domicile of this kind appeared utterly incomprehensible. What sort of home could a boardinghouse make? While the husband was at work, the wife whiled away the tedious hours by sitting in a rocking-chair (a curious American abomination) in a parlor known as the Ladies' Ordinary. Here, she sewed, knitted, read, played piano, or gossiped. With time on her hands and nothing to do, Britons feared that she would inevitably fall prey to temptation and scandal. Mrs. Maury, it is true, was delighted by the divertissements and ease of boardinghouse life; and Reid thought it provided excellent relief from hours of lonely pining.[112] But other travellers could not condemn the practice too strongly. Its popularity among Americans puzzled them. Explanations were not lacking. Buckingham thought it resulted from the lack of houses small enough for only two people.[113]

110 T. C. Grattan, *op. cit.*, II, 59.
111 *Ibid.*, II, 60-69.
112 S. M. Maury, *op. cit.*, 197-198; Hugo Reid, *op. cit.*, 240.
113 J. S. Buckingham, *America*, I, 233.

Others thought that American women preferred hotel life to households of their own, since it relieved them from housework and the worries of the servant problem. Because of the constant contact they had with hotels and boardinghouses during their travels, too many visitors came to regard them as typifying American home life. Mrs. Bishop was one of the few travellers keen enough to realize that there was as much patriarchal home life in America as anywhere in Europe.[114]

Family life in America did not seem all it should be. Men worked late and were dead-tired when they got home. Women had little opportunity for companionship with their husbands. Hence, Mrs. Houstoun charged, wives had a tendency to consider the latter merely as the medium through which dollars found their way to the dressmakers' and milliners' shops.[115] The money that men lavished on their wives astounded many Britons. It led Beste to denounce American wives as lazy, indolent, slovenly, and affected. He warned prospective emigrants that to marry an American girl would mean devoting oneself to " the whining, pining, helpless, lackadaisical affectation of the fine-ladyism which the American sex appear to think so attractive." She would not be above removing the horses from the plough at the busiest time to run off to a social event. Should her husband stop her, he would be kept awake all night with complaints.[116]

Yet this same woman, if necessary, would throw over all luxuries, and accompany her husband without a murmur to the wilderness. She would follow him to sea, or stay awake all night while travelling so that he might rest his head upon her shoulder. Most Britons considered such conduct exemplary. Few would say that American women were not fine wives and devoted mothers.[117] Stirling summarized the travellers' viewpoint succinctly:

114 Mrs. I. L. Bishop, *op. cit.*, 343.

115 Mrs. M. C. J. F. Houstoun, *op. cit.*, I, 184.

116 J. R. D. Beste, *op. cit.*, II, 94-96, 323-324.

117 Mrs. M. C. J. F. Houstoun, *op. cit.*, I, 186; James Robertson, *op. cit.*, 150-151; Mrs. I. L. Bishop, *op. cit.*, 365; J. S. Buckingham, *op. cit.*, I, 55.

I know of no people with stronger domestic affections. The American marries young; he loves his wife and children ... the American pioneer carries his family with him ... the American bagman scours the country in company with his wife ... an American's wife is the peg on which he hangs out his fortune; he dresses her up that men may see his wealth; she is a walking advertisement of his importance. The Englishman loves his house and decks it out when he makes money; the American loves his wife and decks her out for want of a house.[118]

Should mistakes occur in marriage, the remedy was not lacking. Contrary to British custom, divorce in America appeared to be very simple. Divorce laws varied from state to state, New York's being the most stringent, and Illinois' the most lax. Ten days' residence were sufficient to qualify outsiders for divorce in the latter state, however, and many women went there from more stringent states for that purpose. Infidelity and drunkenness were the chief legal grounds for divorce. But other acceptable grounds were numerous, ranging from " joining the Shakers " in Maine, to " any cause which the court might deem proper " in Illinois. In Delaware, Maryland, and Georgia, divorce was left in the hands of the state legislature.[119]

The independence and maturity of American children furnished another surprise for the British visitor. Children ripened early. Majoribanks considered a youth of twelve in America as much a man as one of sixteen in England.[120] Their early training stressed self-reliance. Mrs. Houstoun was astounded when a little fellow of ten was sent off alone at night in a high carriage with a pair of horses, to drive thirty miles and execute a difficult commission. No one, not even the mother, seemed to think the undertaking a dangerous one. As to the necessity of

118 James Stirling, op. cit., 155-159.

119 Alexander Majoribanks, op. cit., 424; Capt. Frederick Marryat, op. cit., second series, II, 26; Harriet Martineau, op. cit., II, 240; D. W. Mitchell, op. cit., 200; J. F. W. Johnston, op. cit., II, 458-459. Johnston listed the grounds for divorce in each state.

120 Alexander Majoribanks, op. cit., 115.

any grown-up person being sent along to take care of the child, Americans would have laughed at the idea.[121] In the cities, children would be found serving customers in the stores with the utmost confidence and self-assurance.[122] But such precocity, some visitors feared, was too often achieved at the loss of parental control. Combe claimed that discipline was lacking in the home, and children did as they pleased. Marryat corroborated this. When a boy refused to obey his mother in Marryat's presence, the father instead of punishing him smiled and commented, "A sturdy republican, sir." [123] The child was too early his own master, agreed Mrs. Maury. No sooner could he sit at a table than he chose his own food; no sooner speak than he argued with his parents. Bad as this might be, countered Thomson, American children were still far more affectionate and respectful towards their parents than was true in British poor or middle-class families. Children were not whipped here, but treated like rational beings. The parents in turn were repaid by the fond endearment and the full confidence of their offspring.[124]

What about the daily manners of Americans towards strangers and each other? Were they really as coarse and as crude as Mrs. Trollope had described? Most visitors who had read the accounts of travellers in the 'twenties and early 'thirties were prepared for the worst. Their own sojourn proved more pleasant than they had expected. Almost invariably they reported that as regards the common courtesies of life, either earlier reports had been gross exaggerations, or else some great improvements had taken place.[125] Instead of the rudeness they

121 Mrs. M. C. J. F. Houstoun, *op. cit.*, I, 48.

122 J. G. Taylor, *op. cit.*, 36.

123 Capt. Frederick Marryat, *op. cit.*, first series, III, 285; George Combe, *op. cit.*, III, 250.

124 S. M. Maury, *op. cit.*, 210; William Thomson, *op. cit.*, 28-29.

125 Mrs. M. C. J. F. Houstoun, *op. cit.*, I, 225; Hugo Reid, *op. cit.*, 47; Robert Playfair, *Recollections of a Visit to the United States and British North America*, 236; R. B. Allardice, *Agricultural Tour in the United States and Canada*, 154; Lady E. C. E. M. Stuart-Wortley, *op. cit.*, 32.

had expected, they had been greeted with politeness and frank hospitality. Americans might dislike Great Britain, and be opposed to British emigration,[126] but when it came to the individual traveller, he was well treated. In fact Americans seemed to lean over backward in their anxiety that foreigners should carry away a favorable impression. In their daily affairs they seemed as courteous and as affable as people of the same class in Britain. Even that arch-conservative, Sir Edward Sullivan, had to admit that his former prejudice against the American people on this score was unfounded. " I do not hesitate to say," he added, " that I met as agreeable women and as gentlemanly men in America as the world can produce." [127] Individually, then, if not in the mass, Americans seemed to be an agreeable people.

[126] See the chapter on Emigration for American nativism.

[127] Sir E. R. Sullivan, *Rambles and Scrambles in North and South America*, vii.

CHAPTER IV

DEMOCRATIC GOVERNMENT

WASHINGTON, D. C., was the American Mecca of the foreign traveller. Sooner or later his footsteps turned towards it, for no trip to the United States was complete without at least a passing glance at the capital of the great republic. To visit America without seeing Washington was like visiting France and skipping Paris, or journeying through England and avoiding London. At least so thought the average Briton, who had no reason to suspect that the capital of the great democracy would differ in relative importance from the capital cities of the Old World.

Alighting from his train in a terminus that one Englishman characterized as " a perfect pigsty," [1] the traveller wiped the last cinder from his eye, and stared about him expectantly. The sight that greeted him was not especially inspiring. The carriage ride to his hotel completed his disillusionment. Accustomed to the crowded streets and age-old edifices of European capitals, he could only stare dejectedly at the great open spaces that surrounded him. The gaunt, half-finished buildings, the desolate emptiness of the Potomac flats, and the vast distances between government buildings gave the city a raw, unfinished flavor that left the visitor despondent and disconsolate. He discovered that Washington was " a capital without a city." [2]

Its favorite title of " The City of Magnificent Distances " in time became corrupted to " The City of Magnificent Intentions." [3] Its location was considered unfortunate, its plan poor. Dickens, in 1842, compared it to London's slum suburb of Pentonville:

[1] W. E. Baxter, *America and the Americans*, 43.

[2] Capt. Frederick Marryat, *Diary in America*, first series, II, 1.

[3] George Moore, *Journal of a Voyage across the Atlantic with Notes on Canada and the United States*, 32.

Burn the (latter) down; build it up again in wood and plaster; widen it a little, throw in part of St. John's Wood; put green blinds outside of all the private houses ... plough up all the roads ... erect three handsome buildings in stone and marble, anywhere, but the more entirely out of everybody's way the better; call one the Post Office, one the Patent Office, one the Treasury; make it scorching hot in the morning and freezing cold in the afternoon, with an occasional tornado of wind and dust; leave a brickfield without the bricks in all central places where a street may naturally be expected: and that's Washington.[4]

Passing years did not remedy the situation. Some time later Major Warburton assailed it as "an architectural joke — a boasting, straggling, raw, uncomfortable failure, of infinite pretension in the plan, wretched and imperfect in the execution." [5] Not even the best friends of the Republic had a kind word for it. Carlisle found Washington "not only stagnant, but retrograde." [6] During sessions it was a place where job-hunters assiduously congregated.[7] Between sessions it resembled a ghost town. To newspapermen, it was a dull place at best.[8]

With his baggage safely deposited at one of the numerous boarding houses, the visitor commenced the inevitable sightseeing tour. The White House, of course, was the capital's chief center of interest.

Entering the White House grounds, the average Englishman was struck by the complete absence of guards, the lack of osten-

4 Charles Dickens, *American Notes*, 300.

5 G. D. Warburton, *Hochelega*, II, 91.

6 Earl of Carlisle, *Travels in America*, 39.

7 Charles Mackay, *Life and Liberty in America*, I, 129.

8 Alexander Mackay, *Western World*, II, 178. Alexander Mackay was the Washington correspondent of the *London Morning Chronicle* during the Oregon controversy. Prior to this he had edited a Toronto newspaper. His book is undoubtedly the best work on America by an English traveller during the period 1836-1860. It provides an excellent summary and analysis of American government and politics (Mackay's chief interest). In this field it is unrivaled, and can be compared only to Tocqueville. Mackay's approach was liberal and sympathetic.

tation, and the simplicity of the building itself. If anything, it resembled an English country club. Its very simplicity was impressive. Even the entourage of the Prince of Wales remarked upon it as " an imposing structure." [9] Only to the nouveau-riche taste of George Moore did it appear meanly furnished.[10]

The ease with which the President could be seen, was most astonishing of all. Although punctilious persons fortified themselves with letters of introduction from prominent politicians or the British Minister, less timorous travellers dropped into the White House with no more introduction than their personal calling cards. To their amazement they discovered that the President was always ready to shake hands and chat briefly with any caller. Chambers told of President Pierce being called from a Cabinet meeting just to shake hands with him.[11] Although this courtesy may have been extended because Chambers was one of England's largest publishers, no one in Washington remarked upon the incident as unusual.

Only a staunch Tory like Major Warburton could find occasion to criticize this custom. He affirmed that it had resulted in the perpetual presence of loungers and political hacks in the Presidential ante-room. The situation was so bad that when he attempted to leave his umbrella in the ante-room before entering the President's office, the negro servant had insisted that he take it along with him, otherwise the umbrella would be stolen ere his return.[12]

But not every Englishman had the temerity to meet the Republican lion in his den. Most of them preferred to meet the President at one of the White House receptions or " levees." The institution of the " levee," at which the President met all who wished to be present, was a great novelty to Europeans.

9 G. D. Engleheart, *Journal of the Progress of the Prince of Wales through British North America and his Visit to the United States*, 81.

10 George Moore, *op. cit.*, 34.

11 William Chambers, *Things as They Are in America*, 265.

12 G. D. Warburton, *op. cit.*, II, 94-95.

These receptions were often enormous in size, sometimes accommodating as many as 3,000 guests.[13] The informality, the equality, and the democratic spirit that characterized these affairs were regarded as typifying the American spirit. Even when " levees " were held in honor of great personages, such as the Prince of Wales, " the doors were open to all comers; the sovereign people came and went as it liked, the Minister of State from his office, and the workmen from his shop; there was no presentation, no order, plenty of hand-shaking and much overcrowding." [14] The President greeted all who approached him, whether foreign ministers, opposition leaders in Congress, or day laborers. Because of the throngs, this greeting was ordinarily limited to a handshake. This last custom had already become so well-established that kindly Charles Mackay could not refrain from commiserating with the President's plight as the greatest handshaker in the country.[15] That the throngs who attended these " levees " were not entirely without ulterior motives became apparent to him when, upon being introduced to President Buchanan, the latter appeared relieved to learn that he was only an Englishman and not another job-seeker.[16]

The traveller's reaction to the " levee " depended upon his previous bias. Dickens aptly expressed the viewpoint of the liberal group when he declared that " the decorum and propriety . . . were unbroken by any rude or disagreeable incident; and every man . . . appeared to feel that he was part of the institution, and was responsible for its preserving a becoming character, and appearing to best advantage." [17] The very propriety of the multitude, however, convinced Tories that the " dregs of society " had been banned. Needless to relate, so undemocratic an action by the titular head of the Democracy merited applause from them.[18]

13 J. S. Buckingham, *America*, I, 288.

14 G. D. Engleheart, *op. cit.*, 81-82.

15 Charles Mackay, *op. cit.*, I, 128.

16 *Ibid.*, I, 219.

17 Charles Dickens, *op. cit.*, 312.

18 Capt. Frederick Marryat, *op. cit.*, first series, II, 7; Mrs. M. C. J. F. Houstoun, *Hesperos*, II, 240.

The President, himself, gave an impression of simple dignity on these occasions. Regardless of the traveller's ideas concerning the role of the Executive, adverse criticism of the President's person was extremely rare. Even Capt. Marryat, who denounced the Executive as " insatiable in its ambition, regardless of its faith, and corrupt in the highest degree," [19] admitted that Van Buren was a clever man, entirely acceptable in personal life.[20] If Grattan, fresh from the courts of European royalty, called Van Buren a rather mediocre fellow of acquired urbanity, Combe reported the latter's manners to be " very agreeable, combining the ease of the gentleman accustomed to the best society with the dignity of public character." [21] The Tory who labeled President Fillmore as a plain, quiet-mannered gentleman who had learned to wear a black coat and hold his tongue, was unique in discussing the person of the Executive in so disrespectful a fashion.[22]

Englishmen never quite got over the shock of seeing the Chief Citizen of the Republic walking, talking, eating, and praying like the average man in the street.

The President walked into the Church unattended by a single servant, took his place in a pew in which others were sitting besides himself and retired in the same manner as he came, without being noticed in any greater degree than any other member of the congregation, and walking home alone . . . like any other private gentleman . . . Everywhere that he passes, he is treated with just the same notice as any other respectable inhabitant.[23]

Not infrequently the traveller found himself more respectful towards the President than the Americans themselves. An officer of the Royal Navy who removed his hat as the Presi-

19 Capt. Frederick Marryat, *op. cit.*, second series, II, 251.

20 *Ibid.*, first series, II, 6.

21 T. C. Grattan, *Civilized America*, I, 171 ; George Combe, *Notes on the United States of North America*, II, 87.

22 Mrs. M. C. J. F. Houstoun, *op. cit.*, II, 240.

23 J. S. Buckingham, *op. cit.*, I, 289-290.

dential carriage drove by was embarrassed to discover that he was the only one to have done so. Such lack of respect moved him to indignation.[24]

The importance of the Presidential office drew attention to the manner in which its incumbent was selected. With such men available as Clay, Webster, and Calhoun, why were nonentities like Harrison, Polk, and Fillmore elected, wondered the English visitor.

Tories raised their usual cry that the masses were too ignorant to make the best choice. It remained for Alexander Mackay to point out that the great figures were too closely associated with sectional views. Hence, the selection of obscurities was necessary in order to prevent the internal split-up of parties. The best nominee was " the one least objectionable to all," for " if admirers were few, so were enemies." [25] Later visitors came to accept this explanation, though they could not condone it.[26]

The danger of a military hero being elected President and then setting up a dictatorship, disturbed many a foreigner. They read the names of General Jackson, General Harrison, General Taylor, and were reminded of Bonaparte and Caesar. The ease with which constitutions had been overthrown on the Continent during 1830, and again in 1848, did not reassure them. Americans seemed too easily dazzled by military exploits. So long as the Presidential term lasted but four years, they were safe. But a second, and possibly a third or fourth term were portent with danger. Both liberals and conservatives agreed that the presidential term should be limited to four years.[27]

Next to the White House and the President, Congress was the most interesting feature of Washington. Upon entering the

---

24 L. B. Mackinnon, *Atlantic and Transatlantic Sketches*, I, 150-151.

25 Alexander Mackay, *op. cit.*, II, 29, 34.

26 Lady E. C. E. M. Stuart-Wortley, *Travels in the United States*, 59; W. E. Baxter, *op. cit.*, 54.

27 J. S. Buckingham, *Eastern and Western States*, I, 501; Alexander Mackay, *op. cit.*, I, 258; II, 345-346; Sir Charles Lyell, *Travels in America*, II, 69; G. D. Warburton, *op. cit.*, II, 257; C. A. Murray, *op. cit.*, II, 186.

portals of the Capitol, English visitors were less impressed by the architecture and statuary than by the courtesy of the government guides and attendants. Chambers, for example, could hardly believe his ears when a guide refused a gratuity on the ground that he was paid by the public for his work.[28] Dickens, familiar with conditions in the British Parliament from his days as a reporter, noted with approval that the public's right to attend and have an interest in the proceedings was fully recognized. " There are no grim door-keepers to dole out their tardy civility by the six pennyworth," he added.[29]

Upon entering the House gallery, the visitor's first impression was that he had inadvertently stepped into a madhouse. Precariously treading a way through the maze of spittoons and expectorations, a variety of odors and noises assailed him as he took a seat. The lack of ventilation, the heat, and the over-crowding raised such a stench that women fainted or became nauseated.[30] Overcoming an initial impulse to flee into the outer air, the traveller gazed wonderingly around him. The scene that greeted his eye was both comic and disillusioning. Below him sat the Representatives of the Sovereign People. Some slept; others whittled; a few, chairs tilted backward and feet on desks, stared intently at the ceiling. On one side, a number were busily engaged in throwing spit-balls. Elsewhere, groups of men were holding informal meetings. Above it all, could be heard reports like pistol shots, made by slapping the desk with a paper to attract the attention of a page-boy. Despite everything, however, the speaker droned futilely on, as oblivious to his surroundings as his fellow-members appeared to be of him. Regardless of whatever else he was doing, every male in the place busily chewed his tobacco plug, and spat vast streams of saliva in every direction.[31]

28 William Chambers, *op. cit.*, 265.

29 Charles Dickens, *op. cit.*, 238.

30 George Combe, *op. cit.*, II, 88.

31 *Ibid.*, II, 88; Mrs. M. C. J. F. Houstoun, *op. cit.*, II, 231.

Though warned by the reports of previous travellers, the visitor was never quite prepared for this. " One might as well harangue an audience below the precipice of Niagara . . . as endeavor to make himself heard in such an indecorous assembly," commented one Englishman, normally favorably disposed towards America.[32] The sight was too much for even the Earl of Carlisle, who contrasting the scene with that of the British Parliament, feared that the spirit of the West, " where members of the Legislature fire off rifles at the Speaker as he sits on the Chair," was invading the House.[33]

" The Chamber of the House of Representative is a fine room, and taking the average of the orations delivered there, it possesses this one great merit—you cannot hear in it," wrote one merciless critic.[34] Most travellers concurred in this, as they considered the oratory to be of a low caliber. Length alone mattered; relevancy was immaterial. " The Bill before the House may be for the better regulation of the Post Office, but that does not deter a member speaking on it from commencing with the discoveries of Columbus, and ending with the political exigencies of his own township," noted the meticulous correspondent of the *London Morning Chronicle*.[35] Regardless of subject, it was alleged, every speech had to be " full of eagles, star-spangled banners, sovereign people, clap-trap, flattery, and humbug." [36] Most speeches were solely for " the record," to be mailed to constituents at government expense under the much-abused franking privilege. This endless stream of nonsense made real work impossible, visitors believed. But this was unimportant, scoffed the critic, as the chief interest of Congress was to assure its own re-election.[37] Considering the small amount

32 W. E. Baxter, *op. cit.*, 51.

33 Earl of Carlisle, *Travels in America*, 82.

34 Capt. Frederick Marryat, *op. cit.*, first series, II, 3.

35 Alexander Mackay, *op. cit.*, I, 298.

36 Capt. Frederick Marryat, *op. cit.*, first series, II, 4-5.

37 Mrs. M. C. J. F. Houstoun, *op. cit.*, II, 232; Capt. Frederick Marryat, *op. cit.*, first series, II, 5.

of business transacted during a session, Grattan could only explain its great length on the basis of the Congressman's desire for the $8 per diem salary.[38]

As for the caliber of the average Congressman, travellers were but little more complimentary. Dickens, who might have been expected to defend these Representatives of the people, was antagonized by their pro-slavery and anti-copyright views. Instead of praising them, he denounced them as " the wheels that move the meanest perversion of virtuous Political Machinery ... (with) despicable trickery at elections; underhanded tamperings with public officers; cowardly attacks upon opponents, with scurrilous newspapers for shields and hired pens for daggers." Their threats and quarrels were greater than " in any civilized society of which we have read." But after his spleen had been vented, even Dickens admitted that Congress did contain some honest men.[39]

Occasionally the critic's imagination would run riot in adding glowing details to an already lurid picture. Such was the case of Mrs. Houstoun, who in direct contradiction to Dickens and other travellers, insisted that bird-calls and animal cries were used to harass opposition speakers.[40] Although this was true of the British Parliament, it was entirely a figment of her imagination as regards Congress.

Those who remained long enough to look under surface appearances, found conditions less alarming. Combe declared that Congressional politicians were no worse than those in Parliament.[41] Alexander Mackay, a newspaperman who understood Washington better than any other Englishman, cautioned that the disorder in Congress was more apparent than real. For when a real crisis arose, order prevailed. Citing as an example the incident in which John Quincy Adams had quoted *Genesis*

38 T. C. Grattan, *op. cit.*, I, 168.

39 Charles Dickens, *op. cit.*, 305-306.

40 Mrs. M. C. J. F. Houstoun, *op. cit.*, II, 23.

41 George Combe, *op. cit.*, II, 180.

to justify American claims to Oregon, he noted that he had seen many farces in Washington, but no tragedies.[42]

Moving on to the other wing of the Capitol, the visitor left behind him the pandemonium and odors of the House, and entered the sedate Senate Chamber. In contrast to the House, the Senate appeared as a dignified orderly assemblage, composed of a remarkable body of men, high in intellectual ability. Here sat Clay, Calhoun, Webster, and the other leading political figures of the nation. This was no circus like the House. Rather, it was a body that would " tolerate no slight of hand tricks . . . to secure a vote one way or another . . . (one) very careful of its reputation." [43] Listening attentively in the gallery, Englishmen were particularly impressed by the Speaker's custom of calling Senators by the names of the states they represented, rather than by their surnames. As the " Senator from Arkansas " replied to the " Senator from Maine," few Englishmen could help but reflect that many of these states, singly, were larger than all England.

But it would be naïve to assume that the physical aspect of the Senate, alone, created the high regard accorded it by the Briton. This was attributable rather to the belief that it was the more conservative body; one to which the country turned for salvation when " the democracy ran mad." Admitting that the Senate was of a higher caliber than the House, liberal observers tended to attribute this to the greater age and experience of its members.[44] But conservatives were quick to retort that the true cause lay in the indirect election of the Senators.[45]

It is illuminating to consider that while Harriet Martineau denounced the Senate as undemocratic, Mrs. Houstoun, archenemy of all things democratic, assured her readers that its debates were conducted with a decorum and dignity not to be

42 Alexander Mackay, *op. cit.*, I, 303.

43 *Ibid.*, I, 311.

44 *Ibid.*, I, 316.

45 Mrs. M. C. J. F. Houstoun, *op. cit.*, II, 235.

surpassed by an European legislature.[46] Not all Tories, however, were willing to be so complimentary even to the conservative arm of a democratic institution. Listening to the debates on the question of paying certain claims to Robert Fulton's heirs, Marryat cynically noted that the Senators were ever anxious to economize on all bills but their own. The rejection of the Fulton claim convinced him that there was little gratitude to be found in a democracy.[47]

State governments received little attention from British travellers. The principal cause for this neglect lay in the multiplicity of state constitutions. As one traveller erroneously remarked, their only similarity to each other lay in their common acceptance of the equality of man.[48] Furthermore, with the exception of Buckingham, few visitors had the interest, time, or patience to travel painstakingly from one state to another to investigate this problem.[49]

What little attention was accorded the states, was almost always monopolized by the discussion of the popular election of judges.[50] This practice was alien to English practice, and aroused great interest. Liberals and conservatives divided sharply on the control of the judiciary by the populace. Conservatives felt that this practice placed judges at the mercy of the electorate, and promoted the interference of politics in the dispensation of justice. That an American should look upon a judge " exactly as he does on a coppersmith and with no more respect," was downright shocking.[51] The low salaries paid to

46 Ibid., II, 235; Harriet Martineau, Society of America, I, 41-42.

47 Capt. Frederick Marryat, op. cit., second series, II, 10-12.

48 W. E. Baxter, op. cit., 49.

49 Buckingham was not particularly interested in this subject either, but his lecture tour took him through every state except Florida and Arkansas. The eight thick volumes on his American travels are encyclopedic in scope, and summarize, among other things, the government of every city and state he visited.

50 See the material on lawlessness in the chapter on Customs and Character for a more complete discussion of this problem.

51 Capt. Frederick Marryat, op. cit., first series, III, 204.

judicial officers failed to attract good men, it was charged, but did provide a sinecure for the dregs of the legal profession. The depth to which the judiciary had fallen was depicted by the Mississippi judge who went from tavern to tavern soliciting votes.[52] Liberals took a pragmatic approach. They claimed that the system worked well in practice, and pointed to the retention of the same judges year after year in Connecticut, despite annual elections.[53]

The Governors of the states also received some attention from travellers. In the late 'thirties and early 'forties, it was noted that (especially in the Western states) there was a trend towards decreasing the power of the Governor and increasing proportionately the power of the Legislature. It was not surprising for Mrs. Houstoun and other conservatives to deprecate such action, but even the liberal Buckingham viewed it with distrust. However, he failed to grasp the true significance of the trend, for he stated that the governorship of Ohio had been transformed into a rubber stamp solely because the Legislature did not like the current incumbent.[54] A decade later all of this had become ancient history. Now, the comparative simplicity of the Governors became a fashionable topic for comment. Special note was made of the Massachusetts governor (N. P. Banks) who had started as a blacksmith, advanced to Speaker of the House, and had lately become an aspirant for the Presidency. Though in past times the Governor had lived regally, this individual, it was noted with wondering admiration, walked daily to the State House and boarded at a public hotel.[55]

But American politics consisted of more than offices and officials. These constituted the skeleton. Political parties and elec-

52 Sir Charles Lyell, *Second Visit to the United States*, II, 213.

53 J. F. W. Johnston, *Notes on North America*, I, 151; George Combe, *op. cit.*, III, 113.

54 J. S. Buckingham, *Eastern and Western States*, II, 335-336; Mrs. M. C. J. F. Houstoun, *op. cit.*, II, 214-215.

55 Charles Mackay, *Life and Liberty in America*, I, 101.

tions formed the flesh and blood. Though the former might interest the political scientist, the latter was apparent to all.

The interest in politics displayed by the average American astounded the foreigner. Politics appeared to be the universal topic of conversation wherever men were gathered together. The multiplicity of elections, federal, state, and local, was all very confusing to the stranger. Dickens recorded with grim humor that directly the acrimony of the last election was over, debate over the next one began. This was " an unspeakable comfort to all strong politicians and true lovers of this country; that is to say, ninety-nine men and boys out of every ninety-nine-and-one-quarter." [56] Other visitors confirmed this, adding that " the number of politicians keeps pace with the Census." [57]

The violence of political discussions and partisanship likewise astonished the newcomer. In 1842, Dickens remarked that on railroad trains quiet people avoided discussing the Presidency because there was an election approaching in 1844.[58] A decade later Chambers noted that " party spirit is . . . the soul of American society—regulating and controlling everything." [59]

It was this last characteristic that led Britons to denounce partisanship as the chief vice of American democracy. They charged that there was erected a tyranny of control based upon absolute party loyalty and discipline, demanding a slavish obedience that no person, public or private, party leader or ward-heeler, Senator or constable, dared offend.

Even so sympathetic an observer as Alexander Mackay deplored this utter absorption of the individual into the party. It had brought about the anomaly that " in the freest country in the world, a man may have less individual freedom of political action or thought, than under many of the mixed governments of Europe." [60] This reflection, however, was mild when com-

56 Charles Dickens, *op. cit.*, 246.

57 Alexander Mackay, *op. cit.*, II, 3.

58 Charles Dickens, *op. cit.*, 246.

59 William Chambers, *op. cit.*, 297.

60 Alexander Mackay, *op. cit.*, II, 33.

pared to the Tory conclusion that " no man can become utterly, hopelessly a slave, but a citizen of a democracy." [61] Despite the inroads on party loyalties made by the slavery question in the 'fifties, partisanship was still strong enough to convince the mild-mannered Baxter that it repressed " freedom of opinion with as high a hand as . . . the Russian Czar." [62]

Party spirit manifested itself most obviously during election campaigns, and these seemed to occur all too frequently. Endless electioneering dominated the nation's political life, and led its public men " to pander to the worst prejudices, the meanest tastes, and the most malignant resentments of the people." [63] Harriet Martineau, who had witnessed the Van Buren election campaign in 1836, staunch democrat though she was, could not restrain her sorrow at the low tone of that campaign. " Nothing can be more disgusting than the contrast between a drawing-room gentleman, at ease among his friends, and the same person courting the people on a public occasion." [64]

But if Miss Martineau was shocked at the duplicity of the politician, conservatives poured out their scorn upon the system which made it necessary for the prospective rulers of the nation to play up to public prejudice. Universal suffrage and political democracy were to blame.

To be a favorite with the people, you must first divest yourself of all freedom of opinion; you must throw off all dignity; you must shake hands and drink with every man you meet, you must be, in fact, slovenly and dirty in your appearance or you will be put down as an aristocrat.[65]

No man with dignity, wealth, or social position would stoop to this. Rather than be dragged through the mire of partisan

61 G. D. Warburton, *op. cit.*, II, 239.

62 W. E. Baxter, *op. cit.*, 56.

63 Earl of Carlisle, *op. cit.*, I, 81.

64 Harriet Martineau, *op. cit.*, I, 88.

65 Capt. Frederick Marryat, *op. cit.*, second series, II, 69-70.

politics, such men preferred to wash their hands of the entire
matter. Not only would they not run for office, but to prevent
arguments with their neighbors many of them refused even to
vote. In some districts not more than half the citizenry exercised the suffrage, and these, it was charged, were chiefly the
idle, the rapacious, and the interested.[66] Furthermore, public
salaries were so low as to attract only the incompetent, the
grafter, and the adventurer who would only be too ready to
serve as the mob's " readiest tool." Sir Charles Lyell summarized the conservative viewpoint succinctly when he informed
his countrymen that " the great evil of universal suffrage is the
irresistible temptation it affords to a needy set of adventurers
to make politics a trade." [67]

Illustrations of the evils of the Spoils System were thrust
upon travellers in unexpected ways. Most amusing of these was
Lady Stuart-Wortley's encounter with a postmaster who could
neither read nor write.[68] T. C. Grattan, Her Majesty's Consul
to Boston, in writing the memoirs of his American assignment,
asserted that corruption existed on a small scale only, for the
American people would not tolerate it if it really amounted to
anything.[69] Other Britons differed with him sharply. The lobby-
ing, log-rolling, and political chicanery of the state legislatures,
especially those in Albany and Harrisburg, were on every visitor's tongue.[70] The equanimity with which Americans accepted
corruption in public office startled them. Miss Martineau had
already noted this in 1836. Later travellers were even more im-

66 G. D. Warburton, *op. cit.*, II, 104.

67 Sir Charles Lyell, *op. cit.*, I, 100; see also Capt. Frederick Marryat,
op. cit., second series, II, 219; G. D. Warburton, *op. cit.*, II, 104; Sir Charles
Lyell, *op. cit.*, I, 99, 101.

68 Lady E. C. E. M. Stuart-Wortley, *op. cit.*, 60.

69 T. C. Grattan, *op. cit.*, I, 335-336.

70 J. S. Buckingham, *America*, II, 321-322, 414-415; J. S. Buckingham,
Eastern and Western States, II, 197-201, 491-494; Mrs. I. L. Bishop, *An
Englishwoman in America*, 415; George Combe, *op. cit.*, II, 33-36, 177;
Charles Mackay, *op. cit.*, I, 100, 129; II, 158, 172; William Chambers, *op. cit.*,
302; Sir Charles Lyell, *op. cit.*, I, 108; Earl of Carlisle, *op. cit.*, 81.

pressed. Alexander Mackay was forced to admit, though he, himself, did not endorse the idea, that he had heard Americans declare that they believed their government to be " the most corrupt on earth." [71]

When it came to election frauds, however, it was generally agreed among travellers that rural voters could be deceived or misled, but not bribed. Election frauds were regarded as purely an urban phenomenon, attributable largely to the Irish electorate.

In view of the fact that the Irish had captured control of Tammany Hall as early as 1820, it is not surprising that even the earliest travellers during our period were cognizant of the problem. Not even the staunchest friends of the Irish attempted to deny that they were a corrupting influence. Beginning in 1836 with Harriet Martineau's account of the Irishman, just landed, who perjured himself and voted nine times, and continuing to Charles Mackay's recital of the New York City election contest of 1857, " when the whole male immigration, landed in the morning from a Cork or Liverpool vessel, voted ere the afternoon for one ticket or the other," this charge was repeated without interruption.[72] Plural voting at the time was comparatively simple since registration laws were either lax or entirely lacking. Travellers noted that Americans were especially indignant at the manner in which the naturalization laws were evaded, often through the connivance of officials affiliated with the dominant party machines.[73] Typical of this was the charge that " there were hundreds of foreigners (principally the labouring Irish) naturalized free of expense by the Jackson party, although they had only just arrived in the country." [74] The ruffianism of Irish hoodlums, " who having obtained the franchise in many instances by making false affi-

71 Alexander Mackay, *op. cit.*, I, 266; see also Harriet Martineau, *op. cit.*, I, 185; Mrs. I. L. Bishop, *op. cit.*, 111; G. D. Warburton, *op. cit.*, II, 235.

72 Harriet Martineau, *op. cit.*, I, 340; Charles Mackay, *op. cit.*, I, 178.

73 J. S. Buckingham, *Eastern and Western States*, I, 493; Alfred Bunn, *Old England and New England*, II, 6.

74 *Uncle Sam's Peculiarities*, I, 229.

davits, consider themselves at liberty to use the club also," [75] did nothing to soothe either native or British susceptibilities. "They are the leaders in all the political rows and commotions," [76] wailed Marryat, paraphrasing the nativists. New York and Philadelphia had the unenviable reputation of being the worst localities in respect to corruption, in the entire country. As late as 1860 the former city was reputedly in the hands of politicians who constituted "the very scum of the Irish population." [77] Although earlier friends of the Irish had blamed this corruption on "faults in the system of registration" or "the cosmopolitan seaport population," [78] travellers after 1840 refused to accept such apologies. The fact that the Irish element almost always supported the ultra-democratic parties, including the New York Loco-Focos of the late 'thirties, did not add to their credit in the eyes of most Englishmen, who traditionally despised them anyway.[79]

The Irish vote was credited with great importance for several reasons. In the first place they controlled or were highly influential in the political machines of the leading cities. This control was entirely out of proportion to their number. Britons viewed Irish influence with suspicion, contempt, and even disgust. Sir Charles Lyell's reflection that the pigs could not be banned from New York streets because their Irish owners had votes and would not stand for it, was typical of this attitude.[80] But more important than the control of any one city was the belief that such control gave to the Irish the " balance of power "

75 Mrs. I. L. Bishop, *op. cit.*, 384.

76 Capt. Frederick Marryat, *op. cit.*, second series, II, 141.

77 William Hancock, *An Emigrant's Five Years in the Free States of America*, 57.

78 Harriet Martineau, *op. cit.*, I, 340; George Combe, *op. cit.*, I, 223.

79 Francis Wyse, *America: Realities and Resources*, III, 51-52; J. G. Taylor, *The United States and Cuba*, 29; J. R. Godley, *Letters from America*, II, 176-177; *Uncle Sam's Peculiarities*, I, 229; Mrs. M. C. J. F. Houstoun, *op. cit.*, I, 179.

80 Sir Charles Lyell, *op. cit.*, I, 249-350.

which had proved the decisive factor in many an election.[81] As far west as Ohio, the emigrant vote was credited with having tipped the scales in favor of the Democrats.[82] As both New York and Pennsylvania were important " doubtful " states in presidential elections, alleged control of these states by the Irish convinced many natives and travellers that these ignorant emigrants actually ruled the country.[83] As a result, the Irish were wooed by both parties, and took advantage of this to extend their powers still further. Johnston, for example, visited a Catholic bazaar in Albany in 1850, and was amazed to find everyone in town patronizing it. Upon inquiry he learned that the Catholic vote was " so strong that nobody who looks for any public office, and no party, dare give them offense. Every one courts them, and thus they continually gain in strength, wealth, and in influence." [84] Some Englishmen went so far as to attribute all anti-British utterances of American public men to the fact that the latter had to throw the bunkum in order to receive the Irish vote.[85]

Wherein lay the secret of Irish success in politics? Their readiness for corruption, their violence at elections, which intimidated the opposition, and their clannishness, were all noted by Britons as factors working in their favor. Amenability to control through such petty patronage as pre-election employment on " pipe-laying " projects in New York, or " reed-cutting " in Savannah, was also recognized.[86] Yet none of these

81 H. S. Tremenheere, *Notes on Public Subjects during a Tour of the United States and Canada*, 124; D. W. Mitchell, *Ten Years in the United States*, 149; Alfred Bunn, *op. cit.*, II, 9; W. E. Baxter, *op. cit.*, 154; Mrs. M. C. J. F. Houstoun, *op. cit.*, I, 179.

82 Sir Charles Lyell, *Travels in North America*, II, 79.

83 Alfred Bunn, *op. cit.*, II, 9; Capt. Frederick Marryat, *op. cit.*, second series, II, 142; D. W. Mitchell, *op. cit.*, 149.

84 J. F. W. Johnston, *op. cit.*, II, 236; see also, Alfred Bunn, *op. cit.*, II, 9; D. W. Mitchell, *op. cit.*, 149-150; J. S. Buckingham, *op. cit.*, I, 567, II, 17; Francis Wyse, *op. cit.*, I, 61.

85 D. W. Mitchell, *op. cit.*, 280; Charles Mackay, *op. cit.*, I, 181.

86 H. S. Tremenheere. *op. cit.*, 124; Sir Charles Lyell, *Second Visit to the United States*, II, 6.

appeared to constitute a sufficiently satisfactory explanation.

English travellers were convinced that the true answer was to be found in their organization—an organization, they believed, that was directed and controlled by the priesthood. " On account of their unanimous subordination to their leaders," the Irish vote was strongest and best organized. In New York, "Archbishop Hughes could rely on them to a man." [87] Hence he had a " greater disposable force at his command than any political leader in the union." [88] The ability of the Catholic hierarchy to control the electorate was affirmed quite frequently. Typical was Baxter's assertion that "in all parts of the country, I heard complaints ... of priests exercising an unconstitutional power over ignorant voters." [89]

Reports of election disorders arising out of the nativist movement were numerous. Travellers took these more seriously than did Americans. Said one of the former concerning one such altercation, " Civil war was declared between the Irish and the lower classes of native citizens." Attempts were made to set fire to Catholic churches. They were prevented only by the presence of Irish guards. In Philadelphia, this Briton noted, a house had been destroyed and many lives lost in a nativist riot.[90] Willingness to believe such tales, seldom witnesed by the author, was influenced not only by the general attitude of hostility towards the Irish, but also by such specific travel incidents as seeing an Irishman flaunting a sign reading, " We will NOT be governed by Americans." [91] Mrs. Bishop, then a sickly young girl, claimed that the New York papers variously announced that from forty-five to seven hundred persons were killed or wounded in the local election disorders of 1854. Irishmen firing on a Know-Nothing assemblage had precipitated three days of

87 D. W. Mitchell, *op. cit.*, 151, 275.

88 J. R. Godley, *op. cit.*, II, 176.

89 W. E. Baxter, *op. cit.*, 155. See also Charles Mackay, *op. cit.*, I, 178 and Alfred Bunn, *op. cit.*, II, 9.

90 *Uncle Sam's Peculiarities*, I, 228, II, 190.

91 J. G. Taylor, *op. cit.*, 30.

fighting, ended only by the calling out of the militia. She, herself, saw two dead bodies, and the walks and roadway of an alley near Five Points slippery with blood. Yet, she reported incredulously, business went on as usual, and her American acquaintances passed it off as " only an election riot." [92]

Aside from the disorders between the Irish and the nativists, American elections appeared surprisingly orderly. Buckingham, who had run for Parliament several times, believed that after the clap-trap of electioneering had passed, elections, even in New York, were conducted with greater decorum and order than any contested election in England. In later years the Know-Nothing disorders and the increasing bitterness over slavery made this less true than it had been at the time of his visit.

The clap-trap of electioneering, with its torch-light parades, its " Hard Cider and Log Cabin " or similar slogans, its electric excitement that occasionally led to campaign parades of " 10,000 boys," [93] all had a tremendous appeal to the visitor. The ludicrousness of the Harrison campaign positively nauseated liberal observers, like Buckingham, who had entertained great hopes concerning the Republic. On the other hand, conservatives were delighted to find such examples of asininity in democratic government. Whenever possible, Englishmen tried to attend campaign rallies to secure " local color." In the late 'thirties Grattan was the honored guest at a Whig rally on Bunker Hill attended by 25,000 New England bluebloods. Shortly thereafter, from the safety of the sidelines, he observed uncouth speakers harangue 5,000 coarse sons of toil at a Loco-Foco meeting.[94] Two decades later his countrymen could still be found attending political rallies, and still remarking, somewhat disappointedly, upon their orderliness. For one special visitor, however, the Americans were obliging enough to pro-

92 Mrs. I. L. Bishop, *op. cit.*, 386. See the chapter on The Face of America for a description of Five Points.

93 George Moore, *Journal of a Voyage across the Atlantic with Notes of Canada and the United States*, 76-77.

94 T. C. Grattan, *op. cit.*, I, 322-323.

vide the desired excitement. The Prince of Wales, during his stopover at St. Louis at the height of the campaign of 1860, had the rare fortune of seeing a knife fight break out when Douglas partisans invaded a Breckenridge meeting.[95] Otherwise, the traveller could report only torchlight parades, tremendous barbeques, florid oratory, and perhaps an occasional pickpocket.

Viewing American government and politics in retrospect, at what conclusion did the English traveller arrive concerning the success of democratic government? Generally speaking, he found very little to praise and much to condemn. Except for slavery, this was the most criticized aspect of American life.

Conservatives advised their countrymen that America only proved once again what history had so often demonstrated in the past, namely, that " no people have as yet been sufficiently enlightened to govern themselves." [96] The foundations of America were rotten, it was affirmed, because the Constitutional Fathers had shown but " the ingenuity of the madman." [97] Contrary to everything they had written, all men were not created equal.

Liberals, although they would not admit that political equality " made the scum uppermost," [98] remained almost as distrustful of it as their conservative colleagues. Though Combe would not go so far as to say that democracy meant the reign " of the oracle of the pot-house, and the ignorant swine-herd of the backwoods," [99] he dolefully admitted that the people's powers exceeeded their educational attainments. Although willing to grant that nothing was beyond the powers of an enlightened electorate, he felt compelled to warn that " one ignorant man is not a fit ruler for a great nation . . . nor are ten million . . . more fit for so doing." [100]

95 G. D. Engleheart, *Journal of Progress of the Prince of Wales through British North America and his Visit to the United States*, 75.

96 Capt. Frederick Marryat, *op. cit.*, second series, II, 247.

97 G. D. Warburton, *op. cit.*, II, 235.

98 Capt. Frederick Marryat, *op. cit.*, second series, II, 240.

99 G. D. Warburton, *op. cit.*, II, 241.

100 George Combe, *op. cit.*, I, 161.

Did a sojourn in America change the traveller's viewpoint concerning democratic government to any appreciable extent? Evidently not! His previous sympathies and prejudices appear to have been the fundamental factor in determining his views. It was natural, for example, that men such as Marryat, Warburton, H. A. Murray, and Sir Berkeley, with aristocratic military backgrounds, should see democracy through jaundiced eyes. On the other hand, reformers like Miss Martineau, Buckingham, and Combe, who had been active in striving to raise the lower classes in England both politically and socially, were predisposed to see the brighter side of the American system. Even if they could not avoid detecting many faults and defects in the democratic Republic, yet they were inclined to seek within each cloud its silver lining.

The persistence of old political prejudices was aptly expressed by the visitor who was candid enough to admit that " I have never had the slightest penchant for republics: I left England strongly biased in favour of our government and institutions, and I returned with all my predilections strengthened." [101] Thus, while conservatives felt that their American tour only confirmed their previous belief that democracy " with every advantage on her side ... has been a miserable failure," [102] liberals persisted in maintaining that " the rise and progress of the United States appears (to be) the greatest and most important fact of the century." [103] But not even the most liberal traveller would go so far as to recommend that England adopt the American system of political democracy. Although some might concede the expediency of democratic government in the United States, all visitors were in full agreement with the clergyman who stated: " Britain...has naught to learn from the present state of American democracy, except to bless God for the more compact and secure fabric of British freedom."[104]

101 Sir E. R. Sullivan, *Rambles and Scrambles in North and South America*, vi-vii.

102 Capt. Frederick Marryat, *op. cit.*, second series, II, 248.

103 W. E. Baxter, *op. cit.*, 70.

104 George Lewis, *Impressions of America and American Churches*, 397.

CHAPTER V

SLAVERY

In the shadow of the Capitol stood a slave mart. To more than one Briton this gave the living lie to the imposing declaration, " All Men are created Free and Equal."

The principle of human bondage was repugnant to most Englishmen. To Buckingham, it seemed as if democratic America assigned exactly the same reason for enslaving negroes, as the Sultan or the Czar for withholding from their subjects those very political liberties of which America was so proud.[1] Certainly the existence of slavery in a land dedicated to freedom, furnished a paradox that merited investigation.

The recent abolition of slavery in the British colonies gave a timeliness to the topic. So did the Texan question, which Englishmen regarded as hinging on the matter of slavery. The occasional clashes between American slave smugglers and British patrols off the African coast, also kept the topic in the foreground.

The traveller's interest, already awakened, was further whetted by the abolitionist controversy in the Union. *Uncle Tom's Cabin* spot-lighted the subject in the 'fifties, and became a by-word in both Europe and America.

Hence no trip to America was complete without some personal investigation of the problem. Even though the visitor might not be able to include an extended tour of the South, at least a side-trip over the border was almost inevitable.

In his naïve eagerness to discuss the matter and secure first-hand information, the traveller often ran into trouble. Thomson, a sickly Scotsman coming to visit a brother in Virginia, argued with his ship captain as to the evils of slavery. Upon landing, word spread that he was an abolitionist. Only the quick intervention of his brother, a slave owner, prevented

[1] J. S. Buckingham, *America*, II, 464-465.

his being tarred and feathered.[2] Ironically, Thomson returned to England an ardent champion of slavery. As early as 1837 Buckingham had noticed that any discussion of slavery in the South was taboo. In Savannah, he was surprised to learn, the word "abolitionist" was more terrible than the name of any murderer.[3] Baxter claimed that a marked change had taken place by 1854 in that the subject was no longer taboo in the Southern press, and that many people, though supporting slavery in public, no longer did so in private. He attributed this change to the quiet propaganda supposedly spread by New England merchants and teachers living in the South.[4] Evidently, belief in this very factor, plus the increasing bitterness of the slavery controversy, made Southerners suspicious of all strangers. English visitors travelling through the South in the 'fifties often felt that they were under surveillance. Stirling, for example, while quietly talking about slavery to a woman, noticed an old gentleman change his seat in the coach so that he could overhear the conversation.[5] From such experiences, travellers learned to keep their eyes open, and their mouths shut.

The visitor had no need to be told when he entered slave territory. The transition was painfully obvious. In the North, all was energy, activity, and enterprise. In the South, ill-built houses going to ruin, fences out of repair, dilapidated railroads, impassable roads, and dirty inns provided a sharp contrast. As compared to the bustling cities of the free states, even Charleston seemed no better than a third-rate town on the banks of the Ohio.[6]

2 William Thomson, *A Trademan's Travels in the United States and Canada*, 168-170.

3 J. S. Buckingham, *Southern or Slave States*, I, 131.

4 W. E. Baxter, *America and the Americans*, 194.

5 James Stirling, *Letters from the Slave States*, 200.

6 W. E. Baxter, *op. cit.*, 175; Charles Mackay, *Life and Liberty in America*, II, 36. See the chapter on The Face of America for further data on the traveller's reaction to the physical appearance of the South.

Nor was the difference between the two sections due to soil or climate alone. The Yank flourished in Georgia as well as in Maine, in New Orleans no less than in Boston. Whenever an improvement was seen in the South, the traveller professed to believe that it was the work of a Northerner.[7] Georgia, to which many Yanks had emigrated, was sometimes called the most progressive state in the South. Lyell told of some New England farmers settled in Virginia who by employing white labor had raised the price of their land from $5 to $40 per acre.[8] Obviously, concluded Englishmen, the difference between the two sections was explicable only on the basis of that peculiar institution, slavery.

A visit to a slave plantation became, therefore, a "must," so far as most travellers were concerned. Riding through the fields where blacks of both sexes, clad in dingy ill-fitting clothes, could be seen pausing in their work momentarily to stare at the stranger, the visitor came to the main house. Its appearance was always disappointing to those who had conjured up visions of luxurious mansions. But the slave quarter did live up to expectations. The typical slave cabin consisted of one room, twelve by fifteen, with a rude wooden bedstead and moss blankets. Sometimes two families resided in one cabin, whose earthen floor was littered with firewood and shavings. In cold weather, half-naked children crouched round the smouldering embers. Poultry walked everywhere. An open ditch took care of the sewage.[9] Small wonder that Miss Martineau called it " something between a haunt of monkeys and a dwelling place of human beings." [10]

Work conditions for the slaves varied widely. Household slaves were well-treated and well-dressed. Even abolitionists would admit that. A personal bond existed between servant

7 W. E. Baxter, *op. cit.*, 175.

8 Sir Charles Lyell, *Second Visit to the United States*, I, 274.

9 F. A. Kemble, *Journal of a Residence on a Georgian Plantation, 1838-1839*, 31.

10 Harriet Martineau, *Society in America*, I, 224.

and master. Furthermore, a nice-looking staff of domestics was a credit to the house. But the field hands were worked for all that could be gotten from them. Conditions were worst in the far South. In the coastal swamps of Georgia, the slaves worked from dawn to dusk, six days a week. A peck of Indian corn a week was the sole food allowance for a grown man, Buckingham reported. A woolen jacket and trouser in winter, and a cotton trouser in summer, was their only clothing.[11] Britons were horrified to hear that on the sugar plantations of the Gulf Coast, negroes would be worked to death in six to eight years, since it was held to be cheaper to " work them off " in that time than to improve working conditions and lower the output. Women worked the same as the men, even to ploughing.[12] In the event of childbirth, the woman had to be back in the fields within three weeks. Excess slaves were hired-out by their masters. In the case of artisans, especially in the border states, it was customary to give the slave a share of his salary, sometimes as high as fifty per cent;[13] the new master, however, was apt to squeeze the last ounce of work from the negro in whose welfare he had no property interest. Rich planters in good times fed their slaves well. But the smaller, poorer proprietors bought broken-down negroes at a low price, fed and housed them poorly, caring little about them as they could easily be replaced.[14] The model plantations, cited by Ulrich B. Phillips and J. D. B. DeBow, in which the field slaves were protected from overwork by the strict regulations laid down by paternalistic masters,[15] were never visited by English travellers. The lat-

11 J. S. Buckingham, *op. cit.*, I, 133.

12 Harriet Martineau, *op. cit.*, I, 224.

13 R. B. Allardice, *An Agricultural Tour in the United States and Canada*, 93-94.

14 Sir E. R. Sullivan, *Rambles and Scrambles in North and South America*, 186.

15 Ulrich B. Phillips, ed., *Documentary History of American Industrial Society*, I, 112-115; J. D. B. DeBow, ed., *The Industrial Resources of the Southern and Western States*, II, 330-333.

ter would doubtless have been surprised to learn of such scientific and humane management on a slave plantation.

To the travellers, professional medical attention for the slaves was unknown. Shortly after her arrival on her husband's plantation, Fanny Kemble paid a visit to the infirmary. Its earthen floor was strewn with wretched women clad in rags. Smoke from a defective chimney filled the room. The shutters were closed, and the room was almost pitch dark. " The poor dingy supplicating sleepers upraised themselves as I cautiously advanced among them; those who could not rear their bodies from the earth raised their piteous beseeching hands." [16] Not even a blanket was available. Medical attention was left to an old negress who acted as nurse.

It was in such surroundings as this that the old worn-out negro awaited his end. Fanny Kemble's portrait of the death of an old slave was in sharp contrast to the kindly paternalism depicted by pro-slavery propagandists. The old negro lay there; " His tattered shirt and trousers barely covered his poor body ... He had nothing under him but a mere handful of straw ... and under his head, by way of a pillow for his dying agony, two or three sticks ... The flies were all gathering around his mouth and not a creature was near him." [17]

Stirling had accepted slave-owners' tales as to the happiness of their slaves until one day in Kentucky he overheard the screams of a female mulatto servant being lashed by his innkeeper for failing to serve Stirling's breakfast on time.[18] Yet not all slave-owners were cruel. Ardent abolitionist though she was, Miss Martineau admitted that " the thoughtfulness of masters, mistresses, and their children about, not only the comforts, but the indulgences of their slaves, was a frequent subject of admiration to me." [19] She went on to tell of a wealthy South

16 F. A. Kemble, *op. cit.*, 215.
17 *Ibid.*, 246.
18 James Stirling, *op. cit.*, 49.
19 Harriet Martineau, *op. cit.*, II, 107.

Carolina master who had refused to leave his plantation during a cholera epidemic, and had nursed his slaves all day with his own hands.[20] But though instances of this kind were not infrequent, most visitors felt they had limited significance since contrary examples could also be cited. Visitors were shocked by the heartlessness of such announcements as, " To be sold immediately, a negro woman and a case of damaged Marseilles soap." [21] Dickens listed a series of newspaper advertisements illustrating the harsh treatment of slaves.

Ran away the negress Fanny. Had on an iron band about her neck. . . . Ran away a negro woman and two children. A few days before she went off, I burned her with a hot iron on the left side of her face. . . . Was committed to jail, a negro man. His back very much scarred by the whip; and branded on the thigh and hips in three or four places. The rim of his right ear has been bit or cut off.[22]

Who could maintain that slaves were well-treated in the face of such evidence? Wyse went even further. He gave extracts from Southern law codes to show what the slave could expect. He cited one section to the effect that seven slaves or more found together on a road without the presence of a white man would be liable to twenty lashes apiece; another stating that should a negro use any but " the most usual route " between two points, he would receive forty lashes.[23] If the slaves were as happy and contented as Southerners claimed, why was there need for such regulations? Why, also, did slaves run away? And why should there be need of bloodhounds on large plantations? Travellers rarely saw a slave actually being punished. But Baxter affirmed that in New Orleans one could watch the whipping of naked, chained slaves as freely as one could enter a reading room or a playhouse.[24] " Shall we whimper over legends of the tortures

20 *Ibid.*, II, 408.

21 Lady E. C. E. M. Stuart-Wortley, *Travels in the United States*, 121.

22 Charles Dickens, *American Notes*, 418-419.

23 Francis Wyse, *America: Realities and Resources*, II, 55-56.

24 W. E. Baxter, *op. cit.*, 185.

practiced on each other by the pagan Indians and smile upon the cruelties of Christian men?" protested Dickens.[25]

Slave auctions had a strange fascination for British visitors. Some, like the abolitionist preacher Ebenezer Davies, deliberately sought them out. Practically all visitors tried to attend one. Southerners did not look upon their presence with favor. When Weld presented a letter of introduction to the editor of *The Richmond Enquirer,* he was welcomed most cordially. But when he requested to be taken to a slave mart, the editor refused on the ground that the spectacle was too revolting to him. Weld accepted this excuse at its face value, and went alone. He found about fifty prospective buyers present. The slaves were led out for inspection from a jail pen in which they were kept. The men were stripped naked and examined carefully. " Marks were criticized with the knowing air assumed by horse-dealers and pronounced to be the results of flogging, vermin and scrofula." The women were examined on the hands, arms, legs, bust, and teeth. If they claimed to have had no children, their bosoms were carefully fondled to check on this. After these preliminaries, the bidding commenced. The opening figure was $500. Bidding was frequently interrupted while the negro was walked up and down, and further examined " precisely like a horse." Finally, there came a mulatto woman with one babe in her arms and two others about three or four years old hanging on to her skirt. Her master (the father of her children) had decided to sell her. They were put up as a unit at $2500. When only $1100 was bid, they were removed from the auction block. Bystanders informed Weld that the woman alone would have brought more, but there was a strong aversion against purchasing white children.[26]

The slaves, themselves, did not seem to mind being sold, and appeared apathetic to their fate. Not infrequently one would call out, " Buy me, master, I am a good field hand and can work

25 Charles Dickens, *op. cit.,* 428.

26 C. R. Weld, *A Vacation Tour in the United States and Canada,* 302-304.

at anything." [27] In Virginia, domestics were sometimes given the opportunity of finding their own new masters. Russell overheard one negress pleading for special privileges from a prospective master, to the effect that her friends and favorites be allowed to visit her. Unable to gain this concession, she finally consented to go and look over her prospective employer's house to see how she liked it.[28]

The break-up of families, the sale of children apart from their parents, the separation of man and wife were extremely revolting to visiting Britons. Though none but Fanny Kemble had actually seen such a separation, they regarded such occurrences as both frequent and inevitable. This was one of the chief evils that they believed to be inherent in the slave system.

The disregard for morality was almost equally revolting to them. Slaves, it appeared, were bred like animals. The aged James Madison nonchalantly informed Miss Martineau that slave women bore as many children as possible, the average being fifteen.[29] In the northern tier of slave states, and especially in Virginia, where cotton culture had declined, visitors reported that the plantations were used as breeding grounds for the slaves needed farther South. Women of less than thirty had ten children. Fanny Kemble, a plantation mistress herself, affirmed rather wildly that " not a girl of sixteen on the plantations but has children, nor a woman of thirty, but has grandchildren." [30] Frequently, masters and overseers cohabited with negresses, and sold their offspring. Weld had been present at one such sale in Richmond. Sullivan witnessed a similar occurrence at New Orleans, where he saw slaves auctioned who were as fair as himself.[31] Fanny Kemble knew an overseer's wife who had the driver string up and lash three women for several days

27 Robert Russell, *North America*, 277.

28 *Ibid.*, 151.

29 Harriet Martineau, *op. cit.*, II, 118.

30 F. A. Kemble, *op. cit.*, 58, 182.

31 Sir E. R. Sullivan, *op. cit.*, 190.

on end, within a month of childbirth, because they had permitted her husband to seduce them.[32] Another planter's wife bitterly informed Miss Martineau that she was but " the chief slave in the harem." [33] A popular tale with travellers was the case of the planter who had several daughters by a slave. He sent them to Europe for their education, and raised them as ladies. His sudden death led the heirs to liquidate his property. It was then discovered that he had never legally manumitted his daughters, and so they were sold into prostitution. Although this story was probably untrue, the large number of the New Orleans brothels containing only quadroons and octaroons lent credence to it. Grattan insisted that in all the slave states, quadroons were deliberately bred for prostitution.[34] Even though he considered the negroes an inferior race, he saw no justification for this. Jefferson was denounced as " a wretch " by Tory visitors on the ground that he had had illegitimate children by his slaves whom he allowed to work on his plantation.[35] This baseless calumny was pounced upon by critics happy to demonstrate by his example that " licentiousness and tyranny have met together; democracy and slavery have kissed each other." [36] Nor could most Britons understand why it was socially permissible for a white man to have children by a negro woman, while for a white girl to cohabit with a negro would be cause for lynching.[87]

Cases of the latter occurred infrequently, but often enough to come to the traveller's attention. Two negroes were burned alive over a slow fire for the attempted rape of a white woman, while Harriet Martineau was in Mobile.[38] Local newspapers

32 F. A. Kemble, *op. cit.*, 227-228.

33 Harriet Martineau, *op. cit.*, II, 118.

34 T. C. Grattan, *Civilized America*, II, 441.

35 Sir E. R. Sullivan, *op. cit.*, 192; Capt. Frederick Marryat, *Diary in America*, first series, III, 55; Mrs. Felton, *American Life*, 56.

36 Mrs. Felton, *op. cit.*, 56.

37 J. S. Buckingham, *op. cit.*, I, 241.

38 Harriet Martineau, *op. cit.*, I, 372.

made no mention of the incident, but she saw to it that the story was circulated when she returned to the North. Some time later another negro lynching, this time in St. Louis, also came to the attention of visitors. These rather isolated cases received attention out of all proportion to their frequency.

Aside from actual lynchings, however, slavery was accused of breeding irresponsibility and lawlessness on the part of the dominant white race. The frequency of dueling, the every-ready pistol, the deadly bowie knife, the hard-drinking, hard-gambling desperadoes were all regarded as largely the off-shoots of the slave system.[39] The economic backwardness of the South was also laid at its door. How could the South improve its economic condition when production was entrusted to the hands of stupid, slow, shiftless negro slaves? As a system, it inevitably brought about " disorder, slovenly negligence, stereotyped adhesion to old methods, disregard of all improvements, costly and un-noticed expenditure and general impoverishment in all that pertained to the cultivation of the soil." [40]

Other evils of slavery were enumerated *ad infinitum*. It had led to internal dissension between the sections that threatened to end in civil war and disunion. It had led to " Bleeding Kansas," with its border ruffians intent upon one object, " the extermination of every Free-Soiler." [41] It had led to complications in foreign affairs, causing among other things the Texan Revolt and the Mexican War. Furthermore, it was creating friction between England and America because of clashes between British patrols and American slavers off the African coast.

Legally, of course, the importation of slaves from Africa had been prohibited since 1808. British visitors pointed out that this trade was being continued clandestinely. The clipper ships, they stated, were particularly suitable for this purpose. Wyse had been aboard a number of these in New York which were " notoriously intended " for black ivory. Such ships sailed under

39 See the section on lawlessness in the chapter on Customs and Character.

40 T. H. Gladstone, *op. cit.*, 219-220.

41 *Ibid.*, 125-126.

American papers to Havana, where the crew was changed. Then the American captain took her to the African coast, and loaded her with slaves. On the return voyage, just before approaching Cuba, he would turn over the ship to another captain sailing under Portuguese papers secured in advance. Thus the slaver had the protection of the American flag on the high seas against British interference. From Cuba the slaves were easily smuggled into Florida and Texas.[42]

Comparison with former slave conditions in the West Indies was inevitable. The general verdict declared American conditions to be worse. But the reasons given to justify this opinion were seldom better than Grattan's naïve assertion that " no well-bred Englishman would dare be a harsh master." [43] Although American masters were declared to be more cruel, no adequate evidence of this was ever given even by men, such as Davies and Phillippo, who were familiar with West Indian conditions.

Yet despite their condemnation of negro slavery on almost every conceivable basis, English travellers were overwhelmingly opposed to abolitionism, also. Those who openly favored the latter were so few as to be counted on one's fingers. Sturge helped runaway slaves to escape on the Underground Railway ; Harriet Martineau defied public opinion by speaking from an abolitionist platform in Boston; Wyse, denouncing the Gag Rule as " a duplicity and a crime," urged emigrants to support the abolitionists. But these three stood almost alone.

In fact they were outnumbered by those visitors who looked upon slavery with favor. One of these, naturalist Amelia Murray, had expressed abolitionist sympathies when she had landed in New England in 1854. But a sojourn in the South changed her views. " We should bestow our compassion on the masters instead of on the slaves," [44] she affirmed. Far from being mis-

42 Francis Wyse, *op. cit.*, II, 69-74.

43 T. C. Grattan, *op. cit.*, II, 417.

44 A. M. Murray, *Letters from the United States, Cuba and Canada*, 195.

treated, the negroes were the merriest, the most contented people she had ever seen. They were only grown-up children. A
domstic in Lynchburg had told her, " Missus, we very like
monkies." She had heard a negro woman who had been offered
her freedom take it as an insult and reply, " I know what the
free niggers are, missus, they are the meanest niggers as ever
was; I hope never to be a free nigger." Obviously, then, Miss
Murray concluded, *Uncle Tom's Cabin* was a libel upon the
slave-owner. Far from being evil, slavery actually established
" permanent and therefore kind relations between labour and
capital." [45] A free negro in Florida, awaiting passage to Liberia,
had assured her that the mass of slaves were unfit for freedom,
and that the African slave trade should be reopened so that more
could be brought away and improved. To abolish slavery because an occasional master was cruel, declared Miss Murray,
would be as logical as to destroy free labor since some bosses
were hard. As for free negro labor, that was as practical as English constitutional government in Ashantee! [46]

Thomson, the Scotch weaver who had narrowly escaped mob
violence as a suspected abolitionist when he first arrived in
the South, became another champion of slavery. He denied
that the slave-owners broke up families. On the contrary, he
insisted, they went out of their way to maintain them. When
slave families were separated, it was chiefly because slaves deliberately married off their own plantation in order to have an
excuse for visiting friends after working hours. The slaves
were not overworked, not even the field hands. " Truth, then,
compels me to say that the planters in general treat their slaves
with great humanity. ... Would to God the aristocracy (of England) would interest themselves half as much to improve the
physical condition of the factory slave in England." [47] He had
seen children of ten and twelve in British factories, working

45 *Ibid.,* 203

46 *Ibid.,* 195-205, 264.

47 William Thomson, *op. cit.,* 191.

twelve hours a day till their hands bled, and he had seen these children whipped when their emaciated limbs could no longer support them to their work. " There is not a planter in America whose blood would not rise and whose arm would not be lifted up to defend even the negroes from such cruelty," affirmed Thomson.[48] Happy was the slave! He had no responsibility, no fear of his children starving, no worry of neglect in sickness or old age, " whereas the labouring men of this boasted country (England) have all the care and responsibility of freemen and none of their valued privileges." [49] Allardice agreed with Thomson that there were many instances of the treatment of English parish apprentices, " the atrocity and horribleness of which would draw tears from the eyes of any slave-owner in Virginia." [50] Both men were won over to slavery principally by its paternalism.

But other factors played their role, also, in gaining pro-slavery adherents. Sir Charles Lyell, for example, whose aristocratic background naturally predisposed him to regard the aristocratic social system of the South with favor, told Lord Acton that he thought well of American slavery because it had done more to elevate the minds of the slaves than had been done by the free North for its poor.[51] He had seen schools for negro slaves in Virginia, Kentucky, and Tennessee, an assertion which Northern friends heard with incredulity. In any case, he felt that the evils of slavery had been grossly overdrawn. The break-up of families, in his opinion, was rare. He, himself, had seen buyers refuse to bid on a woman who had been put on auction without her child. He had known of a widow with five daughters, who refused an opportunity of moving to Richmond, solely out of reluctance to turn over the slaves on her isolated farm to

48 *Ibid.*, 193.

49 *Ibid.*, 195.

50 R. B. Allardice, *op. cit.*, 94.

51 J. E. E. D. Acton, " Lord Acton's American Diaries," *Fortnightly Review*, CX, 917; Sir Charles Lyell, *op. cit.*, I, 129-130, 274.

the mercies of a strange overseer.[52] Such instances, of course, were exceptional, but Lyell professed to believe the contrary.

Mrs. Maury, who had great difficulty with the servant problem in New York, found slavery to be the solution to her troubles. " I like the disposition, I like the service, I like the affection of the slave; I like the bond which exists between him and his master; the union of interests, and the companionship which death alone destroys." [53] When she had spoken to Calhoun about selling a slave, " an involuntary shudder passed over his frame. ' The sale of a slave,' said he, ' I could not look upon '." [54] Small wonder that she admonished the abolitionists to worry about their own poor rather than the negro. Mrs. Houstoun, another aristocratic woman troubled by the servant problem, came to the same conclusion. She threw back the Northern plea of humanity by charging that ninety per cent of all cases of undue severity towards slaves were traceable to ex-Yankee masters. Next she turned upon British abolitionists and pointed out that the English mills would be the first to suffer from the cotton shortage that would inevitably result from liberation.[55]

All pro-slavery adherents agreed with Brothers' statement that to liberate the slave would inflict a curse upon him rather than a blessing. What would be his status as a freeman? Brothers told of the mobs he had seen march through the Philadelphia negro quarter, rioting for three days and nights, tearing down forty houses, looting, and murdering. All of this, he informed his countrymen, had occurred with the full knowledge of the city authorities.[56] Bunn carried this argument still further. He testified that negroes had been barred even from a concert given by a colored singer, the Black Swan, at the Metro-

52 Sir Charles Lyell, *op. cit.*, I, 275, 278, 279, II, 286.

53 S. M. Maury, *An Englishwoman in America*, 193.

54 *Ibid.*, 245.

55 Mrs. M. C. J. F. Houstoun, *Hesperos*, II, 202-212.

56 Thomas Brothers, *The United States of North America. as They Really Are*, 198.

politan House in New York.[57] What better indication could be offered as to the dreadful fate awaiting the liberated negro? Was he not far better off under the paternalism of slavery?

But it remained for Mitchell, who after ten years in the South returned to England and wrote an apology for the Southern position in the Civil War, to expound the extreme pro-slavery argument. Paraphrasing Dew, Harper, and Fitzhugh, he assured Englishmen that the negroes were an inferior race whom slavery had raised from savagery. " From the lazy, murdering, thieving, fetish worshipping African, he has been converted into one of the most useful and productive of the world's laborers." [58] Mankind was not born free, nor equal; neither did it have any inalienable rights. Abolitionism was sheer hypocrisy. Which abolitionist would not see his daughter rather dead than married to a " genuine nigger," however well-dressed or well-educated? Had the Constitutional Fathers succeeded in their ill-advised attempts at abolishing slavery, the entire South would still be an Indian hunting ground. Slavery, he insisted, was a beneficent institution. In his opinion, Britain would do well to establish it in India if it wished to make that area as prosperous as the South.[59]

But these arguments fell on deaf ears so far as the vast majority of English travellers were concerned. They hated slavery as the plague! Why then did they object to abolitionism? Chiefly because they felt it to be an impractical and extremist approach to the problem. Immediate manumission without compensation would be obviously unjust, and would ruin the South. Small wonder, agreed most Britons, that with their fortunes at stake, slave-owners fought liberation tooth and nail. It was

57 Alfred Bunn, *New England and Old England*, 61.

58 D. W. Mitchell, *Ten Years in the United States*, 230.

59 *Ibid.*, 182, 216, 227-251. Although English travellers who upheld slavery paraphrased the doctrines expounded by such Southern apologists as Dew and Harper, they made no direct mention of these men. Anti-slave travellers likewise failed to mention them. Evidently visitors were unfamiliar with the importance of these apologists in formulating the pro-slavery argument.

easy for those without any financial stake, and far removed from the scene of vast negro populations, to talk abstractedly of the moral righteousness of immediate liberation. The unreasonableness and the violence of abolitionist agitation had unified the slave-owners into presenting a common front. Therefore, far from hastening the ultimate end of slavery, abolitionism had simply tightened the collar round the slaves' neck.[60] For every person like Johnston who thought that abolitionist zeal had its value in arousing dormant public opinion,[61] there were a score who regarded abolitionist efforts as misdirected and retarding the day of emancipation. The extent to which abolitionism had solidified the South behind slavery, it was charged in 1844, could be measured by the fact that Calhoun would not have dared call slavery " a glorious institution " twenty years earlier.[62] Abolitionist pressure actually had caused the Slavocracy to change from the defensive to the offensive. Marryat, in 1838, had found many Southerners favoring liberation.[63] But scarcely a slave-owner in the 'fifties would admit as much to a traveller. For this hardening of hearts, Britons held the abolitionists, alone, responsible. Not only had they arrested the anti-slavery movement in the South, but they had intensified sectional bitterness, and caused the shedding of blood in Kansas. " It is wonderful," said Baxter who hated slavery with all his soul, " that men who revere their Bible can listen to the Parkers and Garrisons." [64]

Not only were the abolitionists intemperate and unwise, Englishmen added, but they were hypocrites as well. Until they gave evidence of regarding negroes as human beings by removing the disabilities against them in the North, " abolitionism was a delusion and a snare." [65] What could the visitor think

60 Alexander Mackay, *The Western World*, II, 106.

61 J. F. W. Johnston, *Notes on North America*, II, 486.

62 J. R. Godley, *Letters from America*, II, 73.

63 Capt. Frederick Marryat, *Diary in America*, first series, III, 64.

64 W. E. Baxter, *op. cit.*, 191.

65 William Chambers, *Things as They Are in America*, 359.

when that great abolitionist champion, John Quincy Adams, in discussing the role of Desdemona, assured actress Fanny Kemble " with a most serious expresssion of sincere disgust, that he considered all her (Desdemona's) misfortunes as a very just judgment upon her for having married a nigger." [66] Instead of ranting at the South, said the Briton, let the abolitionists prevent the shameless violation of the rights of the free blacks as men and citizens. Though the status of the free negro had improved somewhat in New England by the 'fifties, in that he was no longer barred from the regular railroad coaches,[67] yet " if a negro had the intellect of a Newton — if he were clothed in purple and fine linen, and if he came as fresh from an Oriental bath and fragrant as Araby's spices—a Northerner would prefer sitting down with a polecat." [68] In the free states a negro dare not show his face outside the gallery set aside for him in the theatre; if sick, he was never admitted to the white man's wards; when praying he must not do it in a white man's church; on most trains he was compelled to ride in the filthy negro car; when dead, gold could not buy him the privilege of being buried in a white man's cemetery. Knowing this, how could abolitionists heap abuse upon the South, where the social position of the negro was far better? Physical repulsion to the negro was certainly stronger in the North, asserted the traveller. Newspaperman Charles Mackay remarked that those who talked loudest of liberty and political equality, turned up their scornful noses at the slightest possibility of contact with a negro.[69] In the South, on the other hand, mothers did not hesitate to suckle their babes at the breast of a negress, nor even to have pet pickaninnies sleep like puppies in their very bedchambers. For that matter, almost every planter admitted one or more female slaves to the intimacy of his bed.[70] So far as the British

---

66 F. A. Kemble, *op. cit.*, 86.

67 James Stirling, *op. cit.*, 53.

68 H. A. Murray, *Lands of the Slave and the Free*, 208.

69 Charles Mackay, *op. cit.*, II, 43.

70 F. A. Kemble, *op. cit.*, 23.

traveller could see, the negro was treated as a dog in both sections, with the exception that " in the South he is sometimes a pet dog, whereas in the North he is always a cur, kicked and booted on every occasion." [71]

If not abolitionism, what was the solution to the slavery question? On this the visitor was hazy. But that sooner or later slavery would be eradicated, he regarded as inevitable.

There appeared to be little likelihood that the whites, either North or South, would ever accord full equality to the negro. Colonization in some tropical clime appeared, therefore, to be the most logical alternative. The efforts of the American Colonization Society and of a number of border states along these lines evoked sympathetic interest. In 1834 Maryland had granted a subsidy of $200,000 for the creation of a Maryland in Liberia, at Cape Palmas. A decade later this colony controlled 1,000 miles of territory, but had only 600 negro colonists. Despite this poor showing, some Britons still remained hopeful.[72] But more of them viewed the project pessimistically. As early as 1836, Harriet Martineau had opposed the entire scheme as unjust and unwise. The negro birthrate, alone, she showed, was greater than the number that could be deported. Southerners favored the scheme, she declared, because it offered an easy means of getting rid of clever and discontented negroes. Let slavery be kept from expanding further, Miss Martineau urged, and it would ruin itself. This would lead to manumission, after which negro and white, she trusted, would learn to live together amicably.[73] Buckingham took a similar view though he doubted whether social equality would be possible for a long time to come.[74] The paucity of the number transported to Liberia became even more noticeable as time passed.

71 Sir E. R. Sullivan, op. cit., 192.

72 J. R. Godley, op. cit., II, 216-217; William Chambers, op. cit., 363.

73 Harriet Martineau, op. cit., I, 356. Later she became an abolitionist, and demanded complete immediate emancipation.

74 J. S. Buckingham, op. cit., I, 574-575.

By 1850 the American Colonization Society had transported a total of only 6,653 negroes, of whom about seventy-five per cent had been liberated solely for that purpose. States like Maryland continued to subsidize their colonization projects. Yet Johnston thought the figures spoke for themselves. Not only was the plan a failure in regard to numbers, but he could see no justice in deporting men from the land of their birth, usually against their wishes.[75] Stirling added still another criticism by pointing out that in the event the project should succeed, the South would thereby lose its sole labor supply.[76]

The colonization project was evidently not practical. What solutions were? Stirling placed his hope in a gradual raising of the intellectual and economic level of the negro. This would decrease prejudice, and prepare the slave for emancipation.[77] Just exactly how this was to be done, he did not say. Religious-minded travellers, especially clergymen, placed their faith in some mystic process of emancipation brought about by " the influence of Christian faith." [78] Most Britons were so convinced of the superiority of free over slave labor that they felt the South had only to be convinced of this to cause it to give up slavery. How to do the convincing, and what the status of the manumitted slave would be, went unanswered.

Other travellers were not so optimistic. Godley was certain that if the colonization scheme failed, insurrection would be inevitable.[79] Marryat was equally positive that sooner or later by desertion, insurrection, or manumission, the slaves would join the Indian tribes in the West. He only prayed that England would keep clear of any servile war that might develop.[80] Alex-

75 J. F. W. Johnston, *op. cit.*, II, 358-361.

76 James Stirling, *op. cit.*, 237-238.

77 *Ibid.*, 239-245.

78 W. E. Baxter, *op. cit.*, 195; F. J. Jobson, *America and American Methodism*, 394.

79 J. R. Godley, *op. cit.*, II, 216-217.

80 Capt. Frederick Marryat, *op. cit.*, first series, III, 78-80.

ander Mackay, who otherwise disagreed with everything Marryat said, also pictured a slave insurrection as inevitable, to be followed by the ultimate expulsion of the slaves from the Continent.[81] No visitor, not even those writing on the eve of the Civil War, believed that emancipation was imminent.

Thus, if the slavery question troubled the minds of Americans, it was a problem for which the British visitor could offer no ready answer. But that some solution must be found, and found soon, became more and more apparent. As early as 1836, C. A. Murray had warned that unless slavery were shortly remedied its " gangrene would spread beyond the reach of medicine." [82] In the next quarter-century the gangrene did spread, until slavery became, in the eyes of the traveller, the most momentous question affecting the United States.[83] Would it lead to the dissolution of the Union? In 1845 Warburton had stated that the South would risk everything rather than surrender on this question.[84] Five years later, Johnston, noting the growing strength of the North, replied that America would never stand for dissolution. Should it occur, regardless of the constitutional questions involved, the majority would " resist such a separation by force of arms and compel the adhesion of the refractory states." [85] The tentacles of the cancer spread steadily over an ever-widening area. In 1856 Stirling remarked that the question no longer centered on the position of the negro, but on the social and economic differences between the North and the South. On the eve of the war, Tallack, a Quaker minister and abolitionist sympathizer, and Reid, a Southern sympathizer, both agreed with Stirling that sectionalism, which had taken on the guise of the slavery question, was now the

81 Alexander Mackay, *op. cit.*, II, 141.

82 C. A. Murray, *Travels in North America*, II, 204.

83 T. C. Grattan, *op. cit.*, II, 409.

84 G. D. Warburton, *Hochelega*, II, 256.

85 J. F. W. Johnston, *op. cit.*, II, 343.

real and more deadly issue.[86] One traveller aptly summarized
the situation:

The South seems to be in that mood of mind which foreruns
destruction: there is a curse upon the land.... The whole South
is like one of her own cotton steamers ... filled from the hold to
the topmost deck with the most inflammable matter; everything
heated up to the burning point, a furious draught blowing from
end to end, and a huge high pressure boiler in her belly pressed
to bursting.[87]

Secession appeared inevitable.

[86] James Stirling, *op. cit.*, 70; William Tallack, *Friendly Sketches in
America*, 227; Hugo Reid, *op. cit.*, 205, 221.

[87] James Stirling, *op. cit.*, 59.

CHAPTER VI

RELIGION

THE coach rumbled to a stop before a New England wayside inn. Driver and passengers dismounted, and entered the bar for a drink while the stage horses were changed. Liquor in hand, the driver walked across the room. As he did so, he noticed a Bible lying on the chimney place. Very deliberately he picked up the Bible, opened it, and in a loud voice read a chapter. The room became quiet; men stood attentive. When he had finished, the usual noise and bustle broke out again.

Godley, who was one of the passengers, though a pious God-fearing man, was amazed. For a moment he thought he was back in the days of the Pilgrims.[1]

Yet this was a land without an Established Church. Religious observance and support were entirely voluntary with the individual. This was a revolutionary innovation so far as the British traveller was concerned. Was voluntary religion conducive to a wholesome religious life? Or did it merely lead to indifference and godlessness?

These and similar questions raced through Godley's mind. He recalled that his friend Grattan had warned him that despite strict observance of religious forms, Americans at heart were indifferent to religion.[2] Yet, here there appeared to be conclusive evidence to the contrary. Godley determined to ascertain the correct answer.

He noted that Americans subscribed to a minister's salary as they did to a fire engine, merely because they regarded it as useful in promoting law, order, and the public welfare. Men argued about politics, slavery, business prospects, the weather. But no one argued about another person's religious beliefs. Godley concluded that Grattan was correct; American religious

1 J. R. Godley, *Letters from America*, II, 124.

2 T. C. Grattan, *Civilized America*, II, 340.

tolerance was at heart only religious indifference. How could a truly religious people tolerate any religion but the true one? As a zealous Anglican, he knew which that was. Never would he, as a conservative politician, permit the voluntary system, a work of the Devil, to displace the Established Church.[3]

Other conservatives agreed with his conclusion, if not with his reasoning. The chief evil in the voluntary system, as they saw it, was the fact that the clergy were dependent upon the congregation for their salaries. This, conservatives feared, led ministers to cater to the whims, fancies, and wishes of their congregations. That the people should control their priests was even less correct than that they should control their judges or their temporal rulers. In other words, the voluntary system meant democracy in religion. To this they were opposed just as clearly as to democracy in government.

Under voluntary religion, conservatives alleged, ministers lost all their dignity, and became the slaves of their congregations.[4] Marryat reported that in some sects travelling laymen made visitations to the churches to check upon the conduct and fidelity of the clergy. After a cursory inspection, the visitors gave advice or admonishment to the minister and prayed with or for him, as they saw fit. " What man of intellect and education could submit to be schooled by shoemakers and mechanics?" demanded the acidulous Marryat.[5]

Dependence upon the congregation for support also meant that the clergy were usually underpaid. J. D. Lewis declared that over half of the Presbyterian clergy had an income of £80 a year or less, and eked out a subsistence by farming or teaching. Decent mechanics earned more than ministers. Hence, he said, it was easy to see why American churches had few outstanding leaders, while the mass of its clergy, especially in rural

3 J. R. Godley, op. cit., II, 124-131.

4 C. A. Murray, Travels in North America, 1834-1836, II, 206; Mrs. I. L. Bishop, An Englishwoman in America, 430; Capt. Frederick Marryat, A Diary in America, first series, III, 98; G. D. Warburton, Hochelega, II, 206.

5 Capt. Frederick Marryat, op. cit., first series, III, 122.

areas, was definitely inferior. Sir Charles Lyell, who had heard an Episcopalian minister in Louisville preach a sermon denouncing the Reformation, was ready to bear witness to this.[6] In the West, Methodist ministers were provided with homes but no salaries. Contributions from members in the form of produce were raised periodically at special parties called " donations." [7] Conditions in the East were much better, but even here the only prelate whom Godley could regard as properly supported was the Episcopal bishop of New York. His income was $6,000, and came from the earnings of invested capital raised by popular subscription.[8] C. A. Murray, master of Queen Victoria's household, agreed that nowhere in America was sufficient provision made for the maintenance of a well-educated clergy.[9]

Moreover, continued critics, even the small expense of contributing to the village church was too great for the poor. Granting that this was still not an acute problem, these Britons insisted that it would become one in the future as the number of the poor increased. Pews in some of the larger churches cost as much as $108 per annum.[10] Voluntary religion was therefore penalizing the poor who were unable to afford the expense. Already there were " millions who had no place of public worship open to them at all," conservatives insisted.[11]

Another criticism leveled at voluntary religion was that it led to the formation of a great many sects, some of them absurd. Not only were all the recognized Protestant denominations represented in America, but many new ones, some bordering on the " lunatic fringe," were constantly being created. " The ease

6 J. D. Lewis, *Across the Atlantic*, 404-405; Sir Charles Lyell, *Second Visit to the United States*, II, 282.

7 William Brown, *America*, 23-24.

8 J. R. Godley, *op. cit.*, II, 42.

9 C. A. Murray, *op. cit.*, II, 205.

10 Capt. Frederick Marryat, *op. cit.*, first series, III, 137-138.

11 G. D. Warburton, *op. cit.*, II, 205; see also Capt. Frederick Marryat, *op. cit.*, first series, III, 153; C. A. Murray, *op. cit.*, II, 206.

with which the Abbé Sieyes promulgated fresh constitutions was a joke to the celerity with which the popular preachers of Boston propound fresh religions," jeered Sir Edward Sullivan.[12] It was not unusual, the critic continued, for some households to contain four or five different persuasions. Children would join other sects just to demonstrate their independence from parental authority. Major Warburton wondered how such families would be reunited beyond the farewell of the grave.[13] Aside from this perplexing problem, the tendency of the Protestant sects to subdivide was paving the way for the triumph of Catholicism, whose unified organization gave it an advantage over the innumerable Protestant sects busy fighting each other.

But despite the innumerable sects, the vast number of churches, and the huge church attendance, Americans at heart were still not truly religious, conservatives charged. In the opinion of one clergyman, long resident in America, the services were attended chiefly by women and old people.[14] In small towns the churches were built of clap-boards so light " that if on wheels, two pair of English post-horses would trot them away to meet the minister." [15] Americans attended church not from zeal for godliness, but from fear of talk by their neighbors. Many joined churches, such as the Unitarian, where conformity would be less rigid and exacting. The state paid great attention to the child's progress in arithmetic so that he might learn how to make money, but in regard to religion, these travellers remarked, the matter was regarded as sufficiently inconsequential to be left entirely up to the parents. It would therefore appear that those who lived in a democracy had wealth, rather than godliness, as their chief pursuit.[16]

12 Sir E. R. Sullivan, *Rambles and Scrambles in North and South American,* 182-183.

13 G. D. Warburton, *op. cit.,* II, 207-208.

14 Henry Caswall, *The Western World Revisited,* 315.

15 Capt. Frederick Marryat, *op. cit.,* first series, III, 99.

16 G. D. Warburton, *op. cit.,* II, 202; Capt. Frederick Marryat, *op. cit.,* first series, III, 142-144.

The superior morality and reverence for religion in Massachusetts was attributable, said Marryat, to the fact that the Church had but recently been disestablished there. Since that had occurred, he stated, churches were empty, and many ministers reduced to great distress.[17] Was any further proof necessary to show the fallacy of voluntary religion and the overwhelming superiority of an Established Church?

More liberal-minded travellers, however, refuted these charges completely. They pointed to the fact that America, though still largely a primitive country, had as many churches as the British Isles; that religious assemblages were being held at one place or another practically all the time; that large donations were constantly being made for religious purposes. America, they concluded, was basically a very religious country. Contrary to the impression given by Marryat, American churches were well-built, neat, light, and airy. In summer, feather fans kept them cool; in winter, stoves and footwarmers kept them comfortably warm. Church music was uniformly superior to that in England, and every congregation did its best to secure a good organ. As compared to the poverty of the Established Churches in Scotland, American churches impressed these visitors as positively luxurious.[18] Church services were always crowded on Sundays. Chapels holding 1,200-2,000 people were filled to capacity. When Baxter attended services in Henry Ward Beecher's church in Brooklyn, over 3,000 persons were present. Churchgoing, reported Maxwell, was all the rage in New York.[19] If Grattan was amused by the coolness with which men lay their heads back on the pew and settled quietly to sleep as soon as the sermon began, at least the high percentage of males in the attendance was in sharp contrast to their paucity

17 Capt. Frederick Marryat, *op. cit.*, first series, III, 140, 142-143.

18 J. S. Buckingham, *America*, I, 191; Alexander Mackay, *The Western World*, III, 276-277; George Combe, *Notes on the United States of North America*, I, 93.

19 W. E. Baxter, *America and the Americans*, 142-143, 145; A. M. Maxwell, *A Run Through the United States*, I, 24.

at English services.[20] As for the women, Miss Martineau had seen so many of them braving hurricanes, frost, and snow to attend sermons that she thought it was overdone.[21] Steamboat captains, a notoriously hard-boiled lot, frequently carried clergymen at half fare or without any payment.[22] Buckingham devoted three pages in small print to an enumeration of the many missions all over the world supported by American voluntary contributions. Who else but a deeply religious people would do this? If the Bible taught religion, then certainly the entire American people were trained in religion from childhood, liberals concluded, inasmuch as every hotel room, every steamboat, every boardinghouse had its Bible.[23]

Most striking of all to British visitors was the puritanical observance of Sunday in America. Only in Scotland had they seen anything like it. In New England, not a railroad train nor a steamboat ran on Sunday. Everywhere in the Union business came to a complete standstill on the Sabbath. Baxter, who had travelled extensively throughout America, swore that nowhere had he seen a single person working at a trade, nor a single store open on Sunday.[24]

Miss Martineau felt that Americans sometimes carried their puritanism too far. She could see no reason for clergymen leaving a gathering when the dancing began. Nor could she see why custom banned them from attending the theatre, or from indulging in a social game of cards. It was this type of thing that made another woman declare that the United States and Scotland were the two most religious spots on earth.[25]

20 T. C. Grattan, *op. cit.*, II, 65; S. M. Maury, *An Englishwoman in America*, 98; W. E. Baxter, *op. cit.*, 140.

21 Harriet Martineau, *Society in America*, II, 346.

22 J. M. Phillippo, *The United States and Cuba*, 248.

23 J. S. Buckingham, *op. cit.*, I, 196-199; James Dixon, *Personal Narrative of a Tour Through Part of the United States and Canada*, 187; W. E. Baxter, *op. cit.*, 147.

24 J. M. Phillippo, *op. cit.*, 252; Mrs. I. L. Bishop, *op. cit.*, 425; W. E. Baxter, *op. cit.*, 147, 153.

25 Harriet Martineau, *op. cit.*, II, 343; Mrs. I. L. Bishop, *op. cit.*, 424.

The charge that the voluntary system muzzled the clergy, was declared absolute nonsense by liberals. Miss Martineau, resenting the fact that most American clergymen in her time were opposed to abolitionism, complained that they were timid, apprehensive of change, and followers of precedent. Far from following the whims of their congregations, she stated, they acted as brakes upon their flocks' radicalism. Alexander Mackay disagreed with her as to the timidity of the clergy, but joined her in declaring that they led rather than followed their congregations. The clergy, he said, were as bold a set of men as could be found anywhere, browbeating their congregations to an extent unknown in England.[26]

Regardless of her theoretical objections, Mrs. Bishop had to admit that in actual practice the clergy were a highly commendable body of men. If less educated than their English brethren, they were more practical. Perhaps the backwoods preacher who told his audience that Jesus was " just another General Jackson," may have been deficient in theology, but his audience understood him better than if he had endeavored to elucidate the Trinity.[27] Beste, a Catholic, told the story of an itinerant preacher who passed through a region destitute of churches and religious interest. Failing to gather more than a half-dozen people at his Sunday meetings, he printed the following handbill:

Religious Notice—The Rev. Mr. Blaney will preach next Sunday in Dempsey Grove, at 10 A.M. and 4 P.M., Providence permitting. Between the services the preacher will run his sorrel mare, Julia, against any nag than can be trotted out of this region for a purse of $100.

People turned out in droves. He preached the morning sermon. Then several planters put up the purse. Another nag was produced. The preacher rode his sorrel to victory amid deafening excitement and acclaim. Everyone remained for the afternoon

26 Harriet Martineau, *op. cit.*, II, 350; Alexander Mackay, *op. cit.*, III, 275.
27 W. E. Baxter, *op. cit.*, 133.

sermon. At its close over two hundred joined up—some from novelty, some for excitement, some because the minister was a good fellow. A flourishing church was thus set up.[28] Such methods though unorthodox appeared to be effective.

Though adherents of the voluntary system admitted that some of these hardworking preachers were underpaid, they felt that the system was still fairer than in England where a few received high salaries and the rest very little. In New York City none received less than $1,000 nor more than $4,000 per annum in salary.[29] True, some of the poor might find it hard to contribute to the pastor's support, but, on the other hand, people appreciated those things best for which they paid. At the same time the efforts of the clergy were enhanced by the knowledge that their own welfare depended upon the size and interest of their flock.[30]

Sects and denominations might be as numerous as ripples on a brook, but no harm came of it, affirmed proponents of the voluntary system. For although scarcely one yard of the brook resembled another, yet it diffused " health and gladness as it rolled along." [31] Some competition between denominations was actually beneficial, since no sect would allow another in the same town to outdo it in buildings, services, or activities. Real struggles between them, these visitors insisted, were non-existent. Rather, cooperation in common interests, such as Sunday School Unions, was much in evidence. Each sect stood upon its respective merits, and every man regarded his neighbor as equal in the eye of Heaven with himself.[32]

It was therefore clearly evident, these visitors concluded, that religion developed most firmly where it was free from state

28 J. R. D. Beste, *The Wabash*, II, 151-152.

29 J. S. Buckingham, *op. cit.*, I, 194.

30 J. R. D. Beste, *op. cit.*, II, 148; George Combe, *op. cit.*, II, 256.

31 J. M. Phillippo, *op. cit.*, 242.

32 Mrs. I. L. Bishop, *op. cit.*, 428; W. E. Baxter, *op. cit.*, 152; S. M. Maury, *op. cit.*, 99.

trammels. Whoever claimed that the voluntary system had failed in America " must speak in ignorance . . . or with wilful perversion of the truth." [33]

Perhaps on no other subject was the division of opinion among travellers so clearly in keeping with their Old World backgrounds as in this matter of voluntary religion. It was not surprising that such conservatives as Marryat, Warburton, Sullivan, C. A. Murray, Grattan, and Godley were vociferously opposed to what they regarded as the destruction of one of the chief pillars of society, the Established Church. Democracy in politics was bad enough; democracy in religion was even worse. Similarly, liberals favoring democracy and opposing an Established Church, took the reverse position. In this group were to be found Buckingham, Combe, Alexander Mackay, Carlisle, Dickens, Phillippo, and Baxter. Catholics and Dissenters, such as Mrs. Maury, Dixon, and Beste, who were likewise opposed to the Established Church in England, though for entirely different reasons, found themselves lined up with the liberals in commending the voluntary system in America. Interestingly enough, while the reactionary Marryat denounced the voluntary system as bordering upon godlessness, that radical thinker on social affairs, Harriet Martineau, felt that the American system did not go far enough, since there were still laws against deists and atheists.[34]

But if there was division among British visitors upon the fundamental question of voluntary vs. established religion, there was unanimity in condemning the current revivalist movement. An itinerant preacher would arrive in some remote town and be welcomed as relieving the religious ennui. He would start the revival. The excitement would spread like wildfire.

Alexander Mackay described a revival meeting which he attended. The lion of the movement was in the pulpit, " sometimes foaming at the mouth " in the midst of his declamations.

33 J. S. Buckingham, op. cit., I, 195.

34 Harriet Martineau, op. cit., II, 317; Capt. Frederick Marryat, op. cit., first series, III, 99, 140, 142-144.

The weaker members of the dense congregation yielded—they became agitated and alarmed—hysterics followed, and some were in tears. Quickly it gained momentum. More and more sought the " anxious seat," and were " born again." Hundreds were converted in a day. Mackay, himself, saw 300 baptized within three hours in a huge tub kept at the foot of the pulpit. Rakes were reclaimed; prodigal sons returned; and hundreds who had been indifferent gave way to fervor. Business was stopped; families neglected. But once the excitement died down, the backsliding was worse than before.[35] Mackay called the effect " appalling." Grattan for once agreed with him. The preachers, " ranting vulgarians . . . scattering threats of damnation and pictures of hell, like men flinging fire-brands into a powder mill," he characterized as " heartless hypocrites living on the weakness and wretchedness of their dupes." [36] The sight of these revival meetings led Harriet Martineau to label American Christianity " a monstrous superstition," [37] while J. D. Lewis denounced them as the animalism of religion—" one gush and all is over." [38]

Closely related to the evangelical sects, in the minds of most travellers, were others bordering on the " lunatic fringe." Of these the Millerites and the Shakers received the widest attention.[39] The former sect had as its main tenet the belief that the world would come to an end on a certain day in 1843. Thousands were converted to this delusion. They sold their homes, gave up their businesses, dressed themselves in white shrouds, and prepared for the coming of Judgment Day. Grattan, who attended a Millerite convention at which over 5,000 people were present, was horrified by the scene.

35 Alexander Mackay, *op. cit.*, III, 268-269.

36 T. C. Grattan, *op. cit.*, II, 343.

37 Harriet Martineau, *op. cit.*, II, 317.

38 J. D. Lewis, *Across the Atlantic*, 407.

39 Brook Farm, Red Bank, and other Transcendentalist or Fourierist experimental communities failed to attact the attention of British travellers.

Everywhere there was singing of hymns in horrid discord, prayers in all gradations of sound, low murmurings, deep howlings, and loud yellings; groups in close converse, single figures in trances, ecstasies and convulsions; contortions of feature and limb, attitudes the most grotesque and unreserved, countenances of fierce energy and imbecile exhaustion.[40]

When the appointed day passed without any unusual occurrence, the leader set a new date. This was repeated twice more. By that time even the most faithful adherents were disillusioned. His followers returned to their former ways, and attempted to salvage the wreckage of their personal and business affairs.

The Shakers were an entirely different type of sect. They lived together in agricultural communities under a rule of strict celibacy. The sect had originated in England, but flourished best in New England and the Middle States. Their name came from the curious dances that characterized their religious services. Their grey shrouds and hoods, the curious shuffling walk, the rhythmic singing and hand-clapping that closed their prayer-services, the still more curious tales circulated about them, all combined to make them a leading tourist attraction. So many visitors did they receive that their meeting houses had special sections reserved for spectators. The service opened with mumbled prayers. Then an elder arose and preached a short sermon directed principally at the visitors. After this the singing and dancing began. Starting slowly with formal movements between the lines of male and female communicants, the dance quickly degenerated into what today would be known as a " jive session." The swaying, gesticulating figures, wrapped in grey shrouds, reminded Miss Martineau of galvanized corpses. Grattan placed them on a scale below that of human beings.[41] That this should go by the name of religion, struck visitors as downright shocking. After the services were over, a short inspection of the community followed which demonstrated the

40 T. C. Grattan, *op. cit.*, II, 350.

41 Harriet Martineau, *op. cit.*, I, 314; T. C. Grattan, *op. cit.*, II, 353.

validity of the Shakers' reputation as excellent farmers and shrewd businessmen. Though accepting all ages and both sexes, most of their converts were women. Dickens, who disliked their puritanism, considered the women so ugly that their celibacy, he felt sure, was not entirely a matter of choice. But Marianne Finch, who had devoted much time and study to Shaker communities, blamed the repulsive appearance of the women upon their dress which, she said, was contrived to conceal all personal advantages.[42] Of the many travellers who visited Shaker communities, Miss Finch remained practically their sole apologist and defender.

In the 'fifties, the Mormons displaced the Shakers and the Millerites as the great American religious curiosity. Their conflicts with the Federal Government, their spectacular migrations, and above all their doctrine of polygamy, brought the Mormons great notoriety. Travellers were somewhat familiar with them from the activity of Mormon missionaries in England. But despite the general curiosity, Salt Lake was much too remote for any except the hardiest and most adventurous travellers to visit. Burton, fresh from explorations in Africa and Arabia, was one of the few who made the hazardous trip. He interviewed Brigham Young, describing him as a gentleman farmer in appearance, without apparent sign of dogmatism or fanaticism. Baked potatoes with buttermilk were his favorite food. On the whole, Burton was favorably impressed by the community. Polygamy, he pointed out, was caused not by licentiousness, but by need for a larger population. As far as he could observe, Mormon women were attached to the practice, having been bribed with promises of Paradise, and subjugated by threats of annihilation. Nor were outside women less willing to accept it, as was evidenced by the many old maids who joined the sect in England and came to Utah to secure husbands. Far from opposing polygamy, he discovered, Mormon women actually boycotted any male with monogamous tendencies, fearing

42 Charles Dickens, *American Notes*, 402-403; Marianne Finch, *An Englishwoman's Experience in America*, 119-120.

that he might turn apostate and thus keep them out of heaven.[43]
For according to Mormon doctrine, women could get to heaven
only through their husbands. Chandless, who had come to Salt
Lake as a teamster and then boarded with a Mormon family,
agreed with Burton that the wretchedness of Mormon women
had been greatly exaggerated. They had never looked forward
to being sole wives, he said, and would rather be the tenth wife
of a rich man than the sole wife of a poor one. No man was
allowed to marry more wives than he could support, and each
wife must have a separate bedroom. Men could get divorces for
adultery alone, whereas women could secure them for any
triviality. He denied that the Mormons were sensualists, pointing out that there were only two brothels in town. These oper-
ated very quietly, and were frequented solely by Gentiles. Public
prostitution was not tolerated; nor was swearing in the streets.

Chandless went on to sketch the government of the community. Brigham Young, regardless of his mild appearance, was
absolute ruler since the spiritual authorities told the people
whom to elect as their temporal leaders. The entire male population were ordained " priests," bound to strict obedience and
unpaid service. At the call of their superiors, they must leave
home and family, and go wherever ordered. He, himself, had
heard these missionaries, after a three-year absence from home,
report to the congregation in the Tabernacle about their work
in places as remote as Denmark and Australia. Despite their
own intensive proselytizing, however, the Mormons were not
intolerant, even permitting preachers of other sects to speak in
the Tabernacle. But after the speaker had finished, an elder
would get up and ridicule him. Relations between the Mormons
and the Federal Government were chronically bad. At a public
dinner Brigham Young had said of General Taylor, " He is
rotting in Hell." When a United States Judge who was present

43 R. F. Burton, *The City of the Saints and Across the Rocky Mountains
to California*, 223-242, 428-432.

objected, Young added, " You'll see him there some day and believe it then." [44]

Other sects and denominations had their chroniclers, too. Many of the British clergymen attending American church conferences discussed the history of their denomination in America in some detail. More often, however, these clerics were so taken up with purely intra-denominational squabbles that their works ignored the broader aspects of religion in America. Discussion of this was left to the layman.

The latter pointed out that the various Protestant denominations in America represented specific economic and social strata in society. One could enter hundreds of Episcopalian churches without seeing a workingman, it was declared, while evangelists preached weekly to thousands. The Methodists and Baptists were considered to be largest in numbers; the Episcopalians the most fashionable; and the preeminence of wealth and intelligence was thought to lay with the Presbyterians.[45] Lyell had believed all Bostonians to be Unitarians, and was surprised to learn that they constituted only a fifth of the population, chiefly its richest citizens. Perhaps it was this that led Dickens to exclaim that if he lived in Boston, he would be a Transcendentalist.[46] Everywhere throughout the Union, and especially in New England, there were large numbers whom Lyell called the " Nothingarians." These were persons who attended Baptist, Methodist, Presbyterian, or Congregational services, depending upon whim or convenience, and were equally inclined to contribute money liberally to any or all of them.[47]

So much for the Protestant denominations. But what about the Catholics? What was their position in America? Long before the vast German and Irish migrations of the 'forties,

44 William Chandless, *A Visit to Salt Lake*, 154-195.

45 W. E. Baxter, *op. cit.*, 134-135; J. R. Godley, *op. cit.*, II, 222; Alexander Mackay, *op. cit.*, III, 260; G. D. Warburton, *op. cit.*, II, 203.

46 Charles Dickens, *op. cit.*, 241. Practically no attention was paid to the Transcendentalists except for a few isolated remarks such as this.

47 Sir Charles Lyell, *op. cit.*, I, 173, 177.

British visitors regarded Catholics as the *bêtes noires* of America. C. A. Murray, in 1836, pointed out that the Catholics in Missouri had gained ground so rapidly that they already outstripped all competition. Buckingham found six of the fifteen schools in St. Louis to be Catholic, in addition to the famous Jesuit college and Sacred Heart convent that gave them overwhelming superiority in higher education. The Catholic clergy far outdid their Protestant brethren in learning, zeal, courtesy, and attention to the lower classes, he warned. In Chicago a similar situation existed, he reported, with three out of five schools being Catholic. Proselytizing went on not only in the West, but also in the Catholic institutions of Boston and Washington, Buckingham added.[48] Marryat was even more alarmed. He thought it quite possible that all America would fall under the fascination of Papal ritual and turn Catholic. Certainly, he concluded, there was no doubt but that the West would do so, inasmuch as Catholics were already in the majority there. Alexander Mackay, otherwise a very sober and tolerant person, was also convinced that the Catholic Church was very deliberately intent upon conquering all America. It had abandoned the East to the Protestants, and was concentrating on the interior. Protestant clergymen arriving in remote frontier areas found Catholic missionaries already well-established. Nor could the frontiersman be blamed for succumbing to the Jesuits, he admitted, when Protestant clergy were not available. Todd expressed fears concerning the activities of the 500 Catholic missionaries reputed to have landed in New York in 1835. He charged that the Church of Rome spent over a million dollars per annum upon propaganda in America. The Scotch Presbyterian minister George Lewis was convinced of the existence of a Jesuit plot to strangle the common schools of St. Louis.[49]

48 C. A. Murray, *op. cit.*, II, 207; J. S. Buckingham, *America*, III, 348-349; J. S. Buckingham, *Eastern and Western States*, III, 119, 121, 263. See also the material on the Irish in the chapter on Emigration.

49 Capt. Frederick Marryat. *op. cit.*, second series, III, 163, 166; Alexander Mackay, *op. cit.*, III, 262-266; H. C. Todd, *Notes upon Canada and the United States*, Addenda, 7; George Lewis, *Impressions of America and American Churches*, 253.

Other equally fantastic charges concerning the nefarious activities of the Catholics were constantly being made.

There is no doubt that most English travellers at this time were intensely allergic to Catholicism on religious grounds. But it should also be noted that they were conversant with the fact that the Church in America had " gathered beneath its banner the most democratic republicans." [50] This meant the Irish laborers, the German agricultural workers, and a smattering of native Democrats and Loco-Focos. This alliance of Catholicism and Democracy made both institutions doubly repugnant to the conservatives.

The tremendous increase in the number and the importance of the Irish after 1845 gave the problem still another twist. It tied up Catholicism with politics and emigration, and, more specifically, with the problems of the Irish in the New World. Many Englishmen were convinced that all the misfortunes of the Irish in America were attributable to the domination exercised over them by the Catholic priesthood. Some visitors went so far as to charge that by controlling the vital Irish vote, the priests wielded a powerful scepter over all America. [51] It was not for nothing, they reasoned, that the reactionary Church of Rome fostered the most radical American democrats in its bosom. If the editor of the *Illustrated London News* became convinced that the anti-British feeling of the Irish-American was " fostered for purposes of ecclesiastical domination and influence," [52] it can be seen that the British were willing to believe the worst about the Catholics.

---

50 C. A. Murray, *op. cit.*, II, 207; see also J. R. Godley, *op. cit.*, II, 174; Sir Charles Lyell, *op. cit.*, II, 291.

51 Alfred Bunn, *New England and Old England*, II, 2-3; Mrs. I. L. Bishop, *op. cit.*, 419; W. E. Baxter, *op. cit.*, 155; Sir Charles Lyell, *op. cit.*, II, 291; John Macgregor, *Our Brothers and Cousins*, 59; Charles Mackay, *Life and Liberty in America*, I, 178; R. Ogden, ed., *Life and Letters of E. L. Godkin*, I, 183. For additional data on the role of the Irish in politics, see the chapters on Democratic Government and on Emigration.

52 Charles Mackay, *op. cit.*, I, 179.

Yet there were those who thought these fears exaggerated and unjustified. To Harriet Martineau the very fact that the Church had reversed its traditional conservatism and now supported democrats in politics demonstrated its ability to conform to American conditions. Others felt that any ascendancy on the part of the Church was bound to be only temporary, since Catholicism was basically at variance with American institutions and ways of thought. Freedom of religion and discussion, they said, was adverse to the influence of the priesthood.[53] This was demonstrated by the large number of defections among second and third generation Americans.[54] But the common schools were generally credited with constituting the most important factor in bringing about a weakening of Church authority.[55] Evidently the Church recognized this also, for it did its utmost, according to British observers, to maintain its own schools. Its success, in 1840, in securing a share of the public funds for parochial schools in New York, dismayed Godley. He regarded this step as the beginning of the end of the separation of Church and State. Though state aid to parochial schools ceased in the following year, the vast majority of Irish children continued to attend the Catholic schools. Yet, if only twenty per cent attended the public schools, stated the Reverend Robert Everest, this number should be sufficient to have the others learn, through contact, proper contempt for " the artifices of the priest." [56]

Catholic visitors, of course, like Beste, Kelly, and Casey, saw nothing wrong in the growth of their Church in America. Evidently, however, they considered it best to ignore the

53 Harriet Martineau, *op. cit.*, II, 323; W. E. Baxter, *op. cit.*, 155.

54 James Robertson, *A Few Months in America*, 158; J. R. Godley, *op. cit.*, II, 172.

55 Charles Mackay, *op. cit.*, I, 182; W. E. Baxter, *op. cit.*, 156; William Chambers, *Things as They Are in America*, 350; J. F. W. Johnston, *Notes on North America*, II, 409; William Hancock, *An Emigrant's Five Years in the Free States of America*, 101; also see the chapter on Education.

56 J. R. Godley, *op. cit.*, II, 32; John Macgregor, *op. cit.*, 59; Robert Everest, *A Journey through the United States and Canada*, 58.

subject in their books. It remained for a Protestant, Mrs. Maury, to undertake a defense of Catholicism. She called Catholicism " the Shield of America," chiefly, it appears, because the priests kept her Irish servants in hand.[57]

While travellers worried about the destruction of the Protestant faith in America by the sinister forces of Rome, another more potent force was preparing to enter the lists to give battle. This was Science. Years before Darwin published his *Origin of Species,* Asa Gray was lecturing on evolution at Harvard. While Sir Charles Lyell was in Boston in 1846, he heard of a Presbyterian minister who had been refused ordination because he would not accept the origin of man as stated in *Genesis.* In the end, Lyell reported, an Independent congregation accepted him as its pastor. Other pastors thereupon endeavored to reach some compromise with him.[58] Johnston, a well-known chemist and agricultural scientist, was shocked at Gray's public lectures on evolution. He felt that speculations of this kind should be restricted to the laboratory because they conflicted with religion. Though Unitarian Boston seemed unperturbed, Johnston warned the clergy that they had better learn some science if they wished to meet the evolutionist on his own ground.[59] However, the controversy of science vs. religion was still in the bud. It remained for a later period to see it blossom forth in its full fury.

57 S. M. Maury, *op. cit.,* 95.

58 Sir Charles Lyell, *op. cit.,* I, 219.

59 J. F. W. Johnston, *op. cit.,* II, 442-447.

CHAPTER VII

EDUCATION

Sir Charles Lyell visited a Boston school. There were 550 girls and nine teachers cramped into three rooms. But each pupil had her own individual fixed seat—a luxury by English standards. The girls looked neat and studious. No trace of corporal punishment was in evidence. The principal beamed as he pointed out the fine quality of the students' work. As a final gesture, Lyell was invited to quiz the pupils himself. Somewhat skeptically he selected Gray's *Elegy in a Country Churchyard*. The excellence of the reading surprised him; the answers to his questions more than satisfied him. He could not have expected more in one of the old English public schools.[1]

Yet this was a school supported by public funds, open to all comers, rich or poor, and without regard to creed. In England and on the Continent, schools with few exceptions were still private and sectarian. After long agitation by educational reformers, Parliament in 1833 had finally granted $100,000 as a subsidy to voluntary schools, run chiefly by religious organizations engaged in common education. The Grants were renewed annually thereafter, and increased in 1839 to $150,000. But, reformers pointed out sarcastically, Parliament had granted $350,000 at the same time for the care of the Queen's horses. Further efforts towards educational progress beat futilely against the Anglican Church's opposition to secular education.

In America, however, the Briton found the principle of popular non-sectarian education to be as firmly established as republicanism itself. Whether he travelled in the North, South, East, or West, the necessity of popular education was everywhere regarded as axiomatic. It was the foundation upon which the entire superstructure of American institutions rested. In a country where political sovereignty was placed in the hands of

1 Sir Charles Lyell, *Second Visit to the United States*, I, 189.

the common man, it was essential that he understand how to exercise it. The state, visitors added, unlike European despotisms based upon force or fraud, had no need to ally itself with ignorance. On the contrary, it found in education its strongest ally.[2] Some opposition to free common school education, it was true, was offered by a small group of men rich enough to send their children to private schools, and hence unwilling to pay for the support of public schools.[3] But the vast majority appeared willing to tax themselves for education to almost any extent. Nor was there any dominant ecclesiastical body, such as the Anglican Church in England, sufficiently powerful to thwart the demands for public education.[4]

Thus it came about that the advantages of education were enjoyed by children of even the poorest class in every inhabited part of the country. At least that was the general impression among British visitors. The provision for schools was so adequate, said Miss Martineau, that the only children to be seen on the streets during school hours were those taking an unauthorized holiday.[5]

The quality of instruction varied, of course, throughout the Union. Travellers believed that educational facilities were best in New England and worst in the South. Johnston pointed out that the education budget of New York State alone was greater than that spent on public education in all England.[6] Even larger expenditures were made by Connecticut and Rhode Island. In 1847, scholarly Alexander Mackay reported that Connecticut alone had 80,000 students in its 1,660 school dis-

2 W. E. Baxter, *America and the Americans*, 157; Alexander Mackay, *The Western World*, III, 225.

3 Hugo Reid, *Sketches in North America*, 257.

4 Alexander Majoribanks, *Travels in South and North America*, 195-196; Sir Charles Lyell, *op. cit.*, I, 231.

5 C. A. Murray, *Travels in North America, 1834-1836*, II, 201; Harriet Martineau, *Society in America*, II, 269.

6 J. F. W. Johnston, *Notes on North America*, II, 491.

tricts, in addition to the thousands attending its academies and colleges.[7]

The largest cities quite naturally had the best schools. Captain Mackinnon considered the Philadelphia school system " among the best in the world." He described it as having one high school, one normal school, 53 grammar schools, 29 secondaries, 130 primaries, and 40 unclassified schools.[8] Girard College, on the northern outskirts of town, was Philadelphia's chief pedagogical tourist attraction. It was an academy supported by a very large endowment left by a philanthropist, Stephen Girard. By the terms of his will it was open only to orphan children. The school's vast buildings of white marble were spectacular and imposing. The instruction, which was strictly non-sectarian, was commended as excellent. In accordance with the terms of the will, clergymen were barred from so much as crossing its threshold. Its teaching positions paid so well, however, that according to Lord Acton it was not infrequent for a minister to renounce his ordination for the sake of securing the post.[9]

The schools of New York, like other things about that city, received more attention from British visitors than any other municipal system. In 1837, Buckingham declared its teachers to be better than those employed in the National and Lancastrian schools of England. The proficiency of the pupils was likewise superior. Most of the schools in his time were private, however, with over 10,000 children attending boarding schools.[10] The establishment of the Board of Education in 1841 changed this situation and gave a marked impetus to free edu-

7 Alexander Mackay, *op. cit.*, III, 234-235.

8 L. B. Mackinnon, *Atlantic and Transatlantic Sketches*, I, 80. Educational statistics were quoted by almost every visitor. But the sources for this data were practically never given, and the discrepancies between the figures quoted were frequently great. Hence, they cannot be regarded as reliable.

9 J. E. E. D. Acton, "Lord Acton's American Diaries," *Fortnightly Review*, CXI, 80.

10 J. S. Buckingham, *America*, I, 203-204.

cation. Godley, shortly thereafter, reported that the quality of the instruction at these schools was " exceedingly good." The instructors were well paid, he was informed, with the men receiving $1,000, and the women primary school instructors $200-$400 per annum. There were even special schools for negro children taught by colored instructors. One of the latter told him that he received $700 a year. The little " blackberries " could read, write, and cipher in a manner that astonished Godley. Both the pronunciation and the caligraphy were infinitely superior to anything he had seen in a similar stratum of society in England.[11] In the 'fifties so many ragamuffin Irish emigrant children attended the public schools in certain districts that special curricula were established for them, patterned on an industrial basis, and known as " Boys Meetings " or " Girls Meetings." Enrollment in these schools, according to Mrs. Bishop who visited them, was restricted to about one hundred each because of the need for personalized attention.[12]

The establishment of the Free Academy in 1847 was rightly regarded by English visitors as affixing the crowning stone in the educational edifice. The Academy (later The City College) was a combination high school, academy, and college. Entrance requirements were surprisingly low by modern standards, but did not seem so to contemporaries, either native or foreign. The applicant for admission had to be at least thirteen years old, with one year of common school education. Passage of a stiff entrance examination in a number of subjects, including history and algebra, was required. The Academy had a library of 3,000 volumes plus 8,000 texts. The principal received a salary of $2,500, but doubled also as professor of moral, intellectual, and political philosophy. Other professors received $1,500, and the tutors $500. By 1854 the Academy had fourteen instructors and 600 students drawn from every rank in society.[13]

11 J. R. Godley, *Letters from America*, II, 33-34.

12 Mrs. I. L. Bishop, *An Englishwoman in America*, 347.

13 H. A. Murray, *Lands of the Slave and the Free*, 118-121; Mrs. I. L. Bishop, *op. cit.*, 437; W. E. Baxter, *op. cit.*, 164.

Other branches of the public school system grew correspondingly in size so that when Mrs. Bishop visited New York in 1854 it had 224 public schools with a total register of 133,831. Twenty-five of these schools were for the colored. An additional 11,000 students attended classes at night. She felt that the system was worthy of the highest praise. The quality of instruction was so good, she said, that even the children of the wealthy merchants attended the public schools.[14] Numerous Catholic parochial schools also existed, patronized chiefly by the Irish. The establishment of the Board of Education in 1841 cut off the state aid they had won in the previous year. However, Lord Acton heard that they evaded the new prohibition against the payment of state funds to religious schools by holding their religious services after the regular school hours.[15] Thus, right down until the Civil War, the majority of the Irish emigrant children continued to attend parochial schools, thereby arousing dire forebodings on the part of English travellers as to the dangers of Romanism in America.[16]

Boston was another city that was complimented for its schools. By the 'fifties it was spending over $330,000 annually for schools, with a school plant costing at least $1,500,000. Visitors were duly impressed. Primary education, they were told, began at the age of four, under women teachers. Boys customarily remained in school till the age of fourteen and girls till sixteen. Female teachers received only $325 per annum in Boston, and one-third to one-half less in the small towns and rural areas nearby. Travellers admitted that this was low, but claimed that male teachers were well paid. Some high school teachers in Boston earned as much as $2,400, they said, which was only $100 less than the Governor's salary.[17] Here, as in New York, Englishmen were surprised to find that even

14 Mrs. I. L. Bishop, *op. cit.*, 347-351, 434-437.

15 J. E. E. D. Acton, *op. cit.*, CXI, 81.

16 See the chapter on Religion for additional data on this problem.

17 W. E. Baxter, *op. cit.*, 160, 163; Sir Charles Lyell, I, 192.

the rich preferred to send their children to the public schools because of the superior instruction.[18] Godley saw boys of twelve studying Ovid and Lucian. The master, in his opinion, was a good scholar. He received a salary of $2,000. The students appeared to be as proficient as those of their age in English private schools.[19]

But the fine salaries, the Latin studies distinguishing the better schools, the fine buildings, and the separate desks were not typical of the country as a whole, Godley warned his countrymen. In the rural areas, education for the greater part of the year consisted only of elementary instruction for the younger children, given by underpaid women teachers. But this situation was alleviated by the numerous college students who secured teaching positions in these communities during the long winter vacation as a means of defraying their college expenses. They received $20 a month, and were boarded by the farmers whose children attended the schools.[20] The inability of smaller communities to pay adequate salaries for male teachers was partially remedied by the establishment of normal schools for the training of women elementary teachers. New England pioneered in this field. By the 'fifties it had built up a surplus of teachers that streamed steadily into the South and West.[21]

Although common school education appeared to be universal throughout the North, this was not true in the South. Phillippo tried to prove statistically that although only one in every thousand white adults was illiterate in New England, the proportion grew to one in every six whites in the South. Godley stated that he had heard Horace Mann declare that from twenty-five to forty per cent of the Southern whites were illiterate. This statement disillusioned him of his earlier belief that all

18 Sir Charles Lyell, *op. cit.*, I, 195.

19 J. R. Godley, *op. cit.*, II, 120.

20 W. E. Baxter, *op. cit.*, II, 100; J. R. Godley, *op. cit.*, II, 120; Robert Russell, *North America*, 98.

21 Hugo Reid, *op. cit.*, 250; J. M. Phillippo, *The United States and Cuba*, 203.

Americans were literate.[22] Though most visitors did not place Southern illiteracy quite so high, a mere glance at the education budgets of the various states revealed the comparatively small amount spent by the Southern states. Miss Martineau pointed out that early marriages were the rule in the South, and this necessarily limited the schooling period, especially for girls. Sons also dropped out of school at an early age in order to go to work on the plantations.[23] Sir Charles Lyell, on the basis of some schools for negroes which he had seen in Kentucky, Virginia, and Tennessee, maintained the extraordinary contention that Southern negro education was superior to that accorded the poor whites in the North. He pointed to the fact that many of the whites had been taught to read by negro nurses, as proof of negro literacy. Mrs. Maury, who like Lyell was basically sympathetic towards Southern society, and who admitted an open preference for the South over any other section, likewise praised Southern education. She claimed it produced less knowledge, but more intuitive thought and wisdom.[24] These fantastic ideas gained no acceptance among other travellers. In their eyes, Southern education was definitely inferior.

In the West, however, the love of education was strong, visitors stated, even though educational facilities were often primitive. In thinly settled areas there might not even be a schoolhouse. In such cases the master lived at one of the farmhouses each week, and held school there.[25] Despite the fact that Oliver called the lack of educational facilities " one of the most serious drawbacks " to emigration to the West, Sturge asserted at this same time (1841) that on a statistical basis even this frontier region stood up as well as any part of Europe in the

22 J. M. Phillippo, *op. cit.*, 202; J. R. Godley, *op. cit.*, II, 122. According to W. E. Dodd, *The Cotton Kingdom*, 115, the actual figure for Southern white illiteracy was seventy per thousand.

23 Harriet Martineau, *op. cit.*, II, 100.

24 Sir Charles Lyell, *op. cit.*, I, 129-130, 275; J. E. E. D. Acton, *op. cit.*, CX, 917; S. M. Maury, *An Englishwoman in America,* 107.

25 William Oliver, *Eight Months in Illinois,* 112.

matter of education.[26] Baxter noted that the Minnesota Territory, still a wild region, already had four seminaries, and had donated 49,000 acres to endow a college at St. Paul.[27] Even in far-off Salt Lake, the Mormons, though outcasts because of their religious practices, maintained the American tradition in education by requiring all children to attend secular schools, tuition free for the poor.[28]

It was inevitable that British travellers, most of whom were well-educated men, should be interested in higher education in America. Phillippo estimated that in 1850 there were 123 colleges in the United States containing 10,000 students and 435 instructors.[29] Although Baxter insisted that Andover, Princeton, Yale, and Auburn occupied a footing of equality with those of Edinburgh and Göttingen, and were superior in theological attainments to Oxford or Cambridge,[30] most colleges were very small and of limited importance. The course of study normally took four years. It included Latin, Greek, mathematics, natural philosophy, rhetoric, English composition, and international and constitutional law. A few of the leading colleges were beginning to introduce the physical sciences and modern languages, also, at this time.

Harvard was generally regarded as the leading American college because of its large endowments, its extensive library, and its distinguished faculty. Yet, in the late 'forties, it had only 300 undergraduates and twenty professors.[31] It was not uncommon for British visitors to present themselves with letters of introduction to the better known men on its faculty. As it was not considered ethical for a traveller to print personal remarks

26 *Ibid.*, 112; Joseph Sturge, *A Visit to the United States*, 211.

27 W. E. Baxter, *op. cit.*, 164.

28 William Chandless, *A Visit to Salt Lake*, 186.

29 J. M. Phillippo, *op. cit.*, 209-211.

30 W. E. Baxter, *op. cit.*, 131.

31 J. F. W. Johnston, *op. cit.*, II, 438. Travellers failed to realize that the University of Virginia, which had nearly a thousand students at this time, was the largest institution of higher education in the country.

about his American hosts and acquaintances, travel books ordinarily omitted such references. But Lord Acton recorded his impressions of Harvard in a private diary that was not published till the twentieth century. He regarded Jared Sparks as " devoid of talent, plodding and honest." *The Life of Washington* was " dry, heavy, far from comprehensive . . . with no other merit than laboriousness." Lord Acton found Longfellow even less impressive. The latter's students did German translation but poorly. As a conversationalist he was disappointing. On the other hand Agassiz elicited high praise, Lord Acton rating him as one of America's foremost men.[32] The Harvard curriculum struck the future historian as too practical. Nothing was studied for its own sake, but only as it would be useful in making a practical man. Thus, rhetoric was studied to aid public speaking; mathematics and science for utility. Little emphasis was placed upon Latin and Greek. " The studies are as languid as in England and the discipline as loose as in Germany," he concluded with disgust.[33] C. A. Murray, another aristocrat, agreed with him. Even if Homer and Plato were not studied, Aristotle and Cicero should be. At very least, Bacon, Montesquieu, Newton, and La Place might be the objects of careful and profound study, Murray insisted. But Miss Martineau criticized Harvard for quite other reasons. A few breezes of democratic inspiration from some country schoolhouse, she said, would do its aristocratic pretensions a world of good.[34]

The conflict between cultural and practical education was being won by the latter in other universities, too, despite the dark forebodings of British visitors. Johnston mentioned the case of Brown University as illustrating this trend. Student enrollment had been dropping so steadily that it appeared that the institution must close. President Wayland, its head, de-

32 J. E. E. D. Acton, *op. cit.*, CX, 931-933.

33 *Ibid.*, CX, 930-933.

34 C. A. Murray, *op. cit.*, II, 209; Harriet Martineau, *op. cit.*, II, 270.

cided the cause for the decline was the university's failure to meet the needs of the community. Thereupon he revised the curriculum in a more practical direction. Modern languages, mathematics, science, and economics were added. Whereas Lord Acton and C. A. Murray, literary men, had championed the humanities, Johnston, a scientist, commended Wayland's action as pointing in the right direction. Similarly, Lyell, the great geologist, was highly pleased at the introduction at Harvard of those very courses in botany, anatomy, chemistry, engineering, and geology which annoyed Lord Acton so greatly.[35]

In the South it was the University of Virginia that drew the traveller's attention. This institution was famous for carrying on the liberal spirit of its founder, Thomas Jefferson. Visitors were amazed to hear that students elected their own courses, and that the professors elected their President from amongst themselves. Salaries were said to be equal for all, being $1,000 per annum plus a house. Visitors were equally surprised to learn that not one student in twenty completed his degree. The others dropped out or took free electives. Its liberal spirit was further illustrated by its practice of rotating the university chaplaincy among ministers of the various Protestant denominations, so that an Episcopalian one year would be followed by a Methodist or Baptist the next. To staunch sectarians like Godley, this was shockingly ungodly.[36]

In the West there was but one college that attracted appreciable attention from the British visitor. This was St. Louis University, a Jesuit school chartered in 1832. Within five years it had a student body of 200, drawn chiefly from Latin-American countries. Boys from ten to sixteen years of age were admitted. The curriculum consisted of a four-year course in either the humanities or practical subjects. Tuition was very low, amounting to only $180 a year, including board and

35 J. F. W. Johnston, *op. cit.*, II, 472, 475-481, 493; Sir Charles Lyell, *op. cit.*, I, 195.

36 J. F. W. Johnston, *op. cit.*, II, 480; J. R. Godley, *op. cit.*, II, 199-200.

lodging. The college's female counterpart was a Sacred Heart convent that offered a course of study which Buckingham considered as duplicating the most fashionable boarding schools of Europe. History, geography, literature, drawing, music, dancing, and languages were included in the curriculum. Tuition was higher than in the boy's college, running to $250 for the year. Although charmed by the reception these institutions accorded him, Buckingham regarded them with misgiving as centers of Catholic propaganda.[37] Later travellers did likewise. It was the Jesuit control rather than the excellence of the schooling that attracted their attention.[38]

Other theological colleges were numerous. Baxter in 1854 estimated their number at forty-four, with 127 professors and 1,449 students.[39] But none of them was sufficiently outstanding or important to arouse much interest among British travellers.

The cheapness of American higher education, however, was a constant surprise to visitors. The University of Virginia, which they considered as the most expensive in the entire country, charged only $350 per annum. H. A. Murray, though strongly opposed to democratic institutions, was moved to admiration when he compared this figure with the champagne dinners, the hunters, the tandems, and the other " necessities " of English university students. " The republican lads go to college to learn something, whereas many papas send their firstborn hope to Oxford and Cambridge to save themselves trouble and keep the youths out of mischief." [40]

But it remained for that sharp critic, Charles Dickens, to hand American colleges the largest bouquet. Regardless of their defects, said he, at least " they disseminate no prejudices; rear no bigots; dig up the buried ashes of no old superstitions; never interpose between the people and their improvement; exclude

37 J. S. Buckingham, *Eastern and Western States*, III, 122-125.

38 See the chapters on Religion, Emigration, and Democratic Government for further data on the attitude towards Catholicism.

39 W. E. Baxter, *op. cit.*, 131.

40 H. A. Murray, *op. cit.*, 320.

no man because of his religious opinions; and, above all, in their whole course of study and instruction, recognize a world ... beyond the college walls." [41]

For those who were unable to have a higher education, but as adults still wished to enlarge their knowledge and improve their minds, there were the Lyceums. Bunn, who toured New England in 1853, reported that practically every village had its lecture hall.[42] Nor was this restricted to that section alone. Johnston, attending some lectures at the Smithsonian Institution, found the lecture halls jammed with capacity audiences of 1,200 to 1,500 people.[43] But not many English visitors, other than those who lectured on the Lyceum circuits, paid much attention to them. Those who did, were deeply impressed by the people's thirst for knowledge. " It is a matter of wonderment ... to witness the youthful workmen, the over-tired artisan, the worn-out factory girl ... rushing ... after the toil of the day is over, into the hot atmosphere of a crowded lecture room." [44] The results attained were another matter. The diversity of subjects and the speed with which one lecture trod upon the heels of another, made it improbable that any of them were well remembered.[45] Regardless of results, however, the visitor considered the intentions admirable.

Having viewed American education in its many aspects over the length and breadth of the land, it was but logical that the traveller should seek to evaluate its success in fulfilling its announced goal, good citizenship. The teaching was generally acknowledged to be thorough and efficient. At very least, practically every white American was literate. By stimulating individual thought rather than emphasizing the mere acquisition of

41 Charles Dickens, *American Notes*, 210.

42 Alfred Bunn, *Old England and New England*, 30.

43 J. F. W. Johnston, *op. cit.*, II, 371.

44 Alfred Bunn, *op. cit.*, 30.

45 Charles Dickens, *op. cit.*, 240; George Combe, *Notes on the United States of North America*, III, 254.

knowledge, travellers stated, the schools were training students early in life to exercise in a rational manner the rights to which they were entitled as American citizens.[46] As a result, on most important social and political questions, " every citizen is found to entertain an intelligent opinion. He may be wrong in his views, but he can always offer you a reason for them." [47] Furthermore, the common schools made possible the assimilation of the emigrant hordes constantly arriving on American shores. The common school system was hailed as the bulwark of Protestantism in preventing the insidious advances of Romanism among the youth.[48] It was also generally credited with inculcating a feeling of equality that tended to prevent the rise of class barriers. A blacksmith grown wealthy had only to wash his hands to enter his new stratum in society. His new associates would be neither so highly cultivated, nor he so poorly educated as to place him in an uncomfortable position.[49]

Not all Britons were so enthusiastic, however. Miss Martineau, while admitting that American schools compared favorably with those of England, deplored the lack of instruction in " political morals." The schools, she complained, gave too superficial an education to train the students adequately for life. Combe, who also had great faith in the efficacy of education as a means for bringing about a better world, was even more disappointed in American education. It was defective, he lamented, in training the individual for self-control and love of the good. Rote learning was being emphasized at the expense of civic leadership. This, he said, was the reason why ignorance was often entrenched in high office.[50]

46 W. E. Baxter, op. cit., 162; J. M. Phillippo, op. cit., 340; Hugo Reid, op. cit., 252; Joseph Sturge, op. cit., 209.

47 Alexander Mackay, op. cit., III, 338.

48 See the chapter on Religion.

49 G. D. Warburton, Hochelega, II, 209.

50 Harriet Martineau, op. cit., II, 269, 279; George Combe, op. cit., I, 162; III, 251, 254.

The strongest attacks on American education came not from over-zealous reformers, but from conservatives and reactionaries who were fundamentally opposed to the entire theory of popular secular education. The sectarians took the lead in this. A secular school, in their opinion, was not only non-religious, it was irreligious. They cried out that the common schools had been reared upon the sacrifice of Christian teaching.[51] Secular education was immoral, demoralizing, inimical to discipline, and encouraging to crime. Mrs. Maury, who had called Catholicism " the Shield of America," pointed to Connecticut which claimed it had less than forty men unable to read at the very time when its crime rate was the highest in the Union, as proof of this. Obviously, then, " before long a Penitentiary will be indispensable wherever there is a free school." [52] Schoolmasters not using corporal punishment were agents of the Devil. Jesuit teachers and methods alone, she maintained, held the key to " the perfection of intellectual and practical education." [53] Godley, though he hated the Catholics, agreed with her in regard to the need for religious control of the schools. He had visited the Philadelphia High School. Despite the competent instructors and well-conducted classes, he regarded the course of study as " an elaborate piece of quackery " because its attention to the physical sciences fixed the mind on material things. Religious instruction was essential to divert the mind from such mundane matters and to stress the fundamental spiritual values, Godley insisted.[54] Another line of attack was the claim that secular education failed to inculcate discipline and obedience towards authority. Marryat charged that discipline in the schools was so lax that the students learned what they wished, and did as they wished. What respect for authority would they have in later life? [55]

51 J. D. Lewis, *Across the Atlantic*, 411.

52 S. M. Maury, *op. cit.*, 110.

53 *Ibid.*, 108.

54 J. R. Godley, *op. cit.*, II, 154-155.

55 H. A. Murray, *op. cit.*, 371 ; Capt. Frederick Marryat, *Diary in America*, first series, III, 287-300.

Conservatives quite naturally tended to deprecate democratic education as too shallow and superficial. Though many were literate, scholars were few.[56] Beste, a Catholic, remarked that despite the imperfect knowledge of the students, their report cards always revealed satisfactory progress. Evidently the teachers taught nothing, and expected nothing.[57]

But it remained for Mitchell, imbued with the Southern theory of superior and inferior peoples, to state the conservative viewpoint most boldly. Popular education, he asserted, trained all for leadership, whereas in reality the majority were fit only to follow. Its chief fruit was the engendering of a distaste for menial work, and an over-estimate of their own ability and importance on the part of the masses. Therefore, he maintained, to educate men on the assumption of the equality of man was sheer folly.[58]

Despite the criticism of over-ambitious liberals and reactionary conservatives, most British visitors thought very highly of American education. Though not perhaps as perfect a system as its founders had expected, yet it was doing a good job. Even observers otherwise sharply critical of democratic institutions agreed that the common school was " one of the glories of America." [59] Its future seemed no less bright. Further advances could be expected since every parent was anxious to improve his children's educational opportunities, and appeared willing to tax himself for this purpose. Nor was there any dominant ecclesiastical body or other vested interest sufficiently powerful to thwart this advance. In so far as the general education of its people was concerned, the United States was not only ahead of any other nation, but appeared destined to maintain its lead for some time to come.[60]

---

56 James Stirling, *Letters from the Slave States*, 24; Capt. Frederick Marryat, *op. cit.*, first series, III, 301; C. A. Murray, *op. cit.*, II, 209.

57 J. R. D. Beste, *The Wabash*, II, 333-334.

58 D. W. Mitchell, *Ten Years in the United States*, 216, 247.

59 Mrs. I. L. Bishop, *op. cit.*, 436; H. A. Murray, *op. cit.*, 377; T. C. Grattan, *Civilized America*, II, 377.

60 Sir Charles Lyell, *op. cit.*, I, 231; Alexander Majoribanks, *Travels in South and North America*, 193, 195-196; J. F. W. Johnston, *op. cit.*, II, 491.

CHAPTER VIII

EMIGRATION

THE 'forties witnessed one of the great periods of human migration. The Irish Famine and the failure of the Revolutions of 1848 brought this movement, already under way, to a new peak, giving it the force of a tidal wave.

Naturally, Englishmen were affected by it. The poor looked with longing inquiry towards the Golden Land. The rich looked also, but their inquiry was tempered with misgiving. The traveller, of necessity, became the chief source of current information on the problem.

Beste, Mrs. Maury, and a few others crossed the Atlantic specifically to look into the matter. Hancock, Brothers, Brown, Oldmixon, and Wyse had actually tried emigration, only to return. Oliver and Regan were still in America when they wrote on the subject. Caird was active as an emigration promoter for the Illinois Central Railroad. Other travellers realized that consideration of the topic would probably increase the circulation of their book. Moreover, emigrants were playing so large a role in American life at this time that few could disregard them entirely.

The poorest English traveller was richer than the average emigrant, and positively wealthy as compared to the Irish emigrant. Conditions, bad enough on the fast packets and liners used by the traveller, were infinitely worse on the emigrant ships. Shipboard conditions may be visualized if one considers that even the better passenger liners were disregarding the Regulations of 1847 which required a minimum of fourteen square feet of space per passenger, with decks not less than six feet apart, and berths at least one-and-a-half feet wide by six feet long.[1]

In the 'thirties, Welsh schooners carrying slate were active in the emigrant trade. A thick layer of sawdust spread over

1 H. P. Fairchild, *Immigration*, 82.

the slate, constituted the floor. The emigrants were herded together worse than cattle, since they did not even have stalls.
Nothing was provided the emigrant except water, and this was
carried in casks on the deck. In bad weather the casks were
frequently swept overboard. Cooking was done on the sawdust.
If adverse winds or calms extended the voyage two or three
months (and this was not infrequent), both food and water
would run low.[2]

The next decade saw some improvement in that the typical
emigrant ship now carried one stove on deck for cooking. But
steerage was much as it had been, and even second class was
scarcely better. Sleeping quarters consisted of a mere trough,
with no division of the sexes. All except first class passengers
were kept confined below deck. Steerage passage was cheap,
however, being only £2, 15s from Liverpool to New York.[3]
The food relief ships that unloaded their cargoes in Ireland, and
then returned to America crowded to the gunwales with starving, ragged humanity, were even worse, being totally unfit for
passenger traffic.

It was not until 1855 that the British government began the
inspection of ship accommodations, and compelled the ship to
provide provisions and do the cooking. Prior to this, each
emigrant had provided his own provisions for the voyage.
All too often, especially in the case of the poverty-stricken
Irish, the emigrant had come on board without food. In such
cases, he either begged, stole, or starved.

Small wonder that small-pox and the dread typhus lurked
in the dark holds of these ships. Deaths at sea were so commonplace, even on luxury liners, that they merited only a curt
notation in travel diaries. The New York State Emigration
Commission calculated that the number of sick on British ships
entering New York harbor was thirty per thousand during
1847-1848. Of 82,000 who sailed for this port in the first half

2 F. C. Bowen, *A Century of Atlantic Travel, 1830-1930*, 21-22.

3 *Ibid.*, 42-43.

of 1847, 947 were buried at sea, and 288 died at quarantine.[4]
The Edinburgh Review set the death toll even higher, 15,000
out of 90,000, or almost seventeen per cent.[5]

English travellers failed to see most of this misery. Confined
to their bunks by seasickness, they seldom had the interest or
fortitude to investigate steerage conditions on the lower decks.
Occasionally one would peek down into the emigrant quarters,
and report that they " behaved exceedingly well " so long as
there was no liquor on board.[6] As for the ships carrying emigrants only, no Englishman capable of writing a book appears
ever to have been a passenger on one. Despite this, however, the
traveller became sufficiently conversant with the hardships
facing the emigrant to lead him to warn the person considering
emigration to pause and reconsider before plunging into an
action which would " expose him to difficulties far greater in
their consequences—more disastrous in their results . . . than
any from which he may possibly have escaped." [7]

The distinction between the travel facilities used by the traveller and the emigrant, was continued to a lesser extent in
America. Travellers who accidentally wandered into the special
emigrant cars that the railroads were beginning to put into
use, were quickly driven out by the stench.[8] Furthermore, large
numbers of emigrants continued to patronize the cheaper canal
transport which the traveller had abandoned in favor of the
speedier railroad. Even on the western river steamers, a special
section, the hot and dangerous aft deck near the boilers, was
assigned to the emigrant trade. There they sat " in the midst
of their bedding, pots and pans, and children with dirty faces,

4 J. B. McMaster, *History of the People of the United States*, VII, 226.

5 S. P. Orth, *Our Foreigners*, 112.

6 Mrs. Felton, *American Life,* 18; Joseph Biggs, *To America in 39 Days
before Steamships*, 20.

7 Francis Wyse, *America: Realities and Resources*, III, 1-2.

8 Mrs. I. L. Bishop, *An Englishwoman in America*, III.

young women and wives with dirty caps, rumpled gowns, and dishevelled hair." [9]

To the British traveller not all emigrants were alike—not by any means. Like the native American, he divided emigrants into groups on the basis of their former nationality. Nor did he consider them as Americans, regardless of naturalization or length of residence. An American, so far as the visitor was concerned, was a native-born son only. Hence, when discussing the absence of poverty and the relative well-being of the populace, the condition of the emigrant was not considered part of the American scene. Thus, many an author who swore that he had never seen a beggar in the United States hastened to add as an afterthought, " except some Irish."

Of the emigrant groups, the Scots and Germans were regarded as the most industrious, the most prudent, and the most successful. The former usually went into trade, while the latter congregated in large agricultural communities, particularly in the Midwest. Both had the reputation for being law-abiding and hard-working.[10] Harriet Martineau, with the Pennsylvania Dutch in mind, alleged that the Germans assimilated slowly.[11] But this was not true of those who arrived after the 'thirties.

English emigrants were relatively few in number, blended into the general pattern of the native population quite easily so far as the visitor could discern, and were not especially colorful or spectacular. Hence, the visiting Briton failed to consider them as a distinctive group. English emigrants at this time did not play an active role in American politics, religion, education, or other institutions. Hence, to a large extent they re-

9 William Thomson, *A Tradesman's Travels in the United States and Canada*, 49.

10 Lady E. C. E. M. Stuart-Wortley, *Travels in the United States*, 91; J. D. Lewis, *Across the Atlantic*, 420; Charles Casey, *Two Years on a Farm of Uncle Sam*, 223.

11 Harriet Martineau, *Society in America*, I, 340.

ceived mention in travel books only insofar as they later wrote of their own experiences.[12]

On the other side of the American Continent, the British visitor ran into the earliest arrivals of another vast emigrant group, the Chinese. Few in number at a time when the need for them was great, prejudice had not yet set in against them. Instead they were regarded as very useful, being " sympathetic, sober, and cleanly, and when treated with proper kindness and indulgence, attached and interested." [13] Above all, they were industrious and never seen idle.

However, it was not the Chinese, nor the Germans, nor the Scots, nor the English, but the Irish emigrant who stole the limelight, so far as the traveller was concerned. The Famine had centered world attention on the Irish. In America, they consti-tuted a large, coherent, and extremely vocal group. What they lacked in wealth, they made up for in colorfulness. They were accused of being the center of all disorders, the dominant force in American politics, the threat to the continued supremacy of Protestantism in America.[14] They were held to be the root and cause of all anti-British feeling on the part of Americans.[15] For the President of the United States to wine and dine Thomas Meagher, a fugitive leader of the abortive Irish Rebellion of

12 Oliver, Nettle, Wyse, Oldmixon, Brothers, Hancock, Brown, and Regan, all came to America with the intention of settling here permanently. Oliver and Regan were the only ones of this group to remain in the United States. The others returned to England after a number of years.

13 William Kelly, *A Stroll through the Diggings of California*, 180.

14 See previous chapters on Democratic Government, Religion, and Education.

15 Charles Mackay, *Life and Liberty in America*, I, 176; James Dixon, *Personal Narrative of a Tour Through Part of the United States and Canada*, 170; Alexander Majoribanks, *Travels in South and North America*, 124-125; William Chandless, *A Visit to Salt Lake*, 50; Alfred Bunn, *Old England and New England*, II, 12; Sir A. A. T. Cunynghame, *A Glimpse at the Great Western Republic*, 113; G. D. Warburton, *Hochelaga*, II, 54; D. W. Mitchell, *Ten Years in the United States*, 283; William Chambers, *Things as They Are in America*, 350; Edmund Patten, *A Glimpse at the United States and Canada*, 27.

1848, was startling. To British visitors, the throngs that crowded Meagher's lectures were alarming; those that bore his carriage through the streets of Boston on their backs were positively nauseating.[16] Such occurrences challenged the Briton's traditional viewpoint as to the inferior status of the Irish. Regardless of personal feelings (for most travellers hated and despised the Hibernians) here was a potent force in American life that merited attention.

Unlike the Germans who moved on to quiet western farms, the Irish remained concentrated in the large cities, especially in the East. By 1850 New York had 133,000 Irish, most poor and many unemployed, crowded into a distinct foreign quarter. This area stretched between Broadway and the Bowery. It was New York's first slum.[17] Entire families lived in one room in the dreary tenements that Collyer had denounced as dens of iniquity back in 1836. The streets were piled high with filth, dirt hills on Centre Street rising four feet in height. Yet no garbage carts visited the area for weeks at a time.[18] Little wonder then that the traveller observed that there was " very little Irish fun left in them; death, languor, listlessness, and disease hovering around them." [19] Bad as these slums were, most visitors admitted that they had seen worse in Dublin and London. The proximity of poverty and opulence in New York, however, gave greater emphasis to the gulf between the two.[20]

While New York had the largest and most important Irish colony in the entire country, similar conditions prevailed elsewhere. In Buckingham's time, New England had been characterized by a comparative absence of foreigners. In 1845 Sir

16 Alfred Bunn, *op. cit.*, II, 12-24.

17 S. P. Orth, *op. cit.*, 113; W. F. Adams, *Ireland and Irish Emigration to the New World from 1815 to the Famine*, 360; see also D. W. Mitchell, *op. cit.*, 147 and Francis Wyse, *op. cit.*, I, 48-49.

18 New York newspaper account, March, 1857, quoted in D. W. Mitchell, *op. cit.*, 147.

19 D. W. Mitchell, *op. cit.*, 145.

20 John Macgregor, *Our Brothers and Cousins*, 58; Mrs. I. L. Bishop, *op. cit.*, 383.

Charles Lyell had calculated that Boston contained only 8,000 Catholics out of a total population of 115,000.[21] During the next decade a radical change took place. The Irish flooded Boston, and overflowed into the nearby mill towns, displacing, finally, the native girls who for a long time had refused to work alongside the Irish because of the latter's dirtiness.[22]

In the middle states, Philadelphia had the largest Irish population after New York. Slum conditions paralleled those in the latter city, even to the presence of the dread cholera.[23] Recurrent riots with the free negroes and the nativists kept the Irish in the public eye. But their creation of labor organizations such as the Molly Maguires (1854) entirely escaped the visitor's attention.

There were not many Irish in the South, but Buckingham had found them working as mill hands in Georgia, and Lyell had seen them engaged on public works in Savannah.[24] It was not until the Famine, however, that the Irish began to appear in appreciable numbers in Southern cities. Baltimore contained the largest colony in the South, yet even here only 15,536 out of 599,860 whites were Irish in 1860.[25] In the Mississippi Valley, New Orleans and St. Louis had many Irish who were employed as firemen on the river steamers. The low wages and the dangerous nature of the work made them preferable to the high-priced slave.[26]

Further north they were found in large numbers in Chicago and Cincinnati. In 1849, visitors calculated that they composed twenty-five per cent of the population of the latter city.[27] They

21 Sir Charles Lyell, *Second Visit to the United States*, I, 189.

22 Mrs. Marianne Finch, *An Englishwoman's Experience in America*, 45.

23 George Combe, *Notes on the United States of America*, II, 53-54.

24 J. S. Buckingham, *Southern or Slave States*, I, 169; Sir Charles Lyell, *op. cit.*, II, 6.

25 D. W. Mitchell, *op. cit.*, 59-61; see also L. F. Schmeckebier, *History of the Know-Nothing Party in Maryland*, 46.

26 William Chandless, *op. cit.*, 50.

27 Ebenezer Davies, *American Scenes and Christian Slavery*, 158.

were to be encountered wherever canal or railroad projects were under way, and as cooks and teamsters on the westbound emigrant wagon trains.[28] Their presence had been noted in Texas as early as 1835,[29] and they were well established in California long before the Gold Rush.[30]

Why did the Irish, a people thoroughly agricultural in background generally refuse to become farmers once they came to America? Why did they crowd together in cities? These questions puzzled the English visitor.

Grattan attributed the phenomenon to the Irishman's gregarious instincts. Buckingham blamed it on the fact that the Irish were habitual drunkards, and the cities had better facilities for obtaining liquor![31] Godkin, an Orangeman who later became editor of *The Nation,* placed responsibility at the door of the Catholic Church. He accused it of vehemently opposing the break-up of the distinct Irish communities since its hold on the emigrants would be loosened once they were scattered.[32] Still others blamed it all on Irish clannishness.

The real explanation was simple enough, but unrecognized by most travellers. The Irish were the " hewers of wood and the carriers of water." They arrived at a time when " foreign labor (was) an article of nearly essential necessity to the progress of the country," [33] because of the vast upsurge of canal, railroad, and industrial construction. Even Marryat conceded that though the most troublesome of emigrants, the Irish were also " the most valuable to the United States." [34] For, as Dickens remarked, "who else would dig, and delve, and drudge,

28 William Chandless, *op. cit.,* 48-49.

29 G. W. Featherstonhaugh, *Excursion through the Slave States,* II, 146.

30 William Kelly, *op. cit.,* 216.

31 T. C. Grattan, *Civilized America,* II, 36; J. S. Buckingham, *Eastern and Western States,* II, 17.

32 R. Ogden, ed., *Life and Letters of E. L. Godkin,* I, 183.

33 Earl of Carlisle, *Travels in America,* 33.

34 Capt. Frederick Marryat, *Diary in America,* second series, II, 139.

and do domestic work, and make canals and roads, and execute great lines of Internal Improvement?" [35] Thus, they secured for themselves "the privilege of monopolizing all the rough and menial employment of every kind, which (was) otherwise set apart as only fitted for the colored population, and which but few Americans could be found to undertake." [36] The Irish settled wherever such work was to be had.

Hence, in New York they were the porters, draymen, bootblacks, newsboys, and general laborers of the city; in New England they were mill hands; in the West they worked as steamboat firemen, teamsters, and cooks; everywhere they could be found as laborers and navvies. Later they became domestics as well. If Maxwell, in 1840, was amused to see an Irish waiter struggling with the intricacies of a French menu, by the 'fifties the Irish had already "dispossessed in a great degree the coloured race" as domestics and hotel servants.[37] This was true in the North only, although some Britons erroneously believed it to be equally true in Baltimore, Washington, Richmond, and other Southern cities.[38] English opinion of the Irish as domestics was extremely low. It was expressed most fluently by Beste, who wrote:

The Irish servants and porters were the nuisance of the United States. Despised by the Americans, themselves despising the blacks; with their bellies full for the first time in their lives; insolent in their looks; extortionate in their demands; oaths in their mouths; free from all restraint of a neighborhood or parish priest; beggars upon horseback.[39]

35 Charles Dickens, *American Notes*, 264.

36 Francis Wyse, *op. cit.*, III, 31; see also Edmund Patten, *op. cit.*, 27.

37 A. M. Maxwell, *A Run through the United States*, II, 140; William Chambers, *op. cit.*, 189.

38 D. W. Mitchell, *op. cit.*, 60-61; James Robertson, *A Few Months in America*, 156; Sir A. A. T. Cunynghame, *op. cit.*, 280.

39 J. R. D. Beste, *The Wabash*, I, 74.

Domestic service was attractive to them since wages and keep were higher than the 40c per hour paid laborers on canal construction.[40] Robertson stated that in 1856 porters were receiving $18-$20 per month, waiters $12-$15, boys $8-$12, and females $7-$12, plus maintenance.[41] These salaries, while not as high as those earned by native Americans, were indisputably more than they had received in Ireland.

Was the status of the Irish improved by migration to America? Few attempted to answer the question directly, the tendency instead being to emphasize their hardships in America. Yet no one denied Grattan's assertion that by migration the Irishman had " infinitely improved over his status in the Old World." [42] Porter, who had become United States Senator from Louisiana; Boyd, who had risen to be an outstanding member of the Massachusetts Legislature; and Read, Commodore of the Philadelphia Navy Yard, were pointed to as illustrating the high positions to which the Irish could rise in their new home.[43] Even if the first generation gained little, the second was certainly improved. Food was cheaper and more plentiful; wages were twice as high as in Ireland; and opportunities for education and advancement were beckoning.[44] Paddy, who had starved in Ireland, now sent remittances home to the Old Country. William Kelly, an Irishman himself, affirmed that on the basis of what he had seen in California, his new property interests would develop the Irishman's interest in peace, progress, law and order.[45] The emigrant's own viewpoint on the subject was aptly expressed in the argument used by the waiter who tried to persuade Warburton's valet to desert his master and remain in America: "As soon as I have done my

40 W. F. Adams, *op. cit.*, 225.

41 James Robertson, *op. cit.*, 155.

42 T. C. Grattan, *op. cit.*, II, 1.

43 *Ibid.*, II, 31-32; James Lumsden, *American Memoranda*, 17.

44 G. D. Warburton, *op. cit.*, II, 54.

45 William Kelly, *op. cit.*, 217.

day's work, I dress in my best clothes and walk about, or go into the smoking room as well as any of them with plenty of money in my pockets." [46]

If the ignorant priest-ridden Irish were thus able to raise themselves in America, what could not a good industrious Englishman accomplish in this land of opportunity? Travellers assured their countrymen that all over America people lived more luxuriously and more richly than in England. Why, even hired laborers in the fields were provided with better fare than thousands of the genteel classes in England! [47] Poverty and beggars were unknown. Combe reported that laborers had comfortable, well-furnished homes, and owned property with the luxuries that went with it. [48] Miss Martineau told of clerks in broadcloth, of factory girls carrying umbrellas, of swineherds wearing spectacles. She had even witnessed a parade of mechanics with " sleek coats, glossy hats, gay watchguards, and doe-skin gloves." [49] In New Orleans the stevedores had demanded and secured two substantial wage increases in four weeks. [50] It was in vain that Bell, returning to England after the Panic of 1837, told of seeing scores of destitute, homeless wretches lying on hulks or under the market sheds in New York and Philadelphia. [51] It was futile for Buckingham to point out that " instances of death, from destruction and want, are much more numerous than I had thought possible in a country like this " where food was cheap and labor well paid. [52] " No man should remain to starve ... who in three weeks may transport himself and his children to a land where he may attain

---

46 G. D. Warburton, *op. cit.*, II, 55.

47 William Chambers, *op. cit.*, 342; see also James Robertson, *op. cit.*, 146-147.

48 George Combe, *op. cit.*, III, 248.

49 Harriet Martineau, *op. cit.*, I, 12, II, 63.

50 James Robertson, *op. cit.*, 222.

51 Andrew Bell, *Men and Things in America*, 229.

52 J. S. Buckingham, *America*, I, 160.

comfort; if not comparative affluence," replied one visitor, pointing to the fact that in America even women received as much as male factory hands in England.[53] Caird, land promoter for the Illinois Central Railroad, emphasized that an emigrant could settle down in Illinois at a total cost of only £6, 7s, including transportation and provisions from Liverpool.[54] Haste, he warned, was necessary ere the opportune moment for property purchases at the low rates caused by the depression of 1857 would pass away forever. Prentice, a radical thinker in economics and politics, whose mind was filled with rosy pictures of the future despite the recent failure of his Manchester newspaper, urged the British bourgeois desiring retirement, but unable to afford it in England, to come to America. He calculated that a mere £200 investment would be sufficient to purchase and stock a twenty-five acre farm which would provide its owner with food and lodging for the rest of his days. If not agriculturally-minded, the retired businessman could earn £64 in interest annually on a £800 investment, and this too could support him in comfort.[55] There was not the least doubt, affirmed one liberal clergyman, that Englishmen could emigrate to the United States " with the certain prospect of advancing their interests in every respect," just so long as they were industrious and sober.[56]

Those who took this advice too literally, and abandoned sheltered homes for wilderness trails, realized their error too late. " To be obliged to live on Indian bread and salt pork. . . to be entirely deprived of a little beer, cider, or wine . . . to be lacking some of the plainest comforts of life, as milk, butter, and cheese . . . to be situated in a place where triflings things, as a little yarn for mending, or soap for washing, could not be

53 J. D. Lewis, *Across the Atlantic*, 420.

54 Sir James Caird, *Prairie Farming in America*, 12.

55 Archibald Prentice, *A Tour in the United States*, 67.

56 Jabez Burns, *Notes of a Tour in the United States and Canada*, 175.

obtained without going a mile or two," [57] was certainly something they had never bargained for or expected.

It was situations like this that led experienced emigrants to warn that "some people appear to think that if they were once across the Atlantic, they would have nothing else to do but to enjoy themselves; but they will find themselves mistaken." [58] The wilderness, as Mrs. Houstoun put it, was "no bed of roses." [59]

Thomson, who had seen a great deal of the United States as an itinerant weaver, felt that British ideas as to the advantages of emigration had been greatly over-rated.[60] After a two-year sojourn, he returned to England. So did a great many others. Some of them capitalized on their experiences by publishing advice for others.[61] It was to be expected that the comments of this group would be more caustic than the glowing eulogies of those travellers who had seen America at arm's length. Yet much of what they said had merit, for at least their testimony was based upon actual experience.

The consensus of opinion among this group was that if labor one must, America offered plenty of room and remuneration for toil. If one had neither rank nor money, if one's income was declining, and one's family increasing, America was the place to go. But if one possessed rank, money, or good prospects, let him by all means stay in England! One Scotch emigrant expressed this sentiment fully when he said, "Tell the people at home, if they are doing well, to stay where they are." [62]

---

57 John Eyre, *The Christian Spectator*, 39.

58 William Oliver, *Eight Months in Illinois*, 251.

59 Mrs. M. C. J. F. Houstoun, *Texas and the Gulf of Mexico*, 198.

60 William Thomson, *op. cit.*, 227.

61 Included in this group were Wyse, Brothers, Oldmixon, Beste, Nettle, Hancock, and Brown.

62 James Stirling, *Letters from the Slave States*, 366; see also S. M. Maury, *An Englishwoman in America*, cxvii; William Oliver, *op. cit.*, 255; J. W. Oldmixon, *Transatlantic Wanderings*, 3.

Despite their own disillusionment with America, none of these writers assumed for a moment that his experiences would keep others from crossing the Atlantic. Bell, who had been in America during the Panic of 1837, was of the opinion that it would be best to let people go so that they might return to appreciate their own country.[63] Less cynical authors, however, were willing to offer such advice as might ease the difficulties confronting emigrants, and prevent serious and dangerous errors.

Paradoxically, the first caution given was a warning against expecting too much in America on the basis of what they had read in travel books. The prospective emigrant " should listen to these details, if not with absolute distrust, at least with some degree of caution." [64] Emigrants who had accepted Mrs. Houstoun's advice to settle in Texas on her assurance that it was a land free of mosquitoes, reptiles, and the " scorching summer heat " prevalent in Canada and the Northern states,[65] would doubtless have agreed with these authors that a little more skepticism would have been invaluable. Kennedy went even futher in his admonition that travel books be read critically. He urged prospective emigrants not only to check various books and guides against each other for accuracy, but also to inquire into the objects of each author in writing his book.[66]

Next, it was emphasized that America was no place for older people who would be liable to fall victim to disease and nostalgia.[67] Let the young emigrate before their habits were formed, and they would like it. What is more, they would succeed! Exile in America was for the young man " with his ax, his rifle, and a few dollars in his pocket." [68]

[63] Andrew Bell, *op. cit.*, 283.

[64] Francis Wyse, *op. cit.*, II, 328.

[65] Mrs. M. C. J. F. Houstoun, *op. cit.*, 193-194.

[66] William Kennedy, *Texas; Topography, Natural History, and Resources*, 48.

[67] Sir James Caird, *op. cit.*, 96; William Thomson, *op. cit.*, 227.

[68] J. W. Oldmixon, *op. cit.*, 4.

Abstinence from drink was essential, considering the ease with which liquor could be obtained in the New World. Otherwise, visitors warned, the young man would meet the early death of a drunkard. It would also be well to take along character testimonials from employers and ministers, as even the worst scoundrel preferred to hire honest and temperate men.[69]

After securing letters of recommendation, the prespective emigrant was urged to sit down, decide upon the approximate location of his new home, and then to purchase through tickets to his destination. For those who would delay purchasing tickets until arrival in America, the terrors that lay in wait for them were set down in detail.

An infamous class of swindlers, called "emigrant runners," meet the poor adventurer on his arrival at New York. They sell him second class tickets at the price of the first class, forged passes, and tickets to take him 1,000 miles, which are only available at the outside of 200 or 300 miles. If he holds out against their extortions, he is beaten, abused, loses his baggage for a time, or is transferred to the tender mercies of the boarding-house keeper, who speedily deprives him of his hard-earned savings. These runners retard the westward progress of the emigrant in every respect; they charge enormous rates for the removal of his luggage from the wharf; they plunder him in railroad-cars, in steamboats, in lodging-houses; and if Providence saves him from sinking into drunkenness and despair, and he can no longer be detained, they sell him a lot in some non-existent locality, or send him off to the West in search of some pretended employment. Too frequently, after the emigrant has lost his money and property, sickened by disappointment and deserted by hope, he is content to remain in New York, where he contributes to increases that "dangerous class" already so much feared in the Empire City.[70]

But America was large and practically unknown to the prospective emigrant. What section would be most suitable for

69 William Hancock, *An Emigrant's Five Years in the Free States of America*, 203; Jabez Burns, *op. cit.*, 175; J. D. Lewis, *op. cit.*, 421.

70 Mrs. I. L. Bishop, *op. cit.*, 445. This recital, though lurid, was not wholly an exaggeration.

him? Though there was some disagreement as to the best location, all travellers were agreed that under no circumstances should the emigrant remain in the cities of the East. For it was here that competition for employment was keenest, the labor supply largest, and opportunities for advancement fewest. It might be wise for the prospective businessman to spend sufficient time in New York to become familiar with American business practices. But all others had best head westward as quickly as possible.

Indiana, Illinois, and Iowa were recomended as the best farm lands, especially after 1848. Improved lands in the East were more expensive; neighbors were more hostile to emigrants; and unprofitable farms alone were placed on sale.[71] Although the exodus from New England occasioned by the Gold Rush made bargains available in that area, this condition was only temporary.[72] Improved farms in semi-settled areas of the Midwest were preferable, as they required less work than unbroken prairie. Of course, those with large families containing many grown ones would find the latter problem less difficult to overcome.[73] In any event it was best to settle in one place rather than to imitate the American frontiersman's habit of looking eternally westward for the El Dorado of better lands.[74] For an inexperienced Englishman to settle too far out in the wilderness was inadvisable and dangerous, since, unlike the American frontiersman, he was no jack-of-all-trades. Furthermore, the prairie regions were very definitely unhealthy, travellers informed their countrymen, largely as the result of diseases generated by nature from the vast quantity of decomposed vegetable matter produced every fall.[75] Even in the more densely

71 J. R. D. Beste, *op. cit.*, II, 313-315.

72 Robert Baird, *Impressions and Experiences of the West Indies and North America*, II, 295.

73 A. J. Pairpoint, *Uncle Sam and His Country*, 331; Archibald Prentice, *op. cit.*, 7.

74 William Oliver, *op. cit.*, 252.

75 Francis Wyse, *op. cit.*, II, 341-343; J. R. D. Beste, *op. cit.*, II, 319.

settled areas, the emigrant was warned, he would encounter everything from colds to cholera, from dysentery to brain inflammations. The summer heat was to be avoided as deadly, everywhere in America. Hence, emigrants should plan to arrive either in the spring or the fall. If summer arrival was unavoidable, the newcomer was advised to wear flannel underwear, avoid cold water, keep out of the sun, and above all to shut out the dangerous night air.[76]

Texas found its best advocate in Kennedy, who extolled it as having the best farming and grazing land in the Western Hemisphere.[77] But slavery barred the path of emigration here as elsewhere in the South. No Briton had the slightest intention of competing with slave labor; few indeed were interested in becoming slaveholders.

Surprisingly enough, British observers reported adversely upon emigration prospects in Canada. Instead, they agreed that the advantages of settling in the United States were far superior to those of Canada. They characterized the latter as "an immense trackless forest, forlorn and forbidding at best." [78]

What about the artisan and the professional man contemplating emigration? Here again the chief injunction was to keep out of the large seaboard cities, and to head for the smaller towns of the interior where wages were high and competition low. Prospects for this more highly skilled group, however, were definitely spotty. While manual laborers made at least fifty per cent more than in England, teachers were so poorly paid that Hancock had known Oxford men glad to take to book hawking. Doctors, on the other hand, made out very well in those portions of the West which were "delightfully unhealthy." Dentists made fortunes, for "nearly everybody has

76 Francis Wyse, *op. cit.*, II, 311-312.

77 William Kennedy, *op. cit.*, 51.

78 R. B. Allardice, *An Agricultural Tour in the United States and Canada*, 63; see also William Oliver, *op. cit.*, 253.

bad teeth." [79] Architects were "not much wanted anywhere," and the same held true of skilled craftsmen in the leather, tanning, and lumbering industries. There existed a tremendous oversupply of clerks.[80] Wyse considered carpenters, shipbuilders, bricklayers, painters, jewellers, and first-rate tailors as having excellent employment possibilities. Not only would these receive high salaries ($8-$12 per week), but they would be assured steady employment. This was true even in far-off California, where such artisans could do better at their old trades than at mining.[81] Machinists, though the highest paid labor ($15 per week), could obtain employment only in the manufacturing centers. Saddlers, coach-makers, and blacksmiths would also find their occupations restricted to certain localities if they wished good wages. Shoemakers were warned that they would have to meet the competition of the New England farmers, who did "home-work" during the long winters. Certain industries, like watchmaking and glassblowing, were non-existent in America. Anyone hoping to secure employment in stores was doomed to certain failure, as foreigners seldom got such jobs.[82]

The emigrant was likewise warned against expecting to find the Americans awaiting him with open arms as a brother, upon his arrival. Rather, he must resign himself to be treated as an alien. Neither naturalization nor length of residence would entirely remove this disability. For the rest of his days, bitterly cautioned the former emigrant, he would be regarded as a legitimate mark for the nefarious designs of his neighbors.[83]

In 1840 Buckingham had noticed that "one of the strongest of the national prejudices of the mass of the people of America, embracing all classes except the highest and most intelligent, is

79 William Hancock, *op. cit.*, 205-209.

80 Francis Wyse, *op. cit.*, III, 11-26.

81 William Kelly, *op. cit.*, 196.

82 Francis Wyse, *op. cit.*, II, 11-26.

83 Andrew Bell, *op. cit.*, 280; Francis Wyse, *op. cit.*, II, 389-401.

a dislike . . . of all foreigners," especially the British.[84] Shortly thereafter, Mrs. Felton was incredulous to find that "generally speaking the Irish meet with a much better reception than the English; so indeed, do all other foreigners."[85] The hostile comments of British travellers undoubtedly had something to do with this. Godley had remarked, in 1842, that the French were welcomer than the English because of their more sympathetic approach. He contrasted Tocqueville with Mrs. Trollope. Certainly the works of Marryat, Dickens, Warburton, and Mrs. Houstoun gained the British few friends in America.

Hatred of the foreigner grew with the passing years. But the avalanche of Irish emigrants that began descending upon America in the 'forties shifted attention from the English emigrant to the Irish. In 1841 visitors already had noted a rising denunciation of "the plague of the Irish."[86] In time this denunciation grew into an uproar, drowning out all reason. The mere fact of being Irish was "almost sufficient to warrant conviction if arraigned before an American Jury."[87] Nor was it uncommon to see Irishmen barred from American-owned stores. When Major Thornton, in 1849, had suggested to an American friend the deportation of negroes as a solution to the slavery problem, the latter, a Bostonian, had retorted that the deportation of the Irish would be preferable.[88]

The emigrants' abysmal poverty, the filth and squalor of the emigrant ships and railroad vans, the terrible conditions of the slums they inhabited, all combined to present them in an unattractive light. The financial burden of maintaining homes and hospitals for the sick and destitute emigrant, which cost New York City $817,336 in 1850 alone, was a heavy one.

84 J. S. Buckingham, *America*, I, 283.

85 Mrs. Felton, *American Life*, 48.

86 Andrew Bell, *op. cit.*, 108.

87 Francis Wyse, *op. cit.*, III, 33.

88 John Thornton, *Diary of a Tour through the United States and Canada*, 87.

Crime in the seaboard cities was on the increase, and emigrants constituted the major part of the prison population in these cities. The Irish, especially, were clannish, boisterous, and only slowly assimilable. Moreover, the speed with which they captured the political machines in such cities as New York, Philadelphia, and Boston, outraged the native-born citizen. Finally, their religion, Catholicism, was worse than anathema to many Americans.

For these and similar reasons, an American nativist movement arose. It first became vocal with the establishment of the Native American Party in 1835. Although it elected a Congressman and numerous local officials, and was blamed as the instigator of the Philadelphia nativist riots of 1844, the party died out shortly thereafter. But the tremendous increase in immigration during the next five years added fuel to nativist sentiment, and finally resulted in the formation of the Know-Nothing Party in 1850. Beginning as a secret organization in New York, it spread throughout the country like wildfire. It was essentially an anti-emigrant movement rather than one directed against a particular nationality. Thus, while anti-Irish in New York, it was chiefly anti-German in Maryland where the Germans more than twice outnumbered the Irish. Its leader, Ned Buntline, was outspokenly anti-British.[89] The party platform called for the stoppage of emigration, the restriction of public office to the native born, and a check upon the spread of " Romanism."

In his viewpoint on nativism, the British traveller was torn between his natural dislike for it as a foreigner, and his approval of it for its anti-Irish stand. Miss Martineau and Grattan attacked nativism for its opposition to emigration. Both of them felt that America should open wide its gates to the poor and oppressed of Europe.[90] Grattan who sympathized greatly

89 L. C. Scisco, *Political Nativism in New York State*, 17; L. F. Schmeckebier, *History of the Know-Nothing Party in Maryland*, 46-47; D. W. Mitchell, *op. cit.*, 269.

90 T. C. Grattan, *op. cit.*, II, 21-22.

with the Irish (being Irish himself) naturally disliked its anti-Irish bias. Stirling, after witnessing the anti-foreign terrorism whereby the Know-Nothings controlled New Orleans, called for the formation of a Vigilante Committee " of angry and energetic foreigners " to put an end to such disorders. Being opposed to democracy, he quite naturally characterized the Know-Nothings as a " pestilent symptom of the gangrene of ultra-democracy." [91] On the other hand, another conservative jeered at American democracy for tolerating nativism which, he was alert enough to point out, was the negation of its basic principle, the equality of man.[92] Mitchell, who had no use for democracy either, snickered as he told how the Know-Nothing leader, Ned Buntline, had once been whipped on Broadway by a prostitute.[93] Evidently, then, though most Englishmen disliked nativism, their reasons for doing so differed widely.

The few who favored it, did so far a single reason only—its anti-Irish policy. In their hatred of the Irish they overlooked the fact that the nativist movement was also anti-British. One Englishwoman went so far as to praise it as the party of true Americanism.[94]

Would nativism prove a serious bar to the success of the English emigrant in America? Travellers thought not! They agreed that although its social manifestations might not always prove pleasant, yet it could not be considered a major handicap. If the emigrant was sober, industrious, and daring, if he was willing to undergo innumerable discomforts and hardships, above all if he could look forward to nothing but poverty at home, let him by all means take his chances on America!

91 James Stirling, *Letters from the Slave States*, 141-144.

92 H. A. Murray, *Lands of the Slave and the Free*, II, 388-389.

93 D. W. Mitchell, *op. cit.*, 269.

94 Mrs. I. L. Bishop, *op. cit.*, 418-420

CHAPTER IX

CONCLUSION

VIEWING their American trip in retrospect, what did travellers think of America as a whole? The tour itself had been one of the great experiences in their lives. In most cases, they returned from America with greater respect for its people than when they had set foot on its soil. Yet, almost invariably, travellers agreed with Lyell that they had " no wish whatever to live in the United States " permanently.[1]

Previous conceptions were modified to a limited extent by travel in America. Occasionally a complete change of viewpoint occurred. The outstanding examples of this were A. M. Murray and William Thomson, both of whom changed from pro-abolitionist to pro-slave on the slavery question. But such instances were rare. The tendency was rather for old viewpoints to be reinforced. Conservatives still felt that American democracy " with every advantage on her side . . . has been a miserable failure," [2] while liberals continued to assert that " the rise and progress of the United States appears (to be) the greatest and most important fact of the century." [3]

All agreed that America's chief advantage lay in the wide diffusion of material well-being among her people, and the comparative absence of poverty and want. But conservatives were quick to interject that this prosperity was due to America's natural resources rather than its democratic institutions. Hence, the prosperity of the populace, they insisted, did not prove the superiority of its institutions.[4] Liberals, on the other hand, habitually coupled the two together. The high level of

1 Sir Charles Lyell, *Second Visit to the United States*, II, 289.

2 Capt. Frederick Marryat, *Diary in America*, second series, II, 248.

3 W. E. Baxter, *America and the Americans*, 70.

4 C. A. Murray, *Travels in North America, 1834-1836*, II, 202; Capt. Frederick Marryat, *op. cit.*, second series, II, 246.

literacy and the common school system were features of American life that were generally admired. But a sharp division of opinion existed as regards American political and religious institutions. Ordinarily, conservatives denounced, while liberals tended to favor them. Slavery, emigration prospects, the customs and character of the American people were also viewed with mixed feelings.

British travellers had little desire to make America conform to English traditions. They had still less desire to transplant American institutions to their own country. Grattan summarized their views succinctly when he stated that although democratic institutions might be best for America, they were still widely inconsistent with the instincts, traditions, and capabilities of European nations. To force them upon the Old World " would be almost impossible and could be effected only at the cost of a struggle more terrible than the object (was) worth." [5]

What would be the future of America? What would be the fate of the Union? Speculation on these questions was inevitable.

Slavery, of course, was the reason most frequently advanced for a split in the Union. Visitors in the 'thirties and 'forties had been confident that the forces of unity would triumph, but by the 'fifties secession seemed more than likely.[6] Aside from slavery, there were other forces, also, which Britons felt tended towards disunity. Chief of these was the growing divergence in sectional interests. The tremendous size of the country, and the lack of adequate transportation and communication facilities between the sections would increasingly accentuate these differences.[7]

Conservatives were convinced that the strain of a long war or a foreign invasion would shatter the loose ties binding the nation together. A military dictatorship would be set up in the

5 T. C. Grattan, *Civilized America*, I, xiii.

6 See the chapter on Slavery.

7 Alexander Mackay, *The Western World*, III, 354.

South, they predicted, while a monarchy would be erected in the North where conditions approximated those in Europe. The West alone would remain a stronghold of democracy. Such disintegration would be most desirable, conservatives believed, inasmuch as a unified America would soon outstrip England.[8]

Liberals thought otherwise. They claimed that if America could be kept from disintegrating, its future prospects were unlimited. There seemed to be almost no limits to its possibilities for territorial expansion. They were confident that some day the United States would extend as far south as Panama— or even Cape Horn. To the North, the absorption of Canada was a foregone conclusion. Instead of a United States of America, the future would see the United Republics of America.[9] Unlike the conservatives, most liberals could see no danger necessarily inherent in this.

As for economic development, no one, not even the conservatives, could see any limit upon her increase in wealth and prosperity. The universal observation regarding her material growth was, " Progress crawls in Europe, but gallops in America." [10] Unless she disintegrated, America seemed destined to become one of the most powerful nations on earth.

In view of this threat to her future supremacy, what should be Britain's attitude towards America? Some visitors urged their mother country to mend her own fences, if she would retain her supremacy. Alexander Mackay, for example, warned that unless England promoted her own industries more zealously, she would seen be outdistanced by her transatlantic sister.[11] Other travellers pooh-poohed such fears, however. Amer-

8 G. D. Warburton, *Hochelega*, II, 256-266; Capt. Frederick Marryat, *op. cit.*, II, 249.

9 Charles Mackay, *Life and Liberty in America*, II, 190-192; J. M. Phillippo, *The United States and Cuba*, 371.

10 Charles Mackay, *op. cit.*, I, v; see also H. A. Murray, *Lands of the Free and the Slave*, 393; A. M. Maxwell, *A Run through the United States*, II, 261.

11 Alexander Mackay, *op. cit.*, III, 358.

ican industry had not even been able to keep up with its own growth in population, Johnston stated. As for competition from American grain, as an agricultural scientist he could assure his countrymen that American wheat exports would decrease rather than increase in the future.[12] Major Warburton, on the other hand, agreed with Mackay that England had been too complacent over the rise of her American rival. She had ignored the fact that the United States regarded Britain as its chief enemy.[13] Grattan, citing his long years of residence in America, confirmed this. He urged that Britain handle America with a firmer hand. "As they despise our praise, let us doubt their promise, avoid giving them credit, and refuse their factory shares and railroad bonds at any price." [14] War between the two nations would be a calamity. But if it came, he agreed with Warburton that the rude waves of democratic America would beat in vain on the rock of England's aristocracy.[15]

Most travellers, however, and particularly the liberals, regarded war between the two nations as not only a calamity, but a meaningless one. Maxwell, the officer in command of the disputed New Brunswick territory in 1841, differed with his friend Grattan completely. Convinced that love and veneration for England was inherent in the breast of every American, Maxwell's trip through the United States was marked by a long series of goodwill speeches. He declared that Britain and America, as allies, could bid defiance to the rest of the earth.[16] With this statement, liberals were in full accord. The lessening of tension between the two nations after 1848 helped promote this attitude. War between the two English-speaking peoples came to be viewed by travellers as fratricidal. One Briton pointed out, in 1857, that European despots would like nothing better than

12 J. F. W. Johnston, *Notes on North America*, II, 335-421.

13 G. D. Warburton, *op. cit.*, II, 265-267.

14 T. C. Grattan, *op. cit.*, II, 180.

15 G. D. Warburton, *op. cit.*, II, 268.

16 A. M. Maxwell, *op. cit.*, II, 260-261.

" to witness the two freest and greatest nations on the globe—
the last asylums of liberty and equality — shedding their
blood." [17] Yet, never were two nations so eminently fitted to
aid and comfort each other in the joint work of civilization.[18]
By 1860, few visitors would quarrel with Dixon's assertion
that " on the peace, harmony, religion, industry and modera-
tion of the Anglo-Saxon peoples in the two hemispheres hang
the destinies of the human race." [19]

[17] J. M. Phillippo, *op. cit.*, 392.

[18] J. S. Buckingham, *Southern or Slave States*, I, Preface; James Stirling,
Letters from the Slave States, 357; J. M. Phillippo, *op. cit.*, 390-392.

[19] James Dixon, *Personal Narrative of a Tour through Part of the United
States and Canada*, 174-175.

CRITICAL BIBLIOGRAPHY

"How do you like America?" has been the standard question put to all newcomers ever since the birth of the Republic. Even though the question was often rhetorical, Americans usually paid some heed to the answer — especially if it was uncomplimentary. Travel works on America, still wet off the printing presses of London, were quickly sent on their way to be reprinted in the New World. The works of Dickens, Marryat, and Miss Martineau, to mention but a few that appeared during the period from 1836 to 1860, were read as avidly in America as in England.

In 1864, H. T. Tuckerman felt that enough had been written about us to merit a book upon the subject of *America and her Commentators*. Reconstruction and expanding industrialism, however, diverted our attention into other channels, so that the ever-growing stream of foreign visitors found us much more complacent about the comments of critics than had been true during pre-war periods. But at the turn of the century, as a new stream of visitors flocked to see the American Colossus, interests in the works of earlier travellers once more revived. Brooks' *How Others See Us* was indicative of this trend. But the number of foreign travel books on America had become so great by this time as to necessitate more specialized studies. The first such study restricted entirely to British travellers was made by E. D. Adams, and appeared as an article in the *Political Science Quarterly* in 1914. Jane L. Mesick followed with a book in 1921 on *The British Traveller in America, 1785-1835*. Since then many others have undertaken studies in this field. Outstanding among them has been Allan Nevins, whose *American Social History as recorded by British Travellers* provides an excellent sourcebook on British travel in America.

Biographical studies of many of the earlier travellers have been appearing in growing numbers, most of them revealing factors that influenced the traveller's viewpoint towards America. Often, too, they contain private letters and similar data which do not appear in the original travel book. In any event, it is essential that something be known of the traveller's background in order to place his work in the proper perspective. The *Dictionary of National Biography* is the best short reference for most British travellers. Other references are also given below. The biographies mentioned under Travel and Travellers, though sufficient for our purposes, constitute only a small part of the many works of this type.

The section on Emigration and American Nativism makes no claim at being definitive. It aims rather to provide a general background, and to serve as a guide for further research. Familiarity with the closely interwoven problems of emigration and nativism is essential for the proper understanding of this period. Travel and emigration frequently went hand in hand. Many travellers were interested in emigration, and not a few emigrants returned to write travel books.

A great many Englishmen visited America between 1836 and 1860. The exact number can never be known, but approximately two hundred and thirty of them published accounts of their travels. Some of these appeared originally in newspapers and periodicals, or as lectures. But so great was the market for books on America that practically every manuscript having any trace of merit or interest sooner or later appeared in book form.

The present bibliography is the most complete one that has appeared on the subject. Although some obscure works may yet be discovered, there is little likelihood of any major addition. The reader is cautioned against confusing American or foreign non-British authors with Britons. This pitfall is perpetually confronting the unwary. It is unfortunate that most bibliographies have fallen into this trap. The works of F. J. Grund (German), Vincent Nolte (German), E. H. D. Domeneck (French), Frederika Bremer (Swedish), and J. C. Haliburton (Nova Scotian) have often been classified as British. The number of Americans listed as British travellers is legion, among them being N. P. Willis, T. L. Nicholls, J. L. Peyton, Charles Lanman, A. E. Silliman, J. K. Townsend, T. J. Farnum, and George Catlin. It should be noted that most bibliographies of travel do not differentiate as to the nationality of the author. In such cases one can safely assume that the works listed are almost entirely by American authors. Neither the author's name nor the place of publication can be accepted as proof of nationality. Many American books were published in England, while the pirating of English works by American publishers was a chronic source of British complaint. Perusal of the book alone provides a sure test. It is also necessary to distinguish between accounts by bona fide travellers, and the treatises or compendiums written by authors who had never visited America. The latter based their accounts entirely upon secondary sources. In this group fall such works as N. W. Senior's *American Slavery* or John Macgregor's *Progress of America from its Discovery by Columbus to the Year 1846*. The latter was written years prior to Macgregor's trip to the United States, and certainly cannot be regarded as a travel book. It is also necessary in considering bibliography to restrict oneself to books narrating trips taken within the years of the selected period. Thus, many an account of a visit made prior to 1836, but printed or reprinted long after that date, must be discarded. Here again actually reading the book is the only sure test. Finally, it should be noted that many British travellers used pseudonyms for one edition and their real names for others, or else published their accounts anonymously until these showed signs of success. Titles also vary, occasionally, from edition to edition. Many bibliographies fail to recognize these factors, and either list the same work several times, or else use one heading or another indiscriminately. For the sake of clarity and uniformity, all works below are listed under the author's real name (when known), with any pseudonym or alias given in parenthesis.

Obviously the English people did not restrict their reading on America solely to the accounts of their own travellers. Continental authors such as Tocqueville were widely read. So were many American authors. To include all such works in this bibliography would be impossible. One type of book, however, was so intimately connected with the problem of travel that it merits special consideration. This was the Tourist and / or Emigrant Guide. It varied greatly in size, scope, and merit from book to book. Sometimes it was only a small pamphlet, like the one written by Vere Foster, which had sold over 250,000 copies at a penny each by 1855. Sometimes it was a solid tome of miscellaneous data, such as Hugh Murray's three volumes on America. Ordinarily these guides contained time-tables, maps, transportation routes, and tourist sights. The larger volumes included, also, brief statistical summaries on population, government, schools, and churches. Those written specifically for sale in Europe simply added some information on crossing the Atlantic. Practically all were written by Americans, though occasionally a British hack-writer would also publish one. British travellers and former emigrants, to be sure, also wrote books designed to aid future travellers and emigrants. But these more properly can be considered as travel accounts, and they have been classified as such in this bibliography. The influence exerted by these Guides is very difficult to ascertain. If we are to use British travel books as a criterion, their influence was negligible. Although most travellers were familiar with the works of previous travellers, hesitating not to quote or criticize them, never once was mention made of the Guides. However, for those readers interested in the subject, a list of all the leading Guides during this period has been appended below.

How did England react to the reports brought back by her citizens from America? This is a study in itself. But a rapid survey of contemporary reviews of these accounts provides a typical cross-section of British opinion. A number of reviews have been listed below. It will be noted that the *Edinburgh Review* consistently espoused a very liberal policy towards the United States during this period. It praised Miss Martineau, reprimanded Dickens, and denounced Marryat. *Blacktsone's Magazine*, on the other hand, maintained the Tory viewpoint, and ardently upheld the views expressed by Sir Edward Sullivan and Major Warburton.

The travel books of Britons who visited America a century ago are no longer in general circulation. In fact comparatively few libraries contain large collections of such works. The New York Public Library has the most complete file. The Library of Swarthmore College has a special collection of British Americana. Columbia University Library and the Library of Congress also have good collections in this field.

1. BRITISH TRAVEL ACCOUNTS

Acton J. E. E. D. "Lord Acton's American Diaries," *Fortnightly Review*, CX, 727-742, 917-934; CXI, 63-83.

While a very young man, Lord Acton visited America as official representative to the New York Exhibition of 1853. He moved in the best social and literary circles of New York, Boston, and Philadelphia, meeting such celebrities as Longfellow, Ticknor, Prescott, and Agassiz. In this private diary, which was not published until after his death, he reveals a snobbish, contemptuous attitude towards American democratic institutions.

Allardice, R. B. (Capt. Barclay). *Agricultural Tour in the United States and Canada.* Edinburgh, 1842.

The author, an unsuccessful claimant for an earldom, and well-known for pedestrian\ walking feats, came to the United States in 1841 to compare its agricultural prospects with those of Canada. He decided in favor of the former as the better field for emigration.

Anonymous. *America Compared with England.* London. 1848.

———— "American Copyright," *Blackwood's Magazine,* LXII, 534-546.

This is merely a letter on that much discussed subject, written from New York in 1847.

———— "American Lions," *Bentley's Miscellany,* IV, 405-412.

Sarcastic comments are made about American heroes. The tone is caustic and flippant.

———— "American Politics," *Blackwood's Magazine,* LXXII, 45-48.

A brief letter written by an Englishman in America (1852).

———— *Domestic Manners of the Americans by Recent Travellers.* Glasgow, 1843.

———— *A Few Days in the United States and Canada.* London, 1846.

———— *Henry, or the Juvenile Traveller; a Delineation of a Voyage across the Atlantic.* London, 1836.

———— *Impressions of the West and South.* Toronto, 1858.

A series of letters on a trip to the United States. They originally appeared in a Toronto newspaper, and were reprinted in book form.

———— "How they Manage Matters in the 'Model Republic,'" *Blackwood's Magazine,* LIX, 439-449, 492-500.

A brief discourse on the United States that is obviously not too friendly.

———— "Journeyings in America by a Young Adventurer," *Chambers' Edinburgh Journal,* I, 262-265, 410-413.

———— *Manners of the Americans.* Glasgow, 1836.

Despite the similarity of titles, this is not by Mrs. Trollope.

———— *New England Tour of his Royal Highness the Prince of Wales.* Boston, 1860.

A chronicle of the Prince's trip through New England during his visit to America in 1860.

———— "Notes of an Emigrant," *Hogg's Instructor,* VII, 177-178, 216-218, 321-323.

Designed to aid the prospective emigrant, but too brief to be of value.

——— " Pedestrian Tour of a Scottish Emigrant in the Middle States of America," *Touts Edinburgh Review*, VI, 381-392, 444-452, 724-734.

After some years in Canada, the author, a Scotsman of good education but slender means, travelled to New York City via Lake Champlain. This is the diary of that trip.

——— *Recollections of a Ramble from Sidney to Southampton*. London, 1851.

The record of a journey between the two cities via South America, Panama, the West Indies, and the United States.

——— *A Sketch of Western Virginia: for the Use of British Settlers in that Country*. London, 1837.

——— *Traits of American Indian Life and Character, by a Fur Trader*. London, 1853.

Sketches by one of the Hudson's Bay Company traders in Oregon.

——— *Transatlantic Rambles by Rugbaean*. London, 1851.

A record of a year of travel in the United States, Cuba, and Brazil.

——— *True Picture of Emigration*. London, 1848.

The experiences of an English emigrant family residing in the United States from 1831 to 1845, narrated by the mother.

——— *Uncle Sam's Peculiarities*. 2 vols., London, 1840.

A virulently anti-democratic work, written in popular dialogue form, that ridicules everything American.

——— *The United States and Canada as seen by Two Brothers, 1858, 1861*. London, 1862.

——— *The United States and Canada in 1859*. London, 1859.

——— *A Young Traveller's Journal of a Tour in North and South America during 1850*. London, 1852.

Ashworth, Henry. *Tour of the United States, Cuba and Canada*. London, 1861.

A brief series of lectures based on a tour during the winter of 1859-1860, which had originally been published in the *Bolton Chronicle*, a newspaper.

Baird, Robert. *Impressions and Experiences of the West Indies and North America in 1849*. 2 vols., London, 1850.

The author is not the American clergyman of the same name who wrote *Religion in America*. Though the treatment of the United States is brief, it is judicious and well balanced.

Ballentine, George. *Autobiography of an English Soldier in the United States Army*. New York, 1854.

Ballentine arrived in America in 1845, and fought in the Mexican War.

Barrow, John. *Facts Relating to Northeast Texas, condensed from notes during a tour through that portion of the U. S. A.* London, 1849.

Baxter, W. E. *America and the Americans.* London, 1855.

The author, educated at the University of Edinburgh and a partner in a mercantile firm, visited the United States in 1846 and again in 1853-1854. In 1855 he became a Whig Member of Parliament, and later rose to prominence as Secretary to the Admiralty and as Privy Councillor. Baxter tried to be fair and impartial in his comments on America, but couldn't repress criticism of things he disliked. His work is a good institutional study, especially on education, religion, politics, and slavery; but it is marred by an anti-Catholic complex.

Bell, Andrews (A. Thomason). *Men and Things in America.* London, 1838.

Bell was an author and translator who spent a year in America during the Panic of 1837. His account is ambling and verbose, with an air of Tory snobbishness. It is not suprising that he was glad to get home.

Benwell, J. *Englishman's Travels in America.* London, 1853.

An ardent abolitionist whose visit to America in 1852 was prompted by a desire to investigate the slavery problem.

Berkeley, Sir G. C. G. F. *An English Sportsman in the Western Prairies.* London, 1861.

Sir Berkeley was a British peer who desired to prove that it was practical to make a hunting trip to America during Parliamentary vacations. He made such an excursion to the Western Plains during the fall of 1859. Though interested chiefly in hunting, Berkeley did not hesitate to point out the manifold evils he saw in American democracy.

Beste, J. R. D. *The Wabash.* 2 vols. London, 1855.

An entire family of wealthy English gentry, including eleven children, toured the Midwest in 1852, ostensibly to investigate emigrant prospects. They spent some time in a settlement on the Wabash. The result was an entertaining tale that portrayed America in a more favorable light than might be expected.

Biggs, Joseph. *To America in 39 Days before Steamships.* Oxford, 1927.

The reprint of the very slender diary of a business trip during the Panic of 1837.

Bill, John. *A Trip to America.* London, 1850.

Bishop, Mrs. I. L. (Bird). *Aspects of Religion in the United States of America.* London, 1859.

———— *An Englishwoman in America.* London, 1856.

Mrs. Bishop, who later became famous as an author and world traveller, first visited America in 1854 as a young woman of twenty-three. She was interested in the amelioration of the poverty and slums of Edinburgh by promotion of emigration to the New World. Her account is mildly sarcastic in tone, but otherwise generally favorable. Her account of New York's educational system is good. The treatment of American politics is definitely hostile.

Booty, J. H. *Three Months in Canada and the United States*. London, 1862.

The diary of a visit in the spring of 1859.

Bromley, Mrs. C. F. K. *A Woman's Wanderings in the Western World*. London, 1861.

The author, who was the daughter of a Member of Parliament, visited the United States in 1853.

Brooks, J. T. *Four Months among the Gold Finders of Alta California*. London, 1849.

Brothers, Thomas, *The United States of North America as They Really Are*. London, 1840.

Written by a corporation lawyer who had been led to emigrate to America by a perusal of Thomas Paine. Financial losses and an unsuccessful venture into politics caused his return to England in 1837 after a residence of fifteen years. Boldly labelling his book as a " cure for radicalism," Brothers proceeded to " debunk" America. The book gained wide notoriety. As a lawyer for banks closed by the Panic of 1837, Brothers wrote on banking and the Panic from first-hand knowledge.

Brown, William. *America*. Leeds, 1849.

Brown, a tavern-keeper in Cleveland and Toronto during 1843-1847, wrote a brief account of living conditions and farming in the Cleveland area, for sale to prospective emigrants.

Buckingham, J. S. *America*. 3 vols., London, 1841.

Buckingham, well-known as a journalist, lecturer, and Whig politician, came to the United States in 1837 on an extended lecture tour after his defeat in the Parliamentary elections of that year. For the next four years he toured the length and breadth of America. In 1841 he published the first part of an encyclopaedic work on his American travels. Though replete in data, the work suffers from a lack of synthesis and interpretation. His liberal views, his active interest in social reforms and the temperance movement were reflected in his attitude towards American institutions.

———— *Eastern and Western States*. 3 vols., London, 1842.

Whereas *America* was devoted largely to first impressions and his tours in the Middle Atlantic States, these volumes narrate his travels in New England and the Midwest.

———— *Southern or Slave States*. 2 vols., London, 1842.

These volumes cover Buckingham's travels in the South, and conclude the series. Though condemning slavery as economically unsound, Buckingham strove to take a balanced view of Southern conditions.

Bunn, Alfred. *Old England and New England.* 2 vols., London, 1853.

The author came to New York City in 1853 following bankruptcy as theatrical manager of Drury Lane. He evidently hoped to recoup his fortunes by writing a work which heaped sarcasm and ridicule upon America.

Burns, Jabez. *Notes of a Tour in the United States and Canada.* London, 1848.

A brief journal of a tour in 1847 by a minister who was an ardent believer in abolitionism and temperance. Except for the slavery question, he was extremely favorable toward the American way of life.

Burton, R. F. *The City of the Saints and Across the Rocky Mountains to California.* London, 1861.

Burton, renowned for his explorations in Arabia and his translation of the *Arabian Nights*, came to America in 1860 to study Mormonism at first hand. His narrative begins with his departure from Missouri, and is devoted almost entirely to his experiences in Utah. It is an excellent sociological study of Mormon institutions and economy. Burton's tolerance is reflected in his conclusions, which are largely favorable. After leaving Utah, he travelled westward to California, and returned to England via Panama.

Caird, Sir James. *Prairie Farming in America.* London, 1859.

An enthusiastic appraisal of Midwest agricultural conditions and emigration prospects by a Member of Parliment and government agricultural expert who visited the area in 1858. Caird's enthusiasm is partially attributable to his being a promoter for the Illinois Central Railroad at the time.

Carlisle, Earl of (G. W. F. Howard). *Travels in America.* New York, 1851.

This is the reprint of a lecture by the famous Whig politician and Cabinet Minister who had visited most of the United States in 1841-1842. Carlisle was very favorably impressed by what he saw in America.

Casey, Charles. *Two Years on a Farm of Uncle Sam.* London, 1852.

Casey was an Irish author who visited the United States in 1849 and again in 1851-1852. Despite the title, the book contains nothing on farming, but is rather a typical tourist travel account. Claiming to present the " between decks " rather than the " poop deck " viewpoint of America, the author is naturally biased in favor of democracy.

Caswall, Henry. *America and the American Church.* London, 1851.

Caswall was an Episcopalian minister who was attached to the staff of Kenyon College, a small British-endowed institution in Ohio, during 1828-1842.

———— *The City of the Mormons.* London, 1842.

The diary of three days spent at Nauvoo, Illinois, in 1842 at the time it was a great Mormon center.

—— *The Western World Revisited.* Oxford, 1854.

In 1853 Caswall returned to America as a delegate to the General Convention of the American Episcopal Church. He revisited Canada and the Midwest, and drew some interesting comparisons between conditions in 1828 and 1854. The major portion of this work, however, is devoted to a religious subject—the General Convention.

Chambers, William. *American Slavery and Colour.* London, 1857.

Though opposed to slavery, Chambers regarded the abolitionists as hypocrites.

—— *Things as They Are in America.* London, 1854.

Chambers had worked his way up from an apprentice to become one of the biggest publishers in England. America impressed him quite favorably during his visit in 1853. The chapter on American railroads is excellent.

Chandless, William. *A Visit to Salt Lake.* London, 1857.

The author journeyed from St. Louis to California by way of Utah, in 1856, as a mule driver. Though skeptical of Mormon religious doctrines, he tried to be impartial. The result is a very entertaining book that also gives a good account of economic and social conditions in Utah and California.

Coke, H. J. *Ride over the Rocky Mountains to Oregon and California.* London, 1852.

Coke crossed the United States in 1850 from Charleston to the Pacific. This is the diary of his experiences while crossing the Plains and the Rockies on horseback.

—— *Tracks of a Rolling Stone.* London, 1905.

Another volume based upon the notes of the 1850 trip.

Collyer, R. H. *Lights and Shadows of American Life.* Boston, 1836.

A forty-page diary of a lecture tour in 1836 by a professor of mesmerism, which contained several vivid sketches of American slum conditions. The author was bitterly hostile, regarding the United States as a den of iniquity ruled by Mammon.

Combe, George. *Notes on the United States of North America.* 3 vols. Edinburgh, 1841.

Combe, a retired businessman and a disciple of phrenology, toured the Northeastern States during 1837-1840, lecturing on phrenology. His fame as a phrenologist gave him access to many leading figures. His journal mixes travel observations with phrenological analyses. His comments reveal a basic sympathy towards the principles of American democracy, but with sharp criticism of the abuses inherent in American politics.

Cornwallis, Kinahan. *Royalty in the New World*. New York, 1860.

The Prince of Wales made a rapid tour of the United States in 1860. Cornwallis was a news correspondent attached to his party. This account of the trip is purely descriptive.

Coulter, John. *Adventures on the Western Coast of South America and California*. 2 vols. London, 1847.

Coulter was a doctor on a whaling and trading ship in the South Pacific. The narrative includes several chapters on California just before the Gold Rush.

Cowell, Mrs. E. M. E. *The Cowells in America*. London, 1934.

The diary of a concert tour to America in 1860-1861, published only recently.

Crowe, Eyre. *With Thackeray in America*. New York, 1893.

A series of pen and ink sketches with a running commentary, by a man who had travelled with Thackeray for six months during his American lecture tour in 1853.

Cunynghame, Sir A. A. T. *A Glimpse at the Great Western Republic*. London, 1851.

The author took leave from his army post in Canada in 1850 and made a whirlwind tour of America, covering 5,300 miles in fifty-three days for £53. Though primarily interested in military establishments, the book is crammed with stories of rail and steamer disasters.

Daubeny, C. G. B. *Journal of a tour through the United States and in Canada, made during the years 1837-1838*. Oxford, 1843.

Daubeny, a naturalist, made the trip in order to carry on some geological investigations. This diary of his travels, printed for distribution to friends only, is well-written and interesting, but of no great value. Although willing to accept democratic institutions in the New World, he strongly opposed their adoption in England.

Davies, Ebenezer. *American Scenes and Christian Slavery*. London, 1849.

This work, first published in *The Patriot*, a London periodical, was written by a British West Indian clergyman and abolitionist preacher who made a 4,000 mile journey through the United States in 1849. Davies deliberately sought out and attended numerous slave auctions. Aside from slavery, he was highly enthusiastic about the status of religion and education in America.

Davis, J. *Mormonism Unveiled*. Bristol, 1855.

A brief account of a journey to Utah with a company of two hundred converts, the author's sojourn there, and subsequently his escape and return to England. Written by an apostate.

D'Ewes, J. *Sporting in both Hemispheres*. London, 1858.

Dickens, Charles. *American Notes*. Boston, 1867.

This is one of the most famous works ever written by an English traveller on America. Dickens visited this country in 1842 while recuperating from a severe illness. He tried to be fair in his estimates, but was outraged by the primitive travelling conditions, and was bitterly hostile towards slavery, the American press, and the lack of copyright protection for foreign authors. His radicalism and over-optimistic expectations merely increased his disappointment at the obvious weaknesses of the Republic. The result was a volume brilliant in vivid descriptions, but at the same time filled with sardonic laughter. American offense at the latter tended to obscure Dickens' basic sympathy towards the United States. His descriptions of American charitable and penal institutions rank second only to his description of travel conditions.

Dix, J. R. *Transatlantic Tracings*. London, 1853.

The author, a surgeon, wrote a series of brief sketches on famous persons and typical scenes encountered on a trip to the United States. The descriptions are poor and exceedingly verbose.

Dixon, James. *Personal Narratives of a Tour Through Part of the United States and Canada*. New York, 1849.

Dixon was a prominent Wesleyan minister who attended the United States Conference in 1847. The major part of his book is devoted to a history of American Methodism. He admired freedom of religion, and regarded the Americans as a highly religious people.

Duff, Alexander. *An Address*. Washington, 1854.

An address delivered before the General Assembly of the Free Church of Scotland, in 1854, upon the Reverend Duff's return from a visit to the United States.

Duncan, Mrs. M. G. (Lundie). *America as I Found It*. New York, 1852.

This account of a trip to America in 1850 has no distinctive feature other than rambling verbosity.

Edge, F. M. *America Today and Yesterday*. London, 1869.

The author reminisces about pre-war America and discusses the prospects for Southern Reconstruction.

———— *Slavery Doomed*. London, 1860.

Edge, who lived in the United States between 1855-1860, devoted the major part of this volume to the slavery questions.

Engleheart, Sir G. D. *Journal of the Progress of the Prince of Wales through British North America and his Visit to the United States*. London, 1860.

The official version of the tour of the Prince of Wales in the fall of 1860, written by a member of the entourage—a private secretary to the Duke of Newcastle.

Everest, Robert. *A Journey through the United States and Canada.* London, 1855.

An interesting but superficial account of a trip to the United States in 1855, written by a late chaplain of the East India Company. While proclaiming an ardent admiration for republicanism, he revealed a strong prejudice against American Catholics.

Eyre, John. *The Christian Spectator.* Albany, 1838.

Eyre was an evangelical clergyman who came to America in 1832 and journeyed to Ohio. After an unsuccessful teaching career, he returned to New York. His travels appear to have consisted of one long battle against greedy, dishonest, and ungodly innkeepers and boarding-house mistresses.

—— *The European Stranger in America.* New York, 1839.

This is a continuation of the previous work, covering Eyre's experiences down to 1838.

Featherstonhaugh, G. W. *A Canoe Voyage up the Minnay Sotor.* 2 vols., London, 1847.

Featherstonhaugh was an Englishman who had made a geological survey of the West for the U. S. War Department in 1834-1835. He was also a member of the British Commission settling the Maine Boundary Dispute in 1842. This book is the diary of an explorative mission in the upper Mississippi Valley in 1835-1836. Although some incidental data on popular manners finds its way into the narrative, the chief interest of the author is devoted to the mineral resources of the area.

—— *An Excursion through the Slave States.* 2 vols. London, 1844.

This work, based upon a trip through the South in 1834-1835, reveals that the author was absolutely opposed to American democratic institutions, but thought highly of her physical resources.

Felton, Mrs. *American Life.* London, 1842.

A brief and rather superficial account of a residence in New York during 1836-1837, written by a wealthy Englishwoman.

Ferguson, William. *America by River and Rail.* London, 1856.

Ferguson was a botanist and entomologist who spent most of his life in Ceylon, where he served for a time as Superintendent of Works. He made an extended trip through the seaboard and Midwestern states in 1855. Though fairly impartial in tone, the author revealed a definite partiality for the wealthy conservative element in America. His interest in American mining resulted in an extensive treatment of this subject, particularly as regards the Midwest.

Finch, Marianne. *An Englishwoman's Experience in America.* London, 1853.

The author was an ardent feminist who came to Boston in 1851 to attend the Sixth Woman's Rights Convention. Next to feminism, her chief interest lay in the Shaker communities—many of which she visited.

Fitzgunne. "A Flying Shot at the United States," *Dublin University Review*, XL, 306-318, 422-436, 582-591, 701-714; XLI, 255-268, 507-519.

Flower, George. *Errors of Emigrants*. London, 1841.

Flower had come to Illinois in 1817 as the leader of an emigrant group. This booklet was written twenty years later to answer the inquiries sent him by prospective emigrants.

Fowler, Reginald. *Hither and Thither*. London, 1854.

This work, written by a barrister who claimed to have spent two years in North America, devotes about two chapters to New York.

Fulton, Deoch, ed. *New York to Niagara, 1836*. New York, 1938.

This is a very brief journal of a trip made by Thomas S. Woodcock, engraver, print publisher, and one time director of the Brooklyn Apprentice Library. Woodcock lived in New York from 1830 to 1846, when he returned to England. The chief value of the journal lies in its observations on business and industrial conditions along the Erie Canal. It was published from the original manuscript by the New York Public Library.

Gladstone, T. H. *An Englishman in Kansas*. New York, 1857.

There is an introduction by F. L. Olmsted to this reprint of letters from Kansas by a kinsman of an ex-Chancellor of the Exchequer. Gladstone had gone there in 1856 as news correspondent for the *London Times*. He was bitterly hostile to the border-ruffians, and gave a first-hand description of "Bleeding Kansas."

Godley, J. R. *Letters from America*. 2 vols. London, 1844.

Godley, a zealous Anglican and a Tory politician, visited America in 1842. His attention was directed chiefly towards American religious and political institutions, which he viewed critically. As regards slavery, he favored the improvement of the economic and legal position of the negro, rather than abolitionism. In later years he became influential in sponsoring Irish emigration to Canada, and in the settlement of New Zealand.

Goodmane, W. F. *Seven Years in America*. London, 1845.

A thirty-two page contrast between Canada and the United States, in which the author maintains that Canada offers superior prospects to the British emigrant.

Gosse, P. H. *Letters from Alabama*. London, 1859.

A series of letters, chiefly related to natural history, based upon a visit to the United States in 1838.

Grattan, T. C. *Civilized America*. 2 vols. London, 1859.

Grattan was the British Consul at Boston during 1839-1846, and was active in settling the Maine Boundary Dispute. Prior to his arrival in America, he had been on intimate terms with the royal houses of Belgium and the Netherlands. This background probably explains why this son of an Irish solicitor gazed with such vast condescension upon the lower classes of the Union. He labeled New England the heart of " civilized America," and had only contempt for the Westerner. Despite these drawbacks, Grattan's work is one of the best of the British travel accounts on America, for he was a keen observer. His chapters on the diplomatic developments of the period are outstanding. It should be noted that this book was written almost twenty years after the events it describes.

Gurney, J. J. *A Journey in North America.* Norwich, 1841.

Gurney was a Quaker minister, a philanthropist, and a writer. He was interested in negro emancipation and penal reform. This is an account of his sojourn in the United States and Canada during 1837-1840, printed for private circulation among his friends.

———— *A Winter in the West Indies.* London, 1840.

A series of open letters addressed to Henry Clay (but directed at the American public) on Gurney's trip to the West Indies in 1840. Their purpose was to focus attention on a defense of abolitionism.

Hall, E. H. *Ho! For the West.* London, 1856.

An emigrant guide to Canada and the Midwest by an Englishman who had resided in Chicago for eight years.

Hall, Marshall. *The Two-Fold Slavery of the United States.* London, 1854.

A discussion of slavery in the United States, with a project for self-emancipation.

Hancock, William. *An Emigrant's Five Years in the Free States of America.* London, 1860.

Hancock, who was probably a businessman, travelled extensively in the North and West during 1852-1857. This account of his experiences is fairly favorable and subtly humorous. The prospects of success for emigrants of various occupations receive special attention.

Harvey, George. *Scenes in the Primeval Forests of America.* London, 1841.

This work consists of plates, drawings, and sketches depicting American woodland scenes.

Head, Sir F. B. *The Emigrant.* London, 1846.

A baronet's reminiscences of a trip to America in 1838; devoted largely to his travel experiences, rather than the subject of emigration.

Henley, T. C. "A Glimpse of Uncle Sam Managing Affairs," *New Monthly Magazine*, CVIII, 1-19.

Several sketches of the functioning of the government at Washington, D. C.

Houstoun, Mrs. M. C. J. F. *Hesperos*. 2 vols. London, 1850.

Mrs. Houstoun travelled extensively in the United States in the early 'forties. Her reactions were based largely upon feminine drawing-room conversations. Her air of Tory condescension was a thin veneer for a deep-rooted hostility towards democratic institutions. She was resentful of the repudiation of state debts following the Panic of 1837. She was one of the few foreigners who outspokenly defended slavery.

—— *Texas and the Gulf of Mexico*. Philadelphia, 1845.

This narrative of a yachting trip to the Gulf Coast in the early 'forties contains some interesting but erroneous data intended for prospective emigrants to the Southwest.

Hussey, H. *The Australian Colonies*. London, 1855.

This is a brief account of a voyage from Australia to the United States via Panama, including a tour through the South in 1854.

James, J. H. (Rubio). *Rambles in the United States and Canada*. London, 1846.

The journey was made in 1845. A short chapter on Oregon is appended.

Jobson, F. J. *America and American Methodism*. London, 1857.

Jobson came to attend the General Conference of the Methodist Church at Indianapolis in 1856. He described the work of the Conference, and gave a detailed history of the Methodist Church in America. Although bitterly hostile to slavery, he thought very highly of the United States.

Johnston, J. F. W. *Notes on North America*. 2 vols. Boston, 1851.

Johnston, a well-known chemist, studied agricultural conditions in Canada and New England during 1849-1850. His observations on this subject were keen. Although most of the work was devoted to Canada, Johnston discussed American economic and social conditions at some length. His comments on American institutions were distinctly favorable.

Kane, Paul. *Wanderings of an Artist among the Indians of North America*. Toronto, 1925.

Kane, who came to America in 1845, spent many years among the Indians of Canada, Oregon, and the Northwest. This volume was brought out by the Radisson Society of Canada.

Kelland, Philip. *Transatlantic Sketches*. Edinburgh, 1858.

This is a reprint of a short lecture on an American trip in 1858.

Kelly, William. *Across the Rocky Mountains from New York to California*. London, 1852.

Kelly was an Irishman who travelled across the Plains to California in the Gold Rush. His book furnishes an excellent account of the difficulties encountered by the Forty-Niners. It is the best contemporary narrative of the Gold Rush by a Briton.

—— *A Stroll through the Diggings of California.* London, 1852.

Once in California, Kelly became a prospector. This book is a vivid portrayal of life in the roaring mining camps.

Kemble, F. A. (Mrs. Butler). *Journal of a Residence on a Georgia Plantation, 1838-1839.* New York, 1863.

Fanny Kemble, a leading English actress, came to the United States in 1832 on a theatrical tour. Two years later she married Pierce Butler, a Southern planter, and retired from the stage. This diary describes life on his plantation, which was located on the Sea Islands of Georgia. Revolted by slave conditions, she gradually became alienated from her husband and finally divorced him in 1848. Her journal is a somewhat jaundiced source on Southern plantation life, but the narrative is replete with vivid descriptions. Though urging manumission, she denied favoring abolitionism.

—— *Journal of a Residence in America.* 2 vols. London, 1835.

This is the journal of her experiences in America prior to her marriage to Mr. Butler.

—— *Records of a Girlhood.* New York, 1878.

—— *Records of Later Life.* London, 1882.

Kennedy, William. *Texas; The Rise, Progress and Prospects of the Republic of Texas.* 2 vols. London, 1841.

Kennedy, secretary to the Earl of Durham, visited the United States during 1838-1839, while on a vacation from his Canadian post. After spending several months in Texas, he returned to England as an active partisan for Texan interests. In 1841 he was appointed British Consul to Galveston, remaining there until 1847. This work is one of the best contemporary histories of the Texan Republic. Geographic and sociologic factors are discussed, in addition to political development.

—— *Texas: Topography, Natural History and Resources.* London, 1841.

This is a reprint of the first volume of the previous work, somewhat expanded. It furnishes excellent geographical data on Texas, county by county, for both naturalist and prospective emigrant.

Lang, J. D. *Religion and Education in America.* London, 1840.

Lang, a clergyman, was so favorably impressed by the voluntary system of religion in America, and by the condition of the American workingman, that he undertook this book as a reply to Capt. Marryat. His sole criticism of America was on slavery.

Lardner, Dionysius. *Railway Economy.* London, 1851.

Lardner had a brilliant reputation as a physicist and writer on scientific subjects. In 1840 he came to the United States for a five-year sojourn. This book is a technical treatise on railroading. It includes an excellent chapter on American canal and railroad transport, embodying the observations made during his visit.

Levinge, R. G. A. *Sketches of Trans-Atlantic Life.* 2 vols. London, 1846.

A light, amusing, and superficial chronicle of a "race through the United States" in 1845, written by a baronet and army officer who had served in the Canadian Rebellion of 1837. Possibly because he was actively interested in promoting emigration to New Brunswick, Levinge omitted any mention of emigration prospects in the United States.

Lewis, George. *Impressions of America and American Churches.* Edinburgh, 1845.

Sent by his church in 1844 to investigate the slavery question in America, this Presbyterian minister and author of numerous religious tracts returned to England a virulent opponent of American innovations. But despite a deep-rooted hostility to political democracy, voluntary religion, and slavery, he still favored emigration to the United States.

Lewis, J. D. *Across the Atlantic.* London, 1851.

Written on the model of Washington Irving's *Sketch Book*, this series of topical sketches claims to be based upon a journey made about 1848. The theme of the book is the defense of the viewpoint expressed by Trollope, Hall, Marryat, and other critics hostile to America.

Linforth, James. *The Route from Liverpool to the Great Salt Lake Valley.* Liverpool, 1855.

A diary of a trip to Utah in 1853. The descriptions of the overland routes and of Mormon customs are interesting, but the chief merit of the book lies in the beautiful engravings it contains. There are thirty such plates.

Lockhart, J. G. *Domestic Manners of the Americans.* Glasgow, 1838.

A number of short excerpts from other travel accounts, largely on the period prior to 1836, collected in a short pamphlet.

Logan, James. *Notes of a Journey through Canada, the United States and the West Indies.* Edinburgh, 1838.

Logan, a Scotch lawyer, went to Canada in 1837 to visit a brother. He continued southward through the United States to the West Indies. Some of his ideas were somewhat fantastic, as for example his belief that the poor health of American women was due to the excessive use of opium.

Lucatt, Edward. *Rovings in the Pacific from 1837 to 1849.* 2 vols. London, 1851.

A description of New Zealand and Oceania, with a glance at California during the Gold Rush, written by a Tahitian merchant.

Lumsden, James. *American Memoranda.* Glasgow, 1844.

A reprint of a series of articles that had appeared in the *Glasgow Argus*, written by a prominent Scotch businessman and philanthropist. Lumsden had toured the eastern seaboard in 1843, and made a number of brief observations on industrial developments.

Lyell, Sir Charles. *Travels in North America.* 2 vols. New York, 1852.

The renowned geologist visited the United States four times. This work is the product of his first trip in 1841-1842. He travelled extensively along both the Atlantic seaboard and the Mississippi, lecturing and making geological observations. The greater part of this journal is devoted to the latter. However, American customs and politics could not help but impinge upon Lyell's consciousness. Though a conservative by background and inclination, his account is distinguished by acute observation, and a deliberate effort towards impartial judgment.

―――― *Second Visit to the United States.* 2 vols. London, 1849.

On his second trip in 1845-1846, Lyell took a far greater interest in American social and economic phenomena. Neither this visit nor the later ones in 1852 and 1853 caused any material change in his attitude towards America as revealed in his first work.

Macgregor, John. *Our Brothers and Cousins.* London, 1859.

Macgregor, a well-known economist, patent attorney, and son of a general, made a summer trip to America in 1859. As might be expected, he was somewhat sarcastic regarding the principle of equality. But though he disliked Americans in most respects, Macgregor held out a welcoming hand to them as brothers in religion, and hence co-workers in controverting the machinations of Romanism.

Mackay, Alexander. *The Western World.* 3 vols. London, 1850.

This is notably the best work on America by an English traveller throughout the entire period from 1838 to 1860. Mackay, a Scotch journalist and political scientist, resided in Canada for several years, editing a Toronto newspaper. Following this, he joined the staff of the *London Morning Chronicle*, and was assigned as its foreign correspondent to cover the Congressional Debates on the Oregon Controversy in 1846. His book provides an excellent summary and analysis of American politics, theoretic and practical. Mackay was well informed, scholarly, and tolerant. He viewed America in a favorable light, and was anxious to interpret its practices for the greater enlightenment of the outside world. Except for an underemphasis upon economic conditions, the book is extremely comprehensive in its scope.

Mackay, Charles. *Life and Liberty in America.* 2 vols. London, 1859.

Charles Mackay had fought in the Napoleonic Wars as a youth. After this he became a well-known songwriter and poet. Turning next to journalism, he rose rapidly. When he came to America in 1857 on a lecture tour, he had become manager of the *London Illustrated News.* American audiences received him enthusiastically. The author was equally favorable towards America. Although not measuring up to the standards set by his namesake, Alexander Mackay, his work revealed many evidences of sharp observation and clear judgment. His most serious error lay in pooh-poohing all fears of a Civil War.

———— *Forty Years' Recollections.* 2 vols. London, 1877 .

Two chapters are devoted to his American visit.

———— *Through the Long Day.* 2 vols. London, 1877.

As in the previous work, some attention is given to his trip, a generation earlier, to the United States.

———— *The Mormons,* London, 1856.

A history of the Mormons based entirely upon secondary sources,
which first appeared as a series of articles in the *Morning Chronicle* in
1850. The following year the articles were collected, and expanded to
book size. Charles Mackay did not visit America until 1857. By that
time his interest in the Mormons had waned. He paid little attention to
them during his sojourn in America.

Mackinnon, L. B. *Atlantic and Transatlantic Sketches.* 2 vols. London, 1852.

A light, chatty work by a captain in the Royal Navy who made a
hunting trip to the West in 1851. It contains many observations upon
the U. S. Navy. Mackinnon's attitude towards America was generally
favorable.

Majoribanks, Alexander. *Travels in South and North America.* London, 1853.

An air of Tory condescension characterizes this account of a visit
in 1852. The author had a tendency to sneer at American ways, but was
forced to admit that the educational system deserved high praise.
Other travellers' works were quoted to an unusual extent.

Marryat, Francis S. *Mountains and Molehills.* London, 1855.

The author tells of his adventures in the California gold mines in 1850.

Marryat, Capt. Frederick. *A Diary in America.* First Series, 3 vols. Second
Series, 3 vols. London, 1839.

This former naval officer and distinguished writer of sea stories came
to America in 1837, ostensibly to investigate democratic government.
The plaudits that greeted his arrival turned to denunciations when he
volunteered his services in suppressing the Canadian Revolt of 1837.
Marryat found little to praise, and much to ridicule in the American
scene. Admitting his disdain for democracy, Marryat used his remarkable
powers of observation and description to heap ridicule upon it. His was
certainly the most virulent attack on American institutions during 1836-
1860. Neither politics, education, religion, nor folkways were spared
the corrosive action of his acid pen.

Martineau, Harriet. *Society in America.* 2 vols. New York, 1837.

Harriet Martineau was also a famous author, but she wrote religious
tracts and economic treatises. Ill and deaf from youth, she dedicated
herself to the cause of humanitarian reform. Her two-year sojourn in
the United States (1834-1836) resulted in an able defense of democratic
institutions. Although admitting that American society failed to live

up to many of the principles upon which it was professedly founded, she foresaw a bright future. However, she did not hesitate to condemn slavery and partisan politics, which she regarded as the bane of the American system.

Harriet Martineau and Capt. Marryat became the two most widely read British authors on America in the period 1836-1860. Each typified a viewpoint: Martineau the liberal, and Marryat the conservative approach.

—— *Retrospect of Western Travel.* 2 vols. London, 1838.

The success of *Society in America* caused Miss Martineau to publish the diary upon which it was based. Written in the form of a journal, this work naturally contained more data on travel conditions. Otherwise there is little else new in it.

—— *The Martyr Age of the United States.* New York, 1839.

Harriet Martineau became an ardent abolitionist in America. This small booklet outlines her arguments in favor of abolitionism. It also contains thumb-nail sketches of the prominent people she met.

—— *The History of American Compromise.* London, 1856.

Another pamphlet outlining the history of the slavery compromises, written from the abolitionist viewpoint.

—— *Autobiography.* 2 vols. Boston, 1877.

Miss Martineau never forgot her early struggles for abolitionism, nor the personalities she met on her American tour. Both are included in her memoirs.

Mather, James. *Two Lectures.* Newcastle, 1840.

Two lectures upon the political institutions of the United States from data procured during a visit.

Maury, S. M. *An Englishwoman in America.* London, 1848.

Mrs. Maury came to the United States in 1846 to improve her health and to investigate emigration prospects for her family of eleven children. Smallpox on board ship led her to start a campaign for improving ship sanitary conditions. In this she was partially successfull. Though claiming to have journeyed 12,000 miles through the United States, the book is devoted largely to New York City. Social affairs, dress, and similar feminine interests dominate the work. Mrs. Maury's attitude was rather supercilious. She upheld slavery, and expressed a preference for Southern life.

—— *Statesman of America in 1846.* Philadelphia, 1847.

This book, an abridged version of her other work, was dedicated to James Buchanan, then Secretary of State, whom she regarded as the ideal American.

Maxwell, A. M. *A Run through the United States*. London, 1841.

Maxwell was the lieutenant colonel in command of the disputed Maine frontier in 1839. He made a trip to Washington, D. C. the following year, while on leave, as the guest of Grattan and of General Winfield Scott. At first very favorably impressed by America, he gradually came under the influence of conservative Americans, and began to repeat their arguments against Jacksonian Democracy.

Mayne, J. T. *Short Notes of Tours in America and India*. Madras, 1869.

Mayne, a cathedral organist in India, made a short tour through New England in 1859. His special interest was American church architecture. Although thoroughly inimical to republicanism, he was willing to admit that not all Americans were bad.

Mitchell, D. W. *Ten Years in the United States*. London, 1862.

The purpose of this book was to explain the causes of the Civil War from the Southern point of view. The author claimed residence in Richmond from 1848 to 1858. Slavery was upheld, and the demagogy of the North bitterly denounced.

Mooney, Thomas. *Nine Years in America*. Dublin, 1850.

A prospectus issued by an emigrant agent.

Moor, A. P. *Letters from North America*. Canterbury, 1855.

Seventy-two pages of letters by a member of St. Augustine's College who visited America in 1853, published in a private limited edition.

Moore, George. *Journal of a Voyage across the Atlantic with Notes on Canada and the United States*. London, 1845.

A brief diary of a three-months' trip in 1844 by one of England's outstanding businessmen and philanthropists, printed for private circulation.

Morgan, H. J. *Tour of the Prince of Wales through British America and the United States*. Montreal, 1860.

A record of the itinerary and speeches of the Prince of Wales during his tour of the United States in 1860.

Morleigh. *Life in the West*. London, 1842.

A journey from London to Wisconsin with stops at various points in the United States; reported in dialogue form.

Morris, M. O. *Rambles in the Rocky Mountains*. London, 1864.

The author spent most of 1858 in the gold mines of Colorado.

Muller, W. (Oliver North). *Rambles after Sport*. London, 1874.

Muller came to the United States on a sports trip in 1860.

Murray, A. M. *Letters from the United States, Cuba and Canada*. New York, 1856.

Amelia Murray was a prominent personage at the British Court. Her chief interest on her American trip in 1854-1855 was natural history, particularly botany. She entered the South as an avowed abolitionist, but left singing paeons of praise in favor of slavery.

Murray, C. A. *Travels in North America. 1834-1836.* 2 vols. New York, 1839.

Charles Murray was also a member of the British Court, acting as Queen Victoria's master-of-household. Later he rose to be a minister and privy councillor. Despite his aristocratic background, he looked with favor upon American ways, even to the extent of falling in love with a New York girl. Murray " went native " and spent a summer living with the Pawnee Indians. The diary of his adventures among them furnishes the most interesting part of the book.

Murray, H. A. *Lands of the Slave and the Free.* 2 vols. London, 1855.

H. A. Murray made up in conservatism for any lack of it on the part of his namesakes. A captain in the Royal Navy, he toured Cuba, the the United States, and Canada in 1855. He condemned egalitarianism most strongly.

Nettle, George. *Practical Guide for Emigrants to North Ameri*ca. London, 1850.

A very brief booklet on the United States, Canada, and Newfoundland by one who claimed to have lived for seven years in these areas.

Nicholls, J. A. *In Memoriam. A Selection of Letters.* Manchester, 1862.

A selection from the letters of J. A. Nicholls, including some from America, published posthumously by his mother for private circulation.

O'Bryan. William. *Narrative of Travels in the United States.* London, 1836.

The author, founder of a religious sect, became a resident of the United States in 1831. His narrative is devoted chiefly to advice for prospective emigrants.

Ogden, P. S. *Traits of American Indian Life and Character.* London, 1853.

Ogden was the chief factor of the Hudson's Bay Company in the Northwest between 1835 and 1854.

Oldmixon, J. W. *Transatlantic Wanderings.* London, 1855.

This is an account of a trip in 1855. The author revisited the scenes of his residence during 1825-1835. Once an emigrant himself, now a captain in the Royal Navy, Oldmixon advised only the poorest laborers to consider emigration to the United States.

Oliphant, Laurence. *Minnesota and the Far West.* Edinburgh, 1855.

Oliphant, Superintendent of Indian Affairs in Canada, made a vacation trip in 1854 around the Great Lakes and across the Western Plains. His descriptions of frontier conditions, of the Indians, miners, and trappers who inhabited the region, are extremely vivid and picturesque. The account first appeared in *Blackwood's Magazine.*

Oliver, William. *Eight Months in Illinois*. Newcastle, 1843.

As a document on the economic history of the Midwest, this little book has few equals. Written by an English emigrant who came to Illinois in 1841, the book is replete with detailed data on farm and frontier life told in an unvarnished but lucid and interesting manner. As regards crops, farming methods, and the rural folkways of the period, the work is unexcelled.

Pairpoint, A. J. *Uncle Sam and His Country*. London, 1857.

A series of topical sketches on the United States and Canada, based on a trip during 1854-1856.

Palliser, J. *The Solitary Hunter*. London, 1857.

A tale of a sporting adventure with a group of fur traders in the Rockies during the summer of 1847.

Patten, Edmund. *A Glimpse at the United States and Canada*. London, 1853.

An interesting but brief account of a trip in the autumn of 1852.

Phillippo, J. M. *The United States and Cuba*. London, 1857.

Phillippo was a missionary to Jamaica who had written a similar compendium on that colony with marked success. This account of America is in topical form, its purpose being to provide a handy compact book for the information of prospective emigrants. Based upon personal observation to a limited extent only, the work is largely the condensation of material from other published sources. The author's attitude was very definitely favorable towards America. Of the numerous guides for emigrants published during this period, Phillippo's is certainly one of the best.

Piercy, Frederick. *The Route from Liverpool to the Great Salt Lake Valley*. Liverpool, 1855.

This is the same work as previously listed under James Linforth who edited it.

Playfair, Hugo. *Brother Jonathan: or the Smartest Nation in all Creation*. 3 vols. London, 1840-1841.

As the title implies, Hugo Playfair was none too sympathetic towards his American cousins. The work has no particular distinction.

Playfair, Robert. *Recollections of a Visit to the United States and the British Provinces of North America*. Edinburgh, 1856.

Robert Playfair was very favorably impressed by America. This may have been partially because as a wealthy man on a vacation tour he used only the best accommodations. His trip was made during 1847-1849. It included a visit to a sister living in Nova Scotia.

Prentice, Archibald. *A Tour in the United States*. London, 1848.

Prentice was a radical in politics, a freetrader in economics, and the manager of a Manchester newspaper devoted to both these causes. His American tour was made in 1848 to recuperate from the effects of his labors in the Anti-Corn League and the failure of his newspaper. As could be expected, his diary favored democracy, temperance, and free trade, but opposed slavery. His chief interest lay in the prospects for emigration and commercial enterprise, both of which he regarded as favorable.

Ranken, George. *Canada and Crimea*. London, 1862.

This diary of a major in the British' Army was published posthumously by his brother. The first part of the work includes the notes of a trip made in 1853 from Canada to the United States.

Regan, James. ·*Emigrant's Guide to the Western States of America*. Edinburgh, 1852.

A highly dramatized tale of life in Illinois in 1842, written largely in dialogue form by an Irish middle-class traveller.

Reid, Hugo. *Sketches in North America*. London, 1861.

A well-written topical compendium of information on the United States, based upon a sojourn during 1859-1860. Reid predicted that secession and civil war were inevitable. He maintained that economic differences—not slavery—was the basic cause for the antagonism between North and South.

Remy, Jules, and Brenchley, Julius. *A Journey to Great Salt Lake*. London, 1861.

Remy, a Frenchman, and Brenchley, an Englishman, visited the Mormons in 1855, and continued overland to California.

Revail, B. H. *Shooting and Fishing in the Rivers, Prairies, and Backwoods of America, 1841-1849*. London, 1865.

Rhys, Capt. H. *A Theatrical Trip for a Wager through Canada and the United States*. London, 1861.

Rhys was an actor who crossed the Atlantic in 1859 to win a bet. This brief diary of his trip is devoted largely to the theater. Its tone is light and jovial.

Richards, R. *The California Crusoe; A Tale of Mormonism*. New York, 1854.

A first-hand account of the Mormon's flight from Nauvoo to Salt Lake in 1846, by an Englishman who later turned apostate and went on to California.

Robertson, James. *A Few Months in America*. London, 1855.

The author, a business man, was chiefly interested in industrial and commercial matters during his visit in 1853-1854. The book is replete with statistical data on these fields. Although his investigations had revealed that America was a poorer country than it first appeared, yet he admitted that the American people as a whole lived far more luxuriously than the English.

Robertson, W. P. *A Visit to Mexico, by the West India Islands, Yucatan, and the United States.* 2 vols. London, 1853.

Only two chapters of this narrative of a trip in 1848 are devoted to the United States.

Ross, Alexander. *The Fur Hunters of the Far West.* 2 vols. London, 1855.

Ross, who had been a fur trapper in the Northwest from the time of the Astor Fur Company, narrated his adventures in Oregon and the Rockies.

Russell, Robert. *North America.* Edinburgh, 1857.

This work is devoted almost entirely to geology, agriculture, and climatology. The author, a well-known naturalist, lectured at the Smithsonian Institution during his visit to America in 1854.

Ruxton, G. F. A. *Adventures in Mexico and the Rocky Mountains.* London, 1847.

Ruxton resigned his commission as a lieutenant while stationed with the British Army in Canada in 1839, and spent the next few years living among the fur trappers and Indians of the Far West. In 1847 he was elected a Fellow in the Royal Geographic and Ethnological Societies on the basis of his works on the West. The above book narrates his adventures on a trip made in 1846 through Mexico and the Rockies. It abounds in bloodcurdling tales of adventure in fighting Indians. The hardships of frontier life in the Southwest are vividly portrayed.

—— *Life in the Far West.* Edinburgh, 1851.

This book first appeared in serial form in *Blackwood's Magazine* following Ruxton's death in St. Louis in 1848. Like the previous work, it was of the Western thriller type, and was restricted entirely to adventure stories concerning the trappers and Indians of the West. Ruxton's works enjoyed great popularity in England. They were the forerunners of the " Cowboy and Indian " story of a later period.

Ryan, W. R. *Personal Adventures in Upper and Lower California.* 2 vols. London, 1850.

A tale of the author's experiences in the California gold mines during 1848-1849.

Shaw, James. *Twelve Years in America.* London, 1867.

This is a reprint of a series of lectures delivered in Ireland in 1866 upon the author's return from a twelve years' sojourn in Illinois. Inasmuch as Shaw was an evangelist, it is not surprising that much of the book is concerned with Methodism and the Methodist Conferences.

Shaw, John. *A Ramble through the United States, Canada, and the West Indies.* London, 1856.

The author, who was a doctor, author, and musician, spent some time in the United States in 1845. His journal consisted of a series of personalized letters on his travel experiences. He endeavored to be amusing in a sarcastic way.

Shaw, William. *Golden Dreams and Waking Realities.* London, 1851.

William Shaw, a former midshipman in the Royal Navy, arrived in California during the Gold Rush on the first boat from Australia. He recounts his adventures on board ship, and his disillusionment upon entering the mining camps.

Sherwell, Samuel *Old Recollections from an Old Boy.* New York, 1923.

The reminiscences of a doctor who came to the United States in 1858 and settled here permanently.

Simpson, Sir George. *Narrative of an Overland Journey Round the World.* 2 vols. London, 1847.

Sir Simpson had been Governor-in-Chief of the Hudson's Bay Company territories. His tour commenced in 1842 and lasted five years. There are three descriptive chapters on the California of the pre-Gold Rush days while it was still a part of Mexico.

―――― *Narrative of a Voyage to Californian Ports in 1841-1842.* San Francisco, 1930.

Sinclair, John. *Sketches of Old Times and Distant Places.* London, 1875.

Reminiscences of a trip to America in 1853 are included.

Slaney, R. A. *Short Journal of a Visit to Canada and the States of America.* London, 1861.

The author, a Member of Parliament, visited America in 1860.

Sleigh, B. W. A. *Pine Forest and Hacmatach Clearings.* London, 1853.

The author was a lieutenant colonel stationed in Canada. Though most of the book is on Canada, there is one chapter on impressions of the United States during a vacation trip in 1852.

Smith, J. R. *A Peep at the Western World.* London, 1863.

The diary of a trip in 1859.

Smith, J. T. *Journal in America.* Metuchen, N. J., 1925.

This is a fifty-page booklet consisting of private notes left by an emigrant who settled in New Jersey in 1837.

Stewart, Samuel. *Travels and Residence.* Belfast, 1842.

Stirling, James. *Letters from the Slave States.* London, 1857.

Although this Scotch author visited almost every part of the United States east of the Mississippi River during 1856-1857, he devoted practically his entire book to the South. He was hostile to both slavery and democracy. The hostility between North and South, he held, was basically due to social differences which expressed themselves by taking opposing sides on the question of slavery. America was only a partial success, for whereas social conditions were improving, political conditions were becoming more corrupt and oppressive.

Stuart-Wortley, Lady E. C. E. M. *Journal of a Tour in North and South America.* London, 1852.

The daughter of a duke, the wife of a baron, Lady Stuart-Wortley wrote poems and travel books. This book, written with interesting simplicity, was the record of a trip in 1849-1850. Though only a small part of the book was on the United States, the author hoped that it would further Anglo-American good will.

—— *Travels in the United States.* New York, 1851.

This volume is devoted entirely to her Ladyship's experiences in America during 1849-1850. Typically feminine in viewpoint, the work is more interesting than valuable. Lady Stuart-Wortley was kindly disposed towards the United States, in a patronizing way.

Sturge, Joseph. *A Visit to the United States.* Boston, 1842.

Sturge, Quaker philanthropist, zealous abolitionist, advocate of Chartism, free trade, and international arbitration, travelled through the Eastern free states with Whittier in 1841. His chief interest was abolitionism, and he interpreted American civilization from that viewpoint.

Sullivan, Sir E. R. *Rambles and Scrambles in North and South America.* London, 1853.

This yachtsman, son of a rear admiral, visited America in 1850. Openly avowing a strong dislike for democracy and republicanism, Sullivan found nothing in the United States to change his previous attitude. Any attempt to introduce American practices into England, he warned, would bring about inevitable ruin. Pithy, pungent, sarcastic, yet interesting, this account became one of the more widely read denunciations of American institutions.

Surtees, W. E. *Recollections of North America.* London, 1861.

Tallack, William. *The California Overland Express: The Longest Stage Ride in the World.* Los Angeles, 1937.

This is a reprint of a series of articles originally appearing in the *Leisure Hour Magazine,* London, 1865. Tallack crossed the United States by stagecoach in 1860, eastbound from San Francisco, on his way home from Australia.

—— *Friendly Sketches in America.* London, 1861.

Tallack was an ardent Quaker. His chief interest in America was the Society of Friends. This book is devoted to the Quakers, emphasis being upon strictly intra-sect problems that concerned them at the time. The author admits a very high opinion of the United States.

Taylor, J. G. *The United States and Cuba.* London, 1851.

In this narrative of an eight-years' sojourn in the United States, Cuba and Ceylon—beginning in 1841—the author, a businessman, proclaimed his intention of debunking America. Actually, the work was fairly favorable and unbiased, except for a deep-seated hatred of the Loco-Focos and the Irish.

Thomson, William. *A Trademan's Travels in the United States and Canada.* Edinburgh, 1842.

Thomson, a Scotch weaver, travelled throughout the United States during 1840-1842 for his health, supporting himself by manual labor. Though he travelled over 5,000 miles, he spent most of his time as a weaver in Ohio. Here he joined a temperance society and a workingman's association. His book is a well-written summary, topically arranged, of the social and economic conditions that would interest the farmer and the tradesman. Thomson was one of the few Englishman who came to the United States an abolitionist and returned a believer in slavery.

Thornbury, Walter. *Criss-Cross Journeys.* 2 vols. London, 1873.

This book is a reprint of articles that had appeared previously in a number of British periodicals. The major part of the work is devoted to the author's trip to the United States during the election campaign of 1860. Thornbury, a journalist, waxed sarcastic about American democracy and manners, reserving his worst barbs for those who would emancipate the negro.

Thornton, John. *Diary of a Tour through the United States and Canada.* London, 1850.

A brief diary by a British major who visited the Northeastern States in 1849. It contains little besides sketches of the many American military men whom he met on his tour.

Todd, H. C. (Traveller.) *Notes upon Canada and the United States.* Toronto, 1840.

This booklet was intended as a guide for tourists and emigrants. Based upon a residence from 1832 to 1840, the notes consist of little more than short, disconnected paragraphs of factual data.

Tremenheere, H. S. *Notes on Public Subjects during a Tour of the United States and Canada.* London, 1852.

The author was well-known in England for his work as a publicist, barrister, school inspector, and poor law commissioner. He made a ten-weeks' tour of the Northern States and Canada in 1851, devoted chiefly to interviewing educators and clergymen on the American system of education. He appears to have made few personal observations, basing his conclusions entirely upon interviews. Admitting the value of popular education, he condemned its non-sectarian nature, and warned England against adopting the American system. There are also chapters on the Press, Secret Ballot, Railways, etc. The viewpoint is Tory.

———— *The Constitution of the United States Compared with our Own.* London, 1854.

This work was written to persuade English reformers that the British Constitution was infinitely superior to the American. It claimed to be an objective analysis of the American system of government, and was based upon *The Federalist*, Supreme Court decisions, and the writings of Justices Story and Kent. Tremenheere's personal observations made during his 1851 tour were kept to a minimum in this work.

Trotter, Mrs. Isabella (Strange). *First Impressions of the New World*. London, 1859.

The diary of a trip made from Boston to St. Louis in 1858 by a wealthy Englishwoman, with her family and servants. It contains some fine descriptions of the cities along her route.

Tuke, J. H. *A Visit to Connaught*. London, 1848.

The author went to Ireland in 1847 to investigate social and economic conditions for a Quaker Relief Committee. He contrasted Irish conditions with the status of the Irish emigrant in America as observed during a trip in 1845.

Turnbull, Jane M., and Marion T. *American Photographs*. 2 vols. London, 1859.

The Turnbull sisters toured the United States, Canada, and Cuba from 1852 to 1857, covering over 26,000 miles. However, their book is disappointingly superficial in that it narrates only the trivialities and incidentals of tourist travel.

Vandenhoff, G. *Leaves from an Actor's Note-book*. London, 1860.

The author, an actor, toured the United States in 1842.

Walpole, Frederick. *Four Years in the Pacific*. 2 vols. London, 1849.

Walpole spent 1844-1848 cruising through the South Pacific as a lieutenant on board a British warship. The major part of his book is devoted to South America and Polynesia, but it also contains some data on California.

Warburton, G. D. *Hochelega*. 2 vols. London, 1846.

Major Warburton, born in Ireland of a wealthy family, was stationed in Canada. This book is a product of his Canadian assignment and a vacation trip to New England in 1844. He was bitterly hostile to all democratic institutions, including popular education, universal suffrage, and voluntary religion.

Warre, Capt. H. *Sketches in North America and the Oregon Territory*. London, 1849.

A volume of huge prints of woodland scenes by a member of the British force sent in 1845 to fortify the mouth of the Columbia River.

Watkin, Sir E. W. *Trip to the United States and Canada*. London, 1852.

Watkin, a British railroad official and future head of the Grand Trunk Railroad of Canada, made a trip to North America in 1851 to recuperate from a breakdown in health. The major part of his journal is devoted to Canada. Watkin warned his countrymen that in the future they would look up to and not down upon the United States.

——— *Canada and the States, 1851-1886.* London, 1887.

Most of this work is devoted to Watkin's numerous trips to America after 1861.

Waylen, Edward. *Ecclesiastical Reminiscences.* London, 1846.

Weld, C. R. *A Vacation Tour in the United States and Canada.* London, 1855.

The author, a barrister and librarian to the Royal Society, was the half-brother of the Weld who had written a well-known book on his travels in America in 1795-1797. Weld regarded this work, based on his own travels in 1854, as the sequel to the earlier one. It is good on social life and slavery.

Wilkie, David. *Sketches of a Summer Trip to New York and the Canadas.* Edinburgh, 1837.

The author was a Scotch traveller and temperance advocate who passed through New York on his way to Canada in 1836. He was not the famous painter of the same name. The book contains little besides descriptions of scenery and sights.

Woods, N. A. *The Prince of Wales in Canada and the United States,* London, 1861.

Another account of the Prince's tour in 1860.

Wyse, Francis. *America: Realities and Resources.* 3 vols. London, 1846.

This was probably the best compendium of information written for use by prospective emigrants during this entire period. In addition to discussing the topography, climate, crops, and industries of each state, there were topical studies on government, slavery, and emigration. Wyse, a businessman who had come to the United States in 1841, included a thorough summary of American business practices. Although ordinarily quite objective, he could not conceal his bitter opposition to slavery and American nativism, nor his lack of enthusiasm for American politics.

2. REVIEWS OF TRAVEL ACCOUNTS IN ENGLISH PERIODICALS

Coke, H. J. "A Ride over the Rocky Mountains to Oregon and California." *Blackwood's Magazine,* LXXI, 187-196.

Dickens, Charles. "American Notes," *Edinburgh Review,* LXXVI, 497-522.

The reviewer warns against taking Dickens' criticisms too literally in view of the fact that he is a popular writer and satirist, untrained in the slow, mature judgment and observation of a foreign people. Furthermore, "it is the nature of an Englishman to think everything ridiculous which contrasts what he has been used to."

Grattan, T. C. "Civilized America," *Frasers Magazine*, LXI, 276-288.

> Hailed as the best work yet written on the United States. Grattan's conservative leanings are accepted as indicating the proper viewpoint.

Johnston, J. F. W. "Notes on North America," *Blackwood's Magazine*, LXX, 699-718.

> The book is praised for containing more varied and valuable information than any published to that time. The reviewer condones Johnston's criticism of American political democracy, but demolishes his argument that Britain has no need to fear the future competition of American agriculture.

Kennedy, William. "The Rise, Progress, and Prospects of the Republic of Texas," *Edinburgh Review*, LXXIII, 241-270.

> Kennedy's impartiality is praised. The reviewer hopes that this work will lead the English to regard the Texan Revolt with satisfaction, and undo their prejudices to the contrary.

Lyell, Sir Charles. "Travels in North America," *Edinburgh Review*, LXXXIII, 129-149.

> The fact that "it exhibits more of the bright side of American character and institutions than ... the panegyrics of the most ardent Democrats who have visited the land of liberty," is attributed to the intellectual company in which Lyell spent much of his time.

Mackay, Charles. "Life and Liberty in America," *Frasers Magazine*, LXI, 276-288.

> The reviewer, probably H. A. Murray, denounces Mackay for libeling his own country for the sake of magnifying the virtues of America, and for being a philo-republican *ad nauseam*.

Marryat, Capt. Frederick. "Diary in America," *Edinburgh Review*, LXX, 123-149.

> Marryat is held to be no more fit to philosophize on democracy than Tocqueville to write sea stories. Marryat's generalizations are condemned as "rash," his ancedotes as "facetious caricature," and his entire work as decidedly inferior to that of Miss Martineau.

—— "Diary in America," *Taits' Edinburgh Magazine*, VI, 553-564.

> This reviewer, on the other hand, praises Marryat as an impartial writer and a quick, penetrating observer.

Martineau, Harriet. "Retrospect of Western Travel," *Edinburgh Review*, LXVII, 180-197.

> Miss Martineau's "intensely democratic spirit" is noted as an important factor in formulating her viewpoint on America.

Murray, C. A. "Travels in North America in 1834-1836," *Edinburgh Review*, LXXIII, 77-84.

Murray is praised for not allowing his intimacy with the British Court to influence the fairness of his account of republican institutions and society.

Shaw, William. "Golden Dreams and Waking Realities," *Blackwood's Magazine*, LXX, 470-487.

A summary of conditions in California during the Gold Rush.

Simpson, Sir George. "Narrative of an Overland Journey Round the World," *Blackwood's Magazine*, LXI, 653-672.

Sullivan, Edward. "Rambles and Scrambles in North and South America," *Blackwood's Magazine*, LXXII, 680-692.

Sullivan is quoted as proof of the veracity of *Uncle Tom's Cabin*. His stand in favor of gradual emancipation, rather than abolitionism, is commended.

Taylor, J. G. "United States and Cuba," *Blackwood's Magazine*, LXIX, 545-563.

Taylor's favorable attitude towards the United States is belittled as superficial and overindulgent.

Trotter, Mrs. I. S. "First Impressions of the New World," *Frasers Magazine*, LXI, 276-288.

The reviewer (probably H. A. Murray) dismisses the work as fit only for very young people desiring to while away a few hours pleasantly.

Warburton, Major G. D. "Hochelega," *Blackwood's Magazine*, LX, 464-474.

The author's conclusion that the United States is unstable and impermanent, is accepted. The reviewer agrees that a peaceful break-up of the Union is the best that can be hoped for. American criticism of the book is a foregone conclusion, it states, inasmuch as Americans will like only such books as give them unqualified praise and set them up as the pinnacle of perfection.

3. TOURIST AND EMIGRANT GUIDEBOOKS

Anonymous. *American Guidebook*. Philadelphia, 1846.

―――― *Emigrants Guide*. Westport, 1832.

―――― *Emigrants Handbook*. New York, 1848.

―――― *The Garden of the World: a Complete Guide to Emigrants*. Boston, 1856.

―――― *Gazetteer of the World*. 14 vols. Edinburgh, 1850-1856.

―――― *Information for Emigrants: North America*. London, 1848.

―――― *New World in 1859*. London, 1859.

―――― *Remarks on the Western States of America*. London, 1839.

―――― *Travellers Guide and Emigrants Directory through the States of Ohio, Illinois, Indiana, and Michigan*. New York, 1836.

―――― *Western Traveller's Pocket Directory and Stranger's Guide*. Schenectady, 1836.

Appleton. *Handbook of American Travel; Guide to the United States and the British Provinces.* New York, 1857.

—— *Illustrated Handbook of American Travel.* London, 1860.

Bronson, Frank S. *Bronson's Travelers' Directory, from New York to New Orleans.* Le Grange, Georgia, 1845.

Colton, J. H. *Emigrants Handbook: or directory and guide for persons emigrating to the United States of America, especially to those settling in the Great Western Valley.* New York, 1848.

—— *Traveler and Tourists' Routebook through the United States of America and the Canadas.* New York, 1854.

—— *The West: Tourist and Emigrants' Guide.* New York, 1851.

Conclin, George. *Book for All Travellers.* Cincinnati, 1855.

Conder, Josiah. *The United States of America and Canada.* 2 vols. London, 1830.

Creuzbaur, R. *Route from the Gulf of Mexica to California, with Directions to Travellers.* Austin, 1849.

Cummings, Samuel. *Western Pilot.* Cincinnati, 1843.

Curtiss, Daniel S. *Western Portraiture and Emigrants Guide; a description of Wisconsin, Illinois, and Iowa.* New York, 1852.

Dana, C. A. *The United States, illustrated in views of city and country with description and historical articles.* New York, 1854.

Dare, C. P. *Philadelphia, Wilmington and Baltimore Railroad Guide.* Philadelphia, 1856.

Davison, G. M. *Travellers Guide.* Saratoga Springs, 1837.

—— *Travellers Guide through the Middle and Northern States and the Provinces of Canada.* New York, 1840.

Disturnell, J. *American and European Railway Guide.* New York, 1851.

—— *Emigrants' Guide to California, Oregon, and New Mexico.* New York, 1849.

—— *Guide between Washington and Boston.* New York, 1846.

—— *Hudson River Guide.* New York, 1848.

—— *New York State Guide.* Albany, 1842.

—— *Northern Traveller.* New York, 1844.

Dwight, Theodore. *Northern Traveller.* New York, 1841.

Fisher, R. S. *New and Complete Statistical Gazetteer of the United States of America.* Colton, 1859.

Foreigner. *Emigration, Emigrants and Know-Nothings.* Philadelphia, 1854.

Foster, Vere. *Work and Wages.* London, 1855.

George. *Emigrants' Guide to the United States and Canada.* London, 1835.

Goodrich, C. A. *Family Tourist; a visit to the principal cities of the Western Continent.* Philadelphia, 1848.

Goodrich, A. T. *New York State Tourist.* New York, 1840.

—— *North American Tourist.* New York, 1839.

Hadley, W. H. *The American Citizen's Manual of Reference.* New York, 1840.

Haskel, D., and Smith, J. C. *Complete Descriptive and Statistical Gazetteer of the United States of America.* New York, 1843.

Hazard, W. P. *American Guide Book*, Philadelphia, 1846.

Holley, O. L., ed. *Picturesque Tourist*. New York, 1844.

James. *Travellers Companion Guide through the West and South to the Gulf of Mexico and the Pacific*. New York, 1853.

Macgregor, John. *Commercial Statistics of America*. London, 1847.

Marcy, R. B. *The Prairie Traveller: a Handbook for Overland Expeditions*. New York, 1859.

Matthew, Patrick. *Emigration Fields: North America, the Cape, Australia and New Zealand*. Edinburgh, 1839.

Mellen, G. *The Book of the United States*. New York, 1839.

Mitchell, S. A. *General View of the United States*. Philadelphia, 1846.

—— *Principal Stage, Steamboat, and Canal Routes in the United States*. Philadelphia, 1834.

—— *Travellers' Guide through the United States*. Philadelphia, 1838.

Murray, Hugh. *The United States of America*. 3 vols. Edinburgh, 1844.

Newhall, J. B. *The British Emigrant's Handbook and Guide to the New States of America*. London, 1844.

—— *A Glimpse of Iowa in 1846*. Burlington, Iowa, 1846.

O'Kelly, Patrick. *Advice and Guide to Emigrants going to the United States of America*. Dublin, 1834.

Peck, J. M. *New Guide for Emigrants to the West*. Boston, 1836.

—— *Travellers Directory for Illinois*. New York, 1839.

Phelps and Ensign. *Travellers Guide*. New York, 1838.

Putnam, G. P. *American Facts*. London, 1845.

Routledge. *American Handbook and Tourist Guide*. London, 1854.

Smith, J. C. *Emigrants Handbook*. London, 1850.

—— *Handbook for Travellers through the United States of America*. New York, 1856.

—— *The Illustrated Handbook; a New Guide for Travellers through the United States of America*. New York, 1846.

Smith, Sidney. *Settlers New Home*. London, 1849.

Stewart, R. *The United States of America*. London, 1852.

Tanner, H. S. *American Traveller*. New York, 1846.

—— *Description of the Canals and Railroads of the United States*. New York, 1840.

Trotter, Alexander. *Observations on the Financial Position and Credit of such of the states of North America as have Contracted Public Debts*. London, 1839.

True, J. P. *Travelers Guide*. Chicago, 1855.

Warner, I. W. *Immigrants Guide*. New York, 1848.

Wetmore, Alphonso. *Gazetteer of the State of Missouri*. St. Louis, 1837.

Wiley, J., and Putnam, G. P. *Emigrant's Guide*. London, 1845.

Williams, W. *Travellers and Tourists Guide through the United States of America*. Philadelphia, 1851.

4. TRAVEL AND TRAVELLERS

Adams, E. D. " The Point of View of the British Traveller in America," *Political Science Quarterly*, XXIX, 244-265.

This is a brief study of the British traveller's viewpoint towards American democracy during 1810-1860. Adams divides this period arbitrarily into decades, and claims that the travel accounts in each decade follow a distinctive trend.

Allibone, S. A. *Critical Dictionary of English Literature and British and American Authors*. 3 vols. Philadelphia, 1874.

Appleton's *Cyclopaedia of American Biography*. 6 vols. New York, 1887.

Armstrong, M. U. *Fanny Kemble*. New York, 1938.

Berger, Max. *American Political Institutions as Seen by British Travellers: 1836-1860*. Columbia University, 1940.

An unpublished Master's thesis devoted to the reaction of the British traveller to such American political institutions as universal suffrage, democratic government, partisanship, and the machinery of government.

Boase, Frederic. *Modern English Biography*. 3 vols. Truro, 1892.

Bowen, F. C. *A Century of Atlantic Travel, 1830-1930*. New York, 1930.

Several chapters are devoted to the sailing ships and steamers crossing the Atlantic during 1830-1860.

Brooks, J. G. *As Others See Us*. New York, 1908.

This is a very superficial and sketchy treatment of the European viewpoint of America during the Nineteenth Century.

Buck, S. J. " Travels and Descriptions (Illinois) 1765-1865," *Illinois State Historical Library, Springfield Collections*, vol. IX.

This bibliography of travel in Illinois lists both American and British travel accounts.

Chace, W. E. *The Descent on Democracy*. University of North Carolina, 1941.

An unpublished doctoral dissertation which studies the observations of British travellers on American Democracy during 1815-1860. Chace concludes that their reaction was overwhelmingly hostile.

Chesterton, G. K. *Charles Dickens, a Critical Study*. New York, 1910.

Cooper, Lane. " Travellers and Observers, 1763-1846," *Cambridge History of American Literature*, I, 185-215, 468-490.

Although the article is devoted chiefly to American travellers, some of the better known foreign travellers are also mentioned.

Dellenbaugh, F. S. " Travellers and Explorers, 1846-1900," *Cambridge History of American Literature*, III, 131-170, 681-728.

The foreign traveller is completely ignored.

Douglas, Antoinette. " Selected List of Original Narratives of Early Western Travel in North America," *St. Louis Public Library Monthly Bulletin*, n. s. XVII, 162-170.

This brief annotated bibliography of travel books on the West, prior to 1875, mentions only a few of the most prominent English accounts.

Driver, L. S. *Fanny Kemble*. Chapel Hill, 1933.

Dunbar, Seymour. *History of Travel*. 4 vols. Indianapolis, 1915.

A standard work that contains an extensive bibliography.

Hamilton, J. D. T. *The South as seen by British Travellers: 1800-1860*. University of Mississippi, 1938.

This unpublished Master's thesis is based upon a very limited number of English travel accounts. Its bibliography is meagre; its conclusions open to question.

Gibbon, Charles. *The Life of George Combe*. 2 vols. London, 1878.

A chapter is devoted to his American sojourn.

Hannay, David. *The Life of Frederick Marryat*. London, 1859.

Hannay pays particular attention to Marryat's motives in coming to America.

Hulbert, A. B. *Pioneer Roads*. Cleveland, 1902-1905.

This work resembles Dunbar, but contains neither citations nor bibliography.

———, *Experiences of Travellers*. Cleveland, 1902-1905.

This is a sequel to *Pioneer Roads*. Except for some quotations from Dickens and C. A. Murray, foreign travellers are disregarded.

Johnson, A. and Malone, D., eds. *Dictionary of American Biography*. 20 vols. New York, 1928-1937.

Kunitz, S. J. and Haycraft, H., eds. *British Authors of the Nineteenth Century*. New York, 1936.

Lane, W. J. *From Indian Trail to Iron Horse: Travel and Transportation in New Jersey, 1620-1860*. Princeton, 1939.

A study of travel routes and travel conditions in New Jersey, based on American sources. Special attention is given to the development of the railroads in the state.

Lyell, Mrs. Charles. *Life, Letters, and Journals of Sir Charles Lyell*. 2 vols. London, 1881.

Lloyd, Christopher. *Captain Marryat and the Old Navy*. London, 1939.

MacGill, C. E., ed. *History of Transportation in the United States before 1860*. Washington, D. C., 1917.

Marryat, Florence. *Life and Letters of Capt. Marryat.* 2 vols. London, 1872.

There are two chapters on his trip to America. The correspondence, though fragmentary, is very revealing.

Mesick, J. L. *The English Traveller in America, 1785-1835.* New York, 1921.

This is the best study on the topic for the period 1785-1835. Mesick treats the entire half-century as an entity, and organizes her material on a topical basis without regard to chronology.

Nevins, Allan. *American Social History as recorded by British Travellers.* New York, 1934.

Nevins has gathered together representative excerpts from British travel accounts. A thumb-nail sketch of the author precedes each excerpt. The travellers are grouped chronologically into several large periods. An introductory study of the trends in each period is particularly valuable. An extensive bibliography is appended.

Ogden, R., ed. *Life and Letters of E. L. Godkin.* 2 vols. New York, 1907.

Godkin, an Ulster Presbyterian who later gained fame as editor of *The Nation*, came to America in 1856 at the age of twenty-five, after service as a war correspondent in the Crimean War. His letters contain interesting though uncomplimentary remarks on the emigrants of the period.

Payne, E. F. *Dickens' Days in Boston.* New York, 1927.

Dickens' writings are correlated with his experiences and acquaintances while in Boston.

Payne, G. H. *England, her Treatment of America.* New York, 1931.

This is a popularly written book based solely upon secondary sources. No mention appears of British travel works on America. English politicians are blamed for the poor relations between the two countries prior to the Civil War.

Phillips, U. B. *A History of Transportation in the Eastern Cotton Belt to 1860.* New York, 1908.

An excellent study of the problem, on a regional basis, with emphasis upon the development of railroads in this area.

Pope-Hennessy, Mrs. Una. *Three English Women in America.* London, 1929.

This work, directed towards popular consumption, consists of biographical sketches of Mrs. Trollope, Harriet Martineau, and Fanny Kemble. There are no citations or bibliography.

Plympton, C. W. " Select Bibliography on Travel in North America," *New York State Library Bulletin Bibliography*, III, 35-60.

A very brief list of titles, chiefly by American authors, covering the entire period of American history.

Rait, R. S. "British Writers on the United States," *Quarterly Review,* CCCCLV, 357-371.

This review, written during World War I, is decidedly sympathetic towards the American resentment of criticism by English travellers. Only a few of the most flagrant critics are discussed. These are countered by expressions of sympathy found in other British works of the period.

Rusk, R. L. *The Literature of the Middle Western Frontier.* 2 vols. New York, 1925.

Some of the better known English travellers are discussed in the chapters devoted to the topic "Travel and Observation." A good bibliography of western guide books and gazetteers is to be found in the second volume.

Ryan, J. P. "Travel Literature as Source Material for American Catholic History," *Illinois Catholic Historical Review*, X, 179-238, 301-363.

Some attention is paid to the British traveller.

Stephen, L. and Lee, S., eds. *Dictionary of National Biography.* 22 vols. London, 1922.

Thomson, P. G. *Bibliography of the State of Ohio.* Cincinnati, 1880.

Tuckerman, H. T. *America and Her Commentators.* New York, 1864.

Although this was the earliest full-fledged treatment of the subject, many of its observations are still valuable.

Turner, R. E. *James Silk Buckingham.* London, 1934.

This is the latest biography of this interesting and widely read traveller.

Tyler, D. B. *Steam Conquers the Atlantic.* New York, 1939.

The story of the development of steam travel on the Atlantic from the *Savannah* to 1880.

Venable, W. H. "Some Early Travellers and Annalists of the Ohio Valley," *Ohio Archaeological and Historical Quarterly*, I, 230-242.

French and American travellers in the Ohio Valley prior to 1845 are considered briefly.

Wagner, H. R. *The Plains and the Rockies.* San Francisco, 1937.

Original narratives of travel and adventure in this region between 1800 and 1865 are annotated, and listed according to the year of their publication.

White, Laura. "The United States in the 1850s as seen by British Consuls," *Mississippi Valley Historical Review*, XIX, 509-536.

This study is based upon the manuscript reports of British Consuls. A comparison of the viewpoints of the Consuls with that of British travellers is very interesting.

Wilkins, W. G., ed. *Dickens in America.* New York, 1911.

Contemporary diaries and newspapers are quoted at length.

Wilson, J. G. *Thackeray in the United States: 1852-1853, 1855-1856.* 2 vols. London, 1904.

Wood, R. G. "Bibliography of Travel in Maine, 1783-1861," *New England Quarterly,* VI, 426-439.

> Though most of the titles are American, some British accounts are included.

5. EMIGRATION AND AMERICAN NATIVISM

Abbott, Edith, ed. *Historical Aspects of the Immigration Problem.* Chicago, 1925.

> Largely a source book on American immigration.

Adams, W. F. *Ireland and Irish Emigration to the New World from 1815 to the Famine.* London, 1932.

> An excellent work on the factors affecting Irish emigration to the United States during the first half of the Nineteenth Century.

Anonymous. "Philadelphia Anti-Catholic Riots of 1844," *American Catholic Historical Researches,* n. s., III, 132-136.

Billington, R. A. *The Protestant Crusade, 1800-1860.* New York, 1938.

> A fine work on the anti-Catholic and nativist movements of the pre-Civil War period. An excellent bibliography is appended.

——— "Tentative Bibliography of Anti-Catholic Propaganda (1800-1860)." *Catholic Historical Review,* XVIII, 492-513.

Brand, C. F. "Know-Nothing Party in Indiana," *Indiana Magazine of History,* XVIII, 47-81, 177-206, 266-306.

Bromwell, W. J. *History of Immigration to the United States.* New York, 1856.

> A collection of statistical tables on emigration to the United States, 1819-1855, based on official government data for each port of entry.

Byrne, Stephen. *Irish Emigration to the United States.* New York, 1874.

Chickering, Jesse. *Immigration into the United States.* Boston, 1848.

> A pioneer effort, brief and inaccurate, but suggestive.

Cole, A. C. "Nativism in the Lower Mississippi Valley," *Mississippi Valley Historical Association Proceedings,* VI, 258-272.

> Almost entirely on the period 1840-1860.

Evangeline, T. M. *Nativism in the Old Northwest, 1850-1860.* Washington, 1936.

Hewitt, W. F. "Know-Nothing Party in Pennsylvania," *Pennsylvania History,* II, 69-85.

Fairchild, H. F. *Immigration.* New York, 1925.

> A standard text.

Hansen, M. L. *Atlantic Migration, 1607-1860.* Cambridge, Mass., 1940.

An excellent work treating the subject largely from its European aspects.

Johnson, S. C. *History of Emigration from the United Kingdom to North America: 1763-1912.* London, 1913.

Kapp, Friedrich. *Immigration and the Commissioners of Emigration of the State of New York.* New York, 1870.

Contains a good account of emigrant conditions aboard ship and in New York, as well as a summary of the laws affecting emigration to that state.

Maguire, J. F. *The Irish in America.* London, 1868.

The author was an Irish Member of Parliament. The work is full, but ill-organized and repetitious.

McGee, T. D'Arcy. *The History of the Irish Settlers in North America.* Boston, 1855.

A panegyric on the Irish race and the Catholic Church, by a violent Anglophobe.

Morehouse, Frances. "Irish Migration of the Forties," *American Historical Review,* XXXIII, 579-592.

A good summary of conditions in Ireland that led to the migration, based upon British government reports.

National Bureau of Economic Research. *International Migrations.* 2 vols. New York, 1931.

Extensive tables and statistics on international migrations, including emigration to the United States.

New York State Assembly. *Report of the Special Committee Investigating the Commissioners of Emigration.* Albany, 1852.

One of the best contemporary accounts of emigrant conditions in New York City.

New York State Commissioners of Emigration. *Annual Reports.* Albany, 1847-1860.

Contain a wealth of data on emigration laws and conditions in the Empire State.

Noonan, C. J. *Nativism in Connecticut, 1829-1860.* Washington, 1938.

O'Driscoll, Felicity. "Political Nativism in Buffalo," *Records of the American Catholic Historical Society,* September 1937.

Page, T. W. "Transportation of Immigrants and Reception Arrangements in the Nineteenth Century," *Journal of Political Economy,* XIX, 732-749.

Schafer, Joseph. "Know-Nothings in Wisconsin," *Wisconsin Magazine of History,* VIII, 3-21.

Schmeckebier, L. F. *History of the Know-Nothing Party in Maryland.* Baltimore, 1899.

Scisco, L. D. *Political Nativism in New York State.* New York, 1901.

A doctoral dissertation based largely on newspaper sources.

Senning, J. P. "Know Nothing Movement in Illinois, 1854-1856," *Illinois Historical Society Journal*, VII, 7-33.

Stephenson, G. M. *History of American Immigration.* Boston, 1926.

A standard work with a fairly good bibliography.

———— "Nativism in the Forties and Fifties, with Special Reference to the Mississippi Valley," *Mississippi Valley Historical Review*, IX, 185-202.

A brief general account dealing chiefly with the Germans.

Stickney, C. *Know-Nothingism in Rhode Island.* Providence, 1894.

Taft, D. R. *Human Migration.* New York, 1936.

A general study of the problem, not too detailed on the period 1836-1860.

Tusca, Benjamin. *Know-Nothingism in Baltimore, 1854-1860.* New York, 1925.

U. S. Census Bureau. *A Century of Population Growth from the first Census of the United States to the Twelfth (1790-1900).* Washington, 1909.

Zwierlein, F. J. "Know-Nothingism in Rochester, N. Y.," *United States Catholic Historical Society Records and Studies*, XIV, 20-69.

INDEX

Abolitionism, 71-73, 108, 110, 114, 118-119, 121-125, 135, 183
Accidents, 41-42, 45, 47-48, 69, 75
Acton, Lord, J. E. E. D., 67n.; on New York Exhibition of 1853, 14-15, 29; on slavery, 120; on education, 149, 151, 153n., 155-156
Adams, J. Q., 94-95, 124
Adams, W. F., 5, 167n., 171n.
Agassiz, A. E., 155
Agriculture, 7, 17, 57; in New England, 35, 177; in the South, 43, 110-111, 117, 178; in the West, 54, 165, 173-174, 177-178; see also Slavery
Alabama, 66; see also Birmingham, Mobile, Montgomery
Albany, N. Y., 37-38, 65, 100, 103
Allardice, R. B. (Capt. Barclay), 84n., 111n., 120, 178n.
Amboy, N. J., 40
American Colonization Society, 119, 125-126
American women: in Lowell mills, 36-37, 79; social distinctions, 59; position of, 54, 76-85; beauty of, 77; poor health of, 78; education of, 78-79; morals of, 79-80; marriage, 80-84; interest in religion, 134; position among Mormons, 140-141
Andover, 154
Anglican Church, 147-148
Anglo-American rivalry, 185-187
Anti-British sentiment, 103, 144, 166, 179-182
Aristocracy, 58-61, 89, 95, 120, 155
Arizona, 18
Atheists, 137
Auburn, 154

Baird, Robert, 177n.
Baltimore, Md., 25, 41, 74, 77, 168, 170
Banking, 72
Banks, N. P., 97
Baptists, 142, 156
Barclay, Capt.; see Allardice
Baxter, W. E., 14; on New York hotels, 26n.; on railroads, 35, 42, 44; on St. Louis, 48-49; on society, 59n.; on justice, 74n.; on American women, 77n., 78; on Washington, D. C., 86n.; on American government and politics, 91n., 93n., 96n., 99, 103n., 104, 107n.; on the Irish, 103n., 104, 144n.; on slavery, 109, 113, 123, 126n.; on religion, 104, 133, 134n.-136n., 137, 142n., 144n.-145n.; on education, 148n., 150n.-151n., 154, 157, 159n.
Beecher, H. W., 133
Bell, Andrews (A. Thomason): on vice, 80; on emigration, 172, 175, 179n.-180n.
Berkeley, Sir G. C. G F., 14, 107; on hunting buffalo, 17, 19, 32
Beste, J. R. D.: on emigration, 13-14, 16, 162, 170, 174n., 177n.; on the Irish, 57, 170; on American women, 82; on religion, 135-137, 145; on education, 161
Bible, 94, 129, 134, 146
Biggs, Joseph, 164n.
Bird, Miss: see Bishop
Birmingham, Ala., 33
Bishop, Mrs. I. L. (Bird), 18n., 23n., 26n.; on society, 59, 60n.; on American women, 76, 77n., 82; on American government, 100n.-102n., 104-105; on Know-Nothings, 104-105, 182; on religion, 130n., 134n., 135, 136n., 144; on education, 150-151, 161n.; on emigration, 18n., 164n., 167n., 176n.
Boardinghouses: see Hotels
Boston, Mass., 15, 32-33, 36, 110; description, 20, 25, 36; telegraphic fire alarm, 30; society, 59, 61; crime, 73; politics, 105, 118, 181; religion, 132, 142-143, 146; schools, 147, 151-152; Irish, 168, 181
Boston Night Watch, 73
Bowen, F. C., 18n., 25n., 163n.
Bremer, Frederika, 22
British West Indies, 108, 118
Brook Farm, 138
Brothers, Thomas, 21; on slavery, 121; on emigration, 162, 166n., 174n.
Brown University, 155-156
Brown, William, 30, 131n.; on emigration, 162, 166n., 174n.
Buchanan, James, 89
Buckingham, J. S., 14, 17, 19; background, 23; on New York, 27; on Lowell, 37; on travel in the South, 43, 45-46, 63; on St. Louis, 48; on Chicago, 52; on egalitarianism, 54-

55, 57; on aristocracy, 61, 63; on American pride, 62; on inquisitiveness, 63; on spitting, 64-65; on drinking, 66, 73; on lawlessness, 68, 70, 73, 74n.; on indifference to human life, 75; on American women, 77, 82n.; on boardinghouses, 81; on American government and politics, 90, 91n., 96-97, 100n.-101n., 103n., 105, 107; on slavery, 108-109, 111, 116, 125; on religion, 133n., 134, 136n., 137, 143; on education, 149, 157; on emigration, 167-169, 172, 179-180; on Anglo-American relations, 187n.

Buffalo, N. Y., 54

Bunker Hill, 36, 105

Bunn, Alfred, 22, 38 n.; on railroad accidents, 41; on American pride, 55, 62n.-63n.; on spitting, 64n.; on drinking, 67n.; on petty crime, 72n.; on the Irish, 101n., 103n.-104n., 144n.; on slavery, 121; on Lyceums, 158

Buntline, Ned, 181-182

Burns, Jabez, 65-66, 173n., 176n.

Burton, R. F., 17, 23, 32, 140-141

Butler, Mrs.: see Kemble

Caird, Sir James, 14; on emigration, 162, 173, 175n.

Calhoun, J. C., 95, 121, 123

California, 17-18, 49-51, 169, 171, 179. See also Gold Rush, Sacramento, San Francisco

Canada, 25, 33, 175, 178, 185-186. See also Montreal

Canals: see Travel in America

Carlisle, Earl of (G. W. F. Howard): on the South, 43-44; on society, 59n.; on Washington, D. C., 87; on Congress, 93; on state governments, 100n.; on religion, 137; on emigration, 169n.

Casey, Charles, 13; on Niagara, 39n.; on accidents, 47; on Catholicism, 145; on emigration, 13, 165

Caswall, Henry, 53, 132n.

Catholicism, 66, 135, 137, 146, 169; fears aroused by, 49, 132, 142-144, 157, 159, 181; and politics, 103-104, 144; weakening of, 145; parochial schools, 143, 145, 151, 157; opposition to secular schools, 145, 151, 160-161; domination by priesthood, 104, 144-145, 169; and nativism, 181-182; see also Germans in America, Irish in America, Jesuits, Nativism, Schools

Chambers, Williams, 14, 61; on American government, 88, 92, 100n.; on slavery, 123, 125n.; on Catholicism, 145n.; on the Irish, 145n., 166n., 170n.; on emigration, 172n.

Chandless, William: on the Mormons, 23, 72-73, 141-142, 154n.; on the Gold Rush, 49; on crime, 72-73; on the Irish, 166n., 168n.-169n.

Channing, Dr. W. E., 36

Charleston, S. C., 33, 43-44, 109

Chicago, Ill., 51-53, 143, 168

Chinese in America, 58, 166

Churches, 17; attendance at, 132-133, 135-136; buildings, 49, 131-133, 136; Mormon Tabernacle, 49, 141; see also the individual sects

Cincinnati, O., 42, 53, 72, 75, 77, 168

Civil War, 117, 122, 126-128

Clergy, 143, 149; control by congregation, 130, 135; education, 131, 135; salary, 130-131, 136; see also the individual sects

Cleveland, O., 53

Clipper ships, 117-118

Collins Line, 17

Collyer, R. H., 27-28, 59, 167

Combe, George, 14, 19, 27, 32, 36; on Hudson River steamers, 38n.; on railroads, 39; on servants, 57n.; on temperance, 67; on election of judges, 75n., 97n.; on American children, 84; on American government, 75n., 90, 94, 97n., 100n., 102n. 106-107; on religion, 133n., 136n., 137; on education, 158n., 159; on emigration, 102n., 168n., 172

Commerce and industry, 16, 43, 165, 177, 185; shipping, 25, 43; shoe manufacturing, 35; Lowell mills, 36-37, 168; in the West, 49-50, 72; in the South, 54, 111, 168; emigrant labor, 165, 168-173; occupations, 178-179; see also Labor, Poverty

Congregationalists, 142

Congress, 91-96; House of Representatives, 92-95; Senate, 95-96

Connecticut, 97, 148-149, 160. See also Norwich

Corruption, 90, 100-103. See also Elections, Patronage

Crowe, Eyre, 21

Cuba, 33, 118

Cunard Line, 18

Cunynghame, Sir A. A. T., 15, 166n., 170n.
Curiosity, 63-64

Darwin, Charles, 146
Davies, Ebenezer, 114, 118, 168n.
DeBow, J. D. B., 111
Deists, 137
Delaware, 83
Democratic Party, 101, 103, 106, 144
Depression of 1857, 173
Dew, T. R., 122
Dickens, Charles, 17, 19; on New York slums, 28; on Lowell mills, 36-37; on canal boat travel, 38; on slavery, 43, 113-114; on St. Louis, 48; on Cincinnati, 53; on inquisitiveness, 63; on spitting, 64; on Washington, D. C., 86-87; on Congress, 89, 92, 94; on elections, 98; on religion, 137, 140, 142; on education, 157-158; on the Irish, 169-170; and anti-British sentiment, 180
Disease, 16, 113, 163-164, 167-168, 175, 177-179
Dissenters, 137
Divorce, 83; among Mormons, 141
Dixon, James, 134, 137, 166n., 187
Dodd, W. E., 153
Drinking, 47, 65-67, 117, 129, 176; and lawlessness, 73; as grounds for divorce, 83; by emigrants, 65-66, 164, 169; see also Temperance
Dueling: see Lawlessness

Egalitarianism, 54-58, 61, 63-64, 74, 89-91, 96-97, 99, 124, 159, 161, 182
Elections, 93-106; conduct of, 66, 101-102, 105-106; of judges, 74, 96-97, 130; frauds, 101-102; role of the Irish, 101-105, 181; influence of the Catholic priesthood, 104, 144-145, 181; see also Partisan spirit, Patronage, Politics, individual parties
Emigrant, 162-182; ships, 162-164; hardships, 167-168, 172-180, 182; opportunities, 171-175, 177-179, 182
Engleheart, Sir G. D., 88-89, 106n.
English in America, 13-14, 16, 165-166, 177
Episcopalians, 131, 142, 156
Everest, Robert, 66, 145
Eyre, John, 174n.

Fairchild, H. P., 162n.

Family life, 80-84; among slaves, 119-121; see also American women, Divorce, Marriage, Morals
Featherstonhaugh, G. W., 169n.
Felton, Mrs., 30; on slavery, 116; on emigration, 164n.; on nativism, 180
Feminism, 17; see also American women
Feuds: see Lawlessness
Fillmore, Millard, 91
Finch, Marianne, 17, 140, 168n.
Fires, 29-31, 73
Fitzhugh, George, 122
Florida, 118
Foreign missions, 134
Foster, Vere, 22
Fourierists, 138
Free Academy, 150
Free negro, 52, 55, 57-58, 88, 119, 121-122, 124, 168, 170; slums, 28; lynching of, 72
Free-Soiler, 117

Garrison, W. L., 71, 123
Georgia, 44, 46, 83, 109-111, 168; see also Savannah
Germans in America, 49, 66, 142, 144, 165, 167, 181
Girard College, 40, 149
Gladstone, T. H., 14, 63-64; on "Bleeding Kansas," 17, 68-69; on slavery, 73n., 117n.
Godkin, E. L., 144n., 169
Godley, J. R., 43n., 102n., 104n.; on slavery, 123n., 125n., 126; on religion, 129-131, 137, 142n., 145; on education, 150, 152, 153n., 156, 160; on nativism, 180
Gold Rush, 16, 18, 49-51, 169, 177
Governors, 97
Grattan, T. C., 17, 23; consul to Boston, 15, 32; on New York hotels, 25-26; on railroad accidents, 41; on servants, 56, 57n.; on aristocracy, 59; on spitting, 64-65; on petty crime, 72; on American women, 81; on American government, 90, 94, 100, 105; on slavery, 116, 118; on religion, 129-130, 133, 134n., 137-139; on education, 161n.; on emigration, 169, 171, 181-182; on nativism, 181-182; on Anglo-American relations, 184, 186
Gray, Asa, 146
Great Lakes, 32, 39-40, 53; see also individual cities and states on the Great Lakes

Hall, Basil, 20
Hancock, William, 16; on New York, 29, 102n.; on Catholics, 102n., 145n.; on emigration, 162, 166n., 174n., 176n., 178, 179n.
Hannay, David., 20n.
Harper, William, 122
Harrisburg, Pa., 100
Harrison, W. H., 91
Harvard, 146, 154-156
Harvey, George, 14
Hotels, 25-27, 57, 97; Astor House, 19, 25-26; Barum's, 26; Mansion House, 26; St. Charles Hotel, 26, 44; St. Nicholas Hotel, 26, 70; Tremont House, 26, 36; Southern inns, 53, 55; boardinghouses, 58, 81-82
House of Representatives: see Congress
Houstoun, Mrs. M. C. J. F., 20, 41n., 47; Cincinnati, 53; on egalitarianism, 54; on aristocracy, 59n.-60n.; on American women, 82; on American children, 83-84; on American government, 89n., 90, 92n.-93n., 94-97, 102n.-103n.; on the Irish, 54, 102n.-103n.; on slavery, 121; on emigration, 174-175; and anti-British sentiment, 180
Howard, G. W. F.: see Carlisle
Hunting, 14, 17, 19, 32

Illinois, 18, 83, 173, 177; see also Chicago
Illinois Central Railroad, 162, 173
Independents, 146
Indiana, 177
Indians, 15, 51, 126
Indifference towards human life, 75-76; see also Accidents, Lawlessness, Mob violence
Inman Line, 17
Inquisitiveness, 63-64
Iowa, 177
Irish famine, 16, 162, 166, 168
Irish in America, 16, 30, 49, 79, 142; condition of, 28, 54, 165, 169-172, 180; occupations of, 37, 54, 56-58, 146, 168-171; as servants, 54, 56-57, 146; drunkenness among, 65-66, 169; lawlessness of, 66, 73, 101-102, 104-105, 166, 181; role in politics, 101-105, 181; domination by priests, 104, 144-145; schools for, 145, 150-151; crossing the Atlantic, 162-164; concentration in cities, 49, 167-171; and nativism, 180-182

Jackson, Andrew, 91
Jefferson, Thomas, 116, 156
Jesuits, 49, 143, 157, 160; see also Catholicism
Jobson, F. J., 17, 22, 54, 126
Johnston, J. F. W., 14; on election of judges, 75n., 97n.; on American women, 80n.; on divorce, 83; on slavery, 123, 126-127; on religion, 103, 145n., 146; on education, 148, 154n., 155-156, 158, 161n.; on Anglo-American rivalry, 186
Judiciary, 64, 70, 74-75, 96-97, 130, 180; see also Dueling, Lawlessness

Kansas, 17, 55, 68-69, 117
Kelly, William, 22-23, 145; on the Gold Rush, 17, 49-51, 179n.; on Chinese emigrants, 166n.; on Irish emigrants, 169n., 171
Kemble, F. A. (Mrs. Butler), 17; on Charleston, 43n.; on dueling, 69-70; on slavery, 110n., 112, 115, 124
Kennedy, William, 175, 178
Kentucky, 46, 48, 69, 112, 120, 153; see also Louisville
Know-Nothings, 68, 104-105, 181-182; see also Nativism

Labor, condition of, 168-174, 177-179
Lardner, Dionysius, 47-48
Lawlessness, 43, 68-75; arson, 30, 73; in the West, 50, 70-71, 93; dueling, 69-70, 117; feuds, 70; election disorders, 66, 88, 102, 106; nativist disorders, 68, 104-105, 182; anti-negro disorders, 71-72, 121; lynchings, 71-72, 116-117; by emigrants, 66, 73, 102, 166, 181; see also Drinking, Judiciary, Mob Violence, Temperance
Lewis, George, 17, 23, 107, 143
Lewis, J. D., 20n.; on religion, 130-131, 138; on education, 160; on emigration, 165n., 173n., 176n.
Liberia, 119, 125-126
Liquor: see Drinking, Temperance
Literacy, 152-153, 158, 161, 183-184
Liverpool, 163, 173
Loco-Focos, 102, 105, 144
Logan, James, 60, 75, 78
Longfellow, J. W., 155
Louisville, Ky., 70, 75, 131
Lowell, Mass., 36-37, 79
Lowell Offering, 37
Lumsden, James, 171n.
Lyell, Sir Charles, 14, 19, 36; on servants, 54; on spitting, 65; on

drinking, 66; on American government, 74n., 91n., 97n., 100, 102, 103n.; on slavery, 110, 120-121; on religion, 131, 142, 146; on education, 147, 148n., 151n., 153, 156, 161n.; on emigration, 168; on living in America, 183

Lynching: *see* Lawlessness

Macgregor, John: on travel conditions, 51n., 55; on Catholicism, 144n.-145n.; on New York slums, 167n.

Mackay, Alexander, 17, 19, 25n., 87n.; on railroad travel, 34, 40n.; on egalitarianism, 34, 40n., 57n., 58, 61; on servants, 57n.; on American pride, 62n.; on American women, 77, 79n.; on American government, 87, 91, 93-95, 98, 101; on slavery, 123n., 127; on religion, 133n., 135, 137-138, 142n., 143; on schools, 148, 159; on sectionalism, 184; on Anglo-American rivalry, 185-186

Mackay, Charles: on the federal government, 87n., 89; on state government, 97, 100n.; on elections, 101, 103n.-104n.; on anti-British sentiment, 103n., 144; on slavery, 109n., 124; on Catholicism, 103n.-104n., 144, 145n., 166n.; on the future of America, 185n.

Mackinnon, L. B., 14, 17; on Chicago, 52n.; on egalitarianism, 90-91; on Philadelphia school system, 149

McMaster, J. B., 164n.

Madison, James, 115

Maine, 67, 83, 110

Majoribanks, Alexander, 31n.; on railroad travel, 34n., 41n.; on servants, 57n.; on crime, 73; on American women, 80; on American children, 83; on education, 148n., 161n.; on anti-British sentiment, 166n.

Mammon, worship of, 42, 58-61, 132

Mammoth Cave, 48

Mann, Horace, 152

Marriage, 80-83, 153; *see also* American women, Divorce, Family life, Morals

Marryat, Capt. Frederick, 14, 17-20, 22, 24, 180; on railroads, 39; on American love of money, 42n.; on travel in the South, 46-47; on stage-coach travel, 51; on egalita-

rianism, 54; on drinking, 65, 67n.; on dueling, 69; on lawlessness, 69, 71n., 72, 74n., 102n.; on American women, 77-80; on divorce, 83n.; on American children, 84; on Washington, D. C., 86n.; on American government and politics, 89n., 90, 93, 96, 99, 100n., 102, 103n., 106n., 107, 183n.; on the Irish, 102, 103n., 169; on slavery, 116n., 123, 126, 127; on religion, 130, 131n.-132n., 133, 137, 143; on education, 160, 161n.; on Anglo-American rivalry, 62, 185n.

Marryat, Mrs. Florence, 22n., 24n.

Martineau, Harriet, 13, 17-19, 23, 30; on railroad travel, 33, 44; on Lowell, 37; on stage-coach travel, 39, 45; on travel in the South, 44-48; on Chicago, 51-52; on society, 58-60; on lawlessness, 70-72; on American women, 37, 76-78; on marriage, 80, 83n.; on American government and politics, 95, 99-101, 102n., 107; on slavery, 73n, 110, 111n., 112, 115-116, 118, 125; on religion, 134-135, 137-139, 145; on education, 78, 148, 153, 155, 159; on emigration, 101, 102n, 165, 172; on nativism, 181

Maryland, 83, 125-126, 181; *see also* Baltimore

Massachusetts, 67, 97, 133, 138; *see also* Boston, Bunker Hill, Lowell

Maury, Mrs. S. M., 16, 64n.; on New York, 29, 30n.; on fire fighting, 30n.; on servants, 57; on American women, 77n.; on boarding-houses, 81; on American children, 84; on slavery, 57, 121; on religion, 134n., 136n., 137, 146, 153, 160; on emigration, 162, 174n.

Maxwell, A. M., 14-15, 19; on railroad travel, 33; on religion, 133; on the Irish, 170; on the future of America, 185n., 186

Mayne, J. T., 76

Meagher, Thomas, 166-167

Mesick, J. L., 7, 20n., 31n.

Methodists, 17, 131, 142, 156

Mexican War, 117

Midwest, 13-14, 32-33, 39-40, 72, 165, 177; rapid growth of, 51-53; *see also* Great Lakes, West, individual cities and states

Millerites, 138-140

Minnesota, 15, 154

Mississippi, 74; *see also* Natchez, Vicksburg
Missouri, 69, 143; *see also* St. Joseph, St. Louis
Mitchell, D. W., 62; on slavery, 21-22, 122; on Boston, 36n.; on drinking, 66n.; on divorce, 83n.; on the Irish, 66n., 103-104, 166n.-168n., 170n.; on anti-British sentiment, 103n.; on education, 161; on nativism, 181n., 182
Mob violence, 71-72, 108-109, 116-117, 119, 121; *see also* Lawlessness
Mobile, Ala., 74, 116
Molly Maguires, 168
Montgomery, Ala., 70
Montreal, 33, 38-39
Moore, George, 14, 86n., 88, 105n.
Morals, 76, 79-83, 115-116, 141, 160, 182; *see also* American women, Divorce, Family life, Marriage
Mormon Tabernacle, 49, 141
Mormons, 17, 23, 32, 49, 58, 72-73, 80, 140-142, 154
Motives for publication, 21-22
Murray, A. M., 14, 32; on polygamy, 58; on temperance, 67n.; on slavery, 118-119, 183
Murray, C. A., 14, 18-19; on Tocqueville, 22n.; on American pride, 63; on American women, 77n., 78-79; on the presidency, 91n.; on slavery, 127; on religion, 130n., 131, 137, 143; on education, 78, 148n., 155-156, 161n.
Murray, H. A., 107; on titles, 61; on crime, 74n.; on slavery, 124; on education, 150n., 157, 160n.-161n.; on nativism, 182; on the future of America, 185n.

Natchez, Miss., 25, 71-72
Native American Party, 181
Nativism, 68, 103-105, 166, 168, 177, 179-182; *see also* Catholicism, Germans in America, Irish in America, Know-Nothings
Navy, 17, 171
Nettle, George, 166n., 174n.
New Brunswick, N. J., 40
New England, 32-33, 105, 139; agriculture and industry, 35-37, 177, 179; oversupply of women, 80; observance of the Sabbath, 134; schools, 148-149, 152; Irish emigrants, 167-168, 170; *see also* individual cities and states
New Hampshire, 66

New Orleans, La., 25, 32-33, 110, 172; description of, 43-44; Know-Nothing riots, 68, 182; Creole women, 77; whipping of slaves, 113; slave auctions, 115; octaroon prostitutes, 116; Irish emigrants, 168
New York Board of Education, 149-151
New York City, 38-40; Exhibition of 1853, 14-15, 29; description of, 25-31; slums, 28, 167, 172; hotels, 25-27, 70; pigs in streets, 29, 102; fires, 29-31; society, 59; Irish, 66, 101-105; liquor stores, 66; police, 68; crime, 70-71, 104-105; judiciary, 74; politics, 101-105; nativism, 103-105, 181-182; slave ships in, 117; religion in, 133, 136, 143; schools, 145, 148-151; emigrant-conditions, 163-164, 167, 170, 176, 180-181
New York State, 38, 83, 103; *see also* Albany, Buffalo, New York City, Niagara Falls
New York State Emigration Commission, 163-164
Newspapers, 68-69, 75, 94, 104, 109, 116-117
Niagara Falls, 33, 38-40
Non-British travellers, 22; *see also* Bibliographical Note, 189-191
Norwich, Conn., 33-34
" Nothingarians," 142

Ogden, R., editor, 169n.
Ohio, 97, 103; *see also* Cincinnati, Cleveland, Sandusky
Oldmixon, J. W.: on servant problem, 57-58; on emigration, 162, 166n., 174n.-175n.
Oliphant, Laurence, 15, 52-53
Oliver, William, 17, 54, 72; on education, 153; on emigration, 162, 166n., 174n., 177n.-178n.
Orth, S. P., 164n., 167n.

Pairpoint, A. J., 177n.
Panic of 1837, 52, 73, 172, 175
Partisan spirit, 98-100; *see also* Elections, Patronage, Universal suffrage
Passaic Falls, N. J., 29
Patronage, 89, 103-104, 168; *see also* Corruption, Elections, Partisan spirit
Patten, Edmund, 166n., 170n.
Philadelphia, Pa., 40; society, 58-59, 61; temperance in, 65; corruption

in, 102; rioting in, 104, 121; poverty in, 172; schools, 149, 160; Irish in, 104, 168, 181
Phillippo, J. M.: on travel costs, 15-16; on American women, 77n.; on slavery, 118; on education, 153n, 154, 159n.; on the future of America, 185n., 187n.
Phillips, U. B., 111
Pierce, Franklin, 88
Pigs, 29, 53, 102
Pittsburgh, Pa., 29
Playfair, Hugo, 84n.
Police, 68, 73; see also Lawlessness
Politics, 97-107; see also Corruption, Elections, Patronage, P a r t i s a n spirit, Universal suffrage, individual parties
Polk, J. K., 91
Polygamy, 58, 140-141; see also Mormons
Poverty, absence of, 55, 165, 171-172, 183
Prentice, Archibald, 16, 41, 173, 177n.
Presbyterians, 130, 142-143, 146
Presidency, 88-91, 97
Presidential "levees," 88-90
Pride, 61-63
Prince of Wales, 13, 19, 88-89, 106
Princeton, 154
Pro-slavery sentiment, 118-122

Quakers, 14, 40, 127

Railroads: see Travel in America
Ranken, George, 14
Red Bank, 138
Regan, James, 162, 166n.
Reid, Hugo, 29n., 81, 84n.; on railroads, 38, 51n.; on lawlessness, 71, 74n.; on slavery, 127-128; on education, 148n., 159n.
Religion, voluntary vs. established, 129-137
Religious revivals, 137-138
Revolutions of 1848, 16, 21, 91, 162, 166-167
Rhode Island, 148
Rhys, Capt. H., 17, 20n.
Richmond, Va., 43, 170
Robertson, James, 16, 61n., 82n.; on cost of travel, 15n.; on railroad accidents, 41; on Catholicism, 145n.; on the Irish, 170n., 171; on emigration, 172n.
Russell, Robert, 115
Ruxton, G. F. A., 17, 32

Sacramento, Calif., 49-50
St. Joseph, Mo., 18
St. Louis, Mo., 15, 51; description of, 48-49; during the Gold Rush, 49; lynching of negro, 72, 117; visit of Prince of Wales, 106; Catholic schools, 49, 143, 156-157; Irish emigrants in, 49, 168; Jesuit plot, 143
St. Louis University, 49, 143, 156-157
Salt Lake City, 49, 140-141, 154
Sandusky, O., 53
San Francisco, Calif., 50
Savannah, Ga., 103, 109, 168
Schmeckebier, L. F., 168n., 181n.
Schools: elementary, 78, 148-149, 151, 184; academies, 78, 147, 149-150; high, 149, 160; industrial, 150; boarding, 149-150, 157; rural, 152-153; Catholic, 49, 143, 145, 151, 156-157; negro, 120, 150-151, 153; Normal, 149, 152; colleges, 49, 143, 149-150, 152, 154-158; seminaries, 154, 157; Lyceums, 158; accomplishments of, 158-161; support for, 148, 161; secular vs. sectarian, 145, 151, 160-161; teachers, 147, 149-157, 160-161, 178
Scisco, L. D., 181n.
Scots in America, 16, 108, 165, 174
Scott, General Winfield, 54
Sectionalism, 127-128, 184
Senate: see Congress
Servants, 54-58, 121
Shakers, 83, 138-140
Slave: auctions, 114-116; women, 111, 114-115; plantation, 110-112, 115-117, 119-120; breeding, 115-116; smuggling, 117-118
Slavery, 94, 99, 105, 108-128; evil effects of, 43, 69, 73, 109-110, 117, 178; and lawlessness, 73, 117; as a divisive force, 184; see also Slave
Smithsonian Institution, 158
South, 43, 54, 109; health conditions in, 16, 43-44, 46; travel conditions in, 18, 42-48, 76, 109; description of, 43-48; agriculture in, 43, 110-111, 117, 178; hotels in, 44-46; food in, 46-47; commerce and industry in, 54, 111, 168; spitting in, 65; child marriages in, 80; schools in, 148, 152-153, 156; Irish in, 168; future of, 184-185; see also Slave, Slavery, Travel in America, individual cities and states
Sparks, Jared, 155
Speculation, 51-53

Spitting, 35, 39, 50, 64-65, 92

Spoils System: *see* Corruption Elections, Partisan spirit, Patronage

Stage-coaches: *see* Travel in America

State governments, 96-98, 100

Steamboats, river: *see* Travel in America

Stirling, James, 52n.; on lawlessness, 68, 72n.-73n.; on American women, 82-83; on slavery, 109, 112, 124n., 126-128; on education, 161n.; on emigration, 174n.; on the Know-Nothings, 182; on Anglo-American relations, 187n.

Strange, author: *see* Trotter

Stuart-Wortley, Lady E. C. E. M., 20, 22, 84n.; on Pittsburgh, 29n.; on love of money, 42n.; on New Orleans, 44n.; on stage-coach travel, 45; on dueling, 69; on the presidency, 91n.; on the Spoils System, 100; on slavery, 113n.; on emigration, 165n.

Sturge, Joseph, 66n., 79; on slavery, 73n., 118; on education, 153-154, 159n.

Sullivan, Sir E. R., 14, 62n., 107; on New Orleans, 44n.; on American manners, 85; on slavery, 111n., 115, 116n., 125; on religion, 132, 137

Sunday, observance of, 134-136

Sunday School Unions, 136

Tallack, William, 14, 51, 127-128

Taylor, J. G., 64n.; on American eating habits, 27n.; on American children, 84n.; on the Irish, 102n., 104n.

Taylor, Zachary, 91, 141-142

Teaching: *see* Schools

Temperance, 66-67, 73; *see also* Drinking

Tennessee, 120, 153

Texan Revolt, 108, 117

Texas, 15, 108, 118, 169, 175, 178

Thackeray, W. M., 21

Theatre, 17

Thomason, A.: *see* Bell

Thomson, William, 13-14, 54; on mob violence, 71n., 72; on disregard for human life, 75; on American women, 78; on American children, 84; on slavery, 108-109, 119-120, 183; on emigration, 165n., 174, 175n.

Thornbury, Walter, 29n.

Thornton, John, 180

Titles, 60-61

Tobacco: *see* Spitting

Tocqueville, Alexis de, 22n., 87n., 180

Todd, H. C. (Traveller), 143

Transatlantic travel, 17-18, 51, 162-164

Transcendentalists, 138, 142

Travel in America: costs, 15-16, 26, 163; motives, 13-20, 32; time spent in America, 18-20, 31; routes, 25, 31-33, 36-40; by canal, 38-40, 64, 164, 169; by railroad, 13, 18-19, 33-42, 44, 51, 55, 75-76, 86, 109, 124, 134, 164, 169; by stage-coach, 14, 18, 39, 44-45, 51, 55, 76-77, 129; by river steamboat, 33, 38, 44, 47-48, 51, 55, 63, 69, 75, 134, 164-165, 168; *see also* Hotels

Traveller, author: *see* Todd

Tremenheere, H. S., 17, 23, 103n.

Trollope, Mrs. Frances, 20, 53, 84, 180

Trotter, Mrs. Isabella (Strange), 15, 57

Turnbull, J. M. and M. F., 15, 17

Uncle Tom's Cabin, 108, 119

Underground Railway, 118

Union, future of the, 184-187

Unitarians, 132, 142, 146

United Republics of America, 185

Universal suffrage, 73, 98-100, 106-107; *see also* Egalitarianism, Elections, Politics, Partisan spirit, Patronage

University of Virginia, 154n., 156-157

Utah, 17-18, 23, 140; *see also* Salt Lake City

Van Buren, Martin, 90

Vermont, 66

Vice: *see* Morals

Vicksburg, Miss., 71

Virginia, 108, 110, 115, 120, 153; *see also* Richmond

Warburton, G. D., 14; dislike for democracy, 20, 60; on servants, 57; on inquisitiveness, 63n.; on drinking, 65n.; on American government, 87-88, 91n., 100n.-101n., 106n., 107; on slavery, 127; on religion, 130n.-131n., 132, 137, 142n.; on education, 159; on the Irish, 166n., 171-172; on nativism, 166n., 180; on Anglo-American rivalry, 185-186

Washington, D. C., 32-33, 40-41, 86-96, 143, 170

Watkin, Sir E. W., 14

Wayland, President of Brown University, 155-156

Weld, C. R., 30n., 52n., 53, 72n.; on disregard for human life, 42, 70-71; on aristocracy, 60n.; on slavery, 114-115

West, 15, 18, 54-55, 74, 126: health conditions in, 16, 177-178; travel conditions in, 18, 48-53, 65; commerce and industry in, 49-50, 72; agriculture in, 54, 165, 173-174, 177-178; egalitarianism in, 54-55, 74, 185; judiciary in, 55; drinking in, 65; scarcity of women in, 80; politics in, 97, 106; religion in, 143; schools in, 49, 143, 152-154, 156-157; Irish in, 49, 168, 170; *see also* Great Lakes, Midwest, individual cities and states

Whigs, 105

White House, 87-89

Wisconsin, 52-53

Wyse, Francis: on the Irish emigrant, 102n.-103n., 167n., 170n.; on slavery, 113, 117-118; on emigration, 162, 164n., 166n.-167n., 170n., 174n.-175n., 177n.-178n., 180n.

Yale, 154

Young, Brigham, 49, 72-73, 140-142